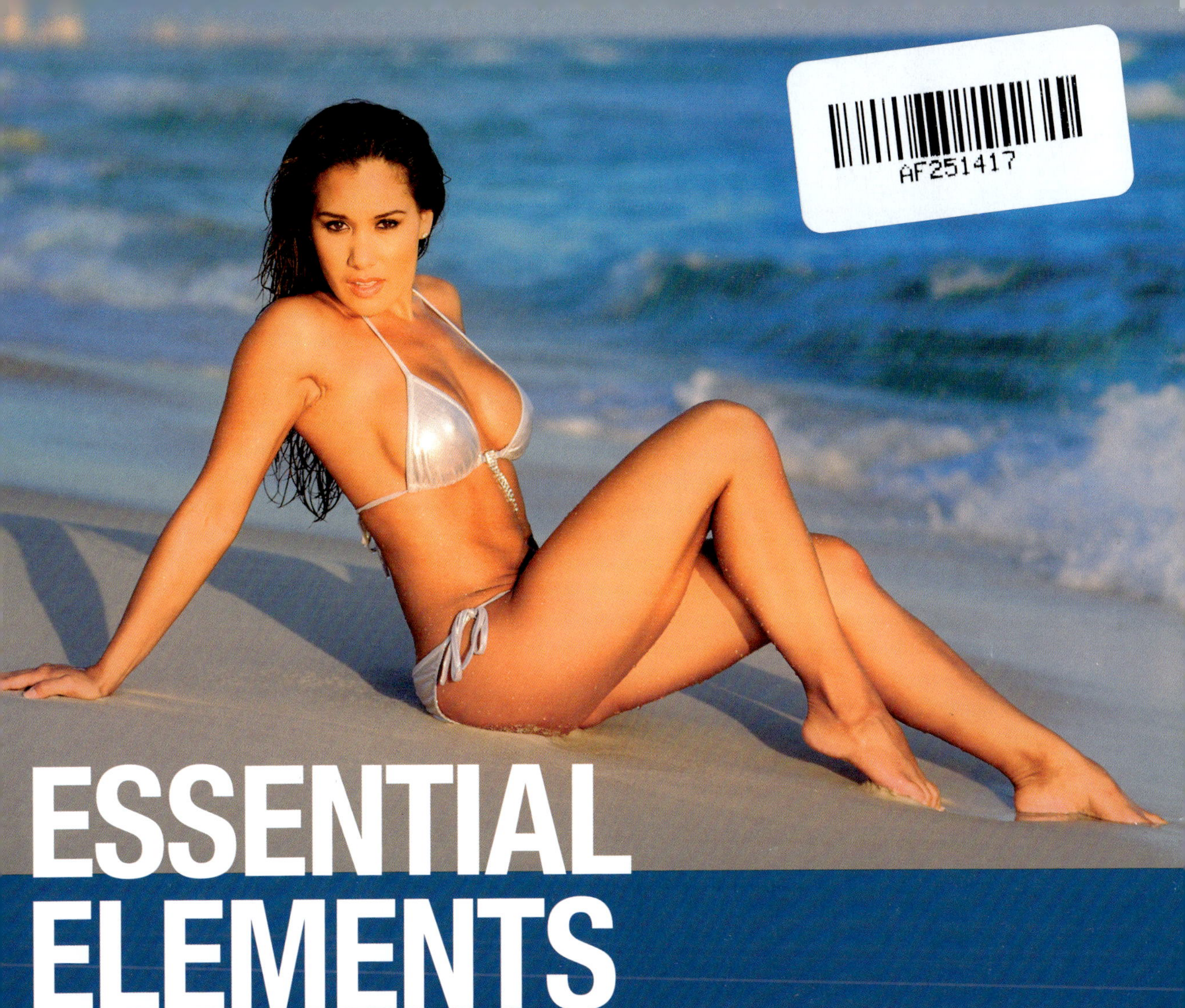

ESSENTIAL ELEMENTS

of PORTRAIT PHOTOGRAPHY

Lighting and Posing Techniques to Make Everyone Look Their Best

Bill Israelson

AMHERST MEDIA, INC. ■ BUFFALO, NY

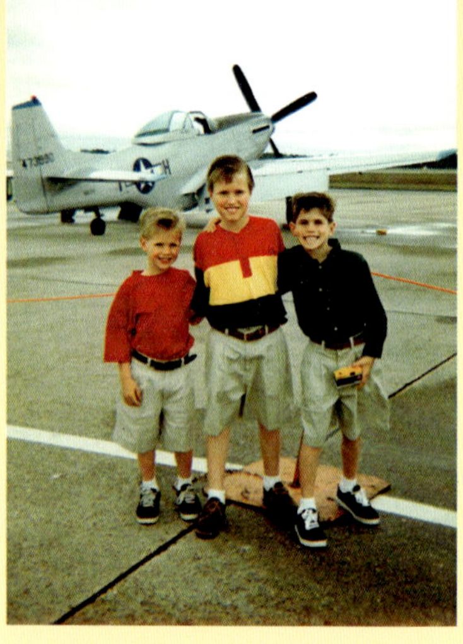
The "Three Amigos," circa 1994.

Dedication

This book is dedicated to my loving family—my wife Katherine and beloved sons Christopher, Jeffrey, and Steven.

Acknowledgments

I wish to thank all those who appear in this book. Without you, the book would be far less interesting! A sincere thank you also goes out to my wife Katherine, who supported the development of this book by coordinating the logistics and administration of the photographic shoots. I am grateful for her never-ending patience.

Published by:
Amherst Media, Inc.
P.O. Box 586
Buffalo, N.Y. 14226
Fax: 716-874-4508
www.AmherstMedia.com

Publisher: Craig Alesse
Senior Editor/Production Manager: Michelle Perkins
Editors: Barbara A. Lynch-Johnt, Harvey Goldstein, Beth Alesse
Editorial Assistance from: Carey A. Miller, Sally Jarzab, John S. Loder
Associate Publisher: Kate Neaverth
Business Manager: Adam Richards
Warehouse and Fulfillment Manager: Roger Singo

ISBN-13: 978-1-60895-751-4
Library of Congress Control Number: 2014933303
10 9 8 7 6 5 4 3 2 1

Check out Amherst Media's blogs at: http://portrait-photographer.blogspot.com/
http://weddingphotographer-amherstmedia.blogspot.com/

Contents

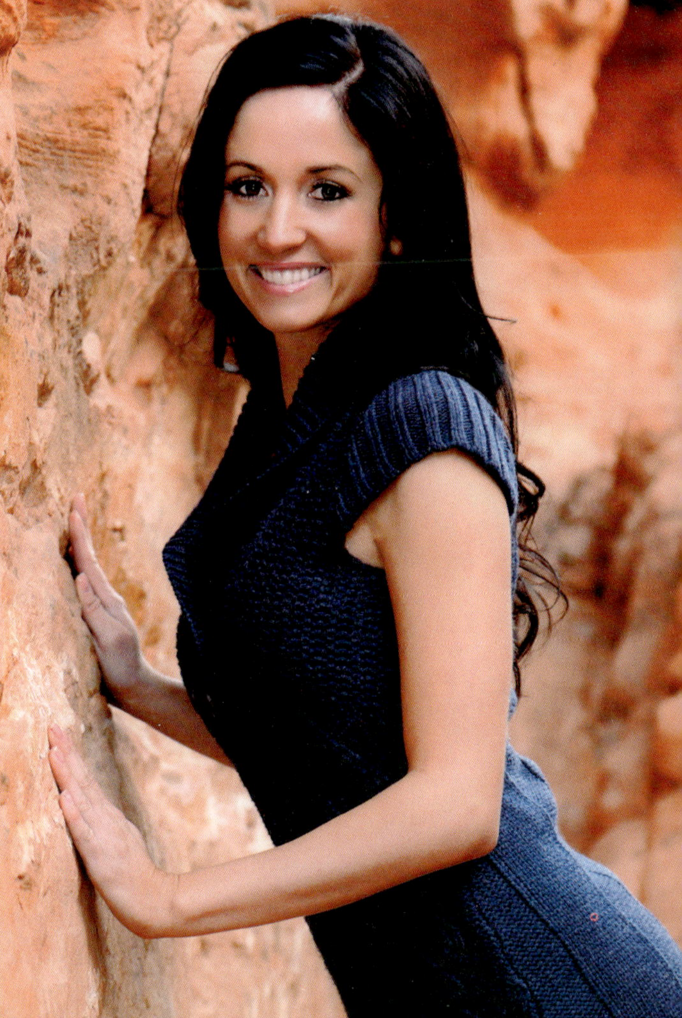

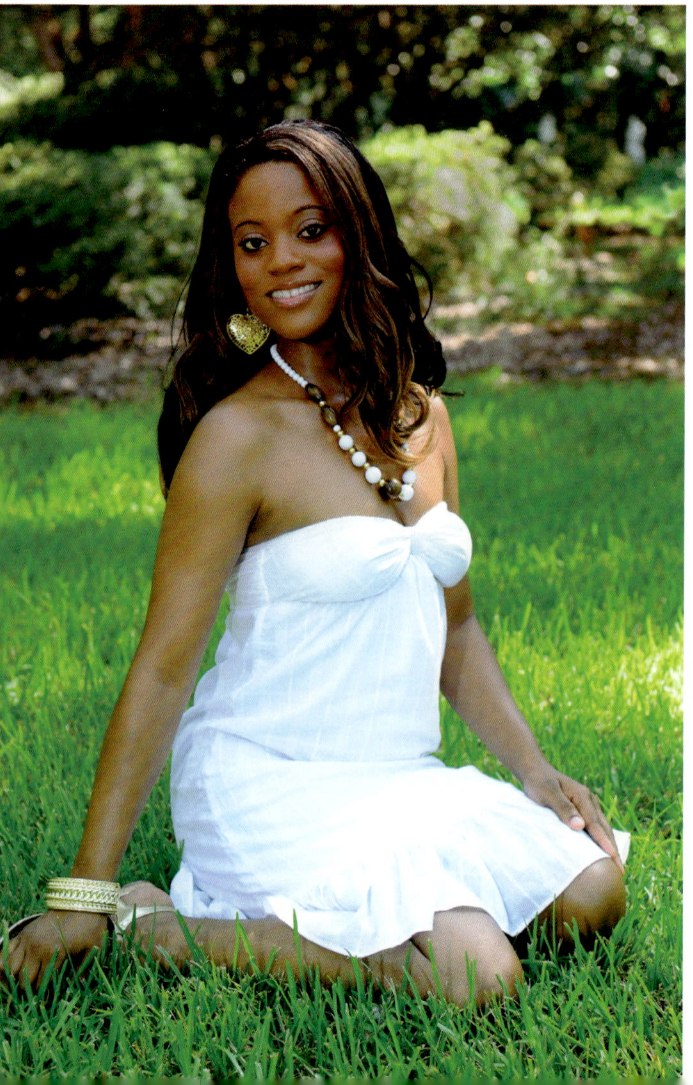

5. Studio Portraits 96

6. Indoor Portraits 114

7. Practice, Practice, Practice 120

Author Biography

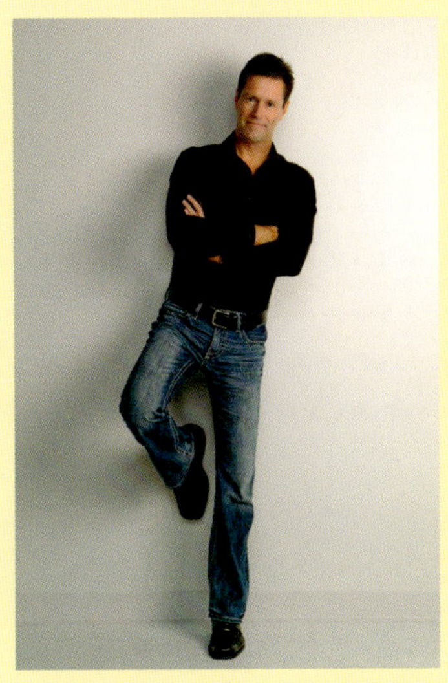

Author photo courtesy of Katherine Israelson.

Bill Israelson is a portrait and wedding photographer based in the Panama City/Destin Florida area. He operates a state-of-the-art studio and is happy to go the distance, work as hard as he can, and do whatever it takes to satisfy his customers.

As a young teen in the '70s, Bill used his dad's Minolta SRT-101 35mm SLR, which soon became his go-to camera for high-school yearbook work and taking photos of friends. His photography journey had begun, and Bill had been "bitten." Since then, photography has been his strongest interest. Throughout the 1980s and '90s, Bill employed a Pentax ME Super 35mm SLR with a variety of Tamron lenses to photograph family, friends, and events. After years of producing thousands of negatives, Bill went digital—and professional—in 2006.

Bill currently conducts photography workshops ranging from the fundamentals to advanced lighting techniques. Rarely is he seen without a camera strapped to his shoulder. He is the real deal—an enthusiast, perfectionist, and, above all, a passionate photographer.

Look for Bill's work at www.williamisraelson.com.

Introduction

The Goal of This Book

The goal of this book is to help you greatly increase the quality and beauty of your photography. The book covers the essential elements of portrait photography—from common mistakes to the needed equipment, we lay a foundation of how to use the tools of the trade. We then get into a discussion about the point of portrait photography and the art and skill of photographing people to ensure that they look their very best. Perhaps the most important idea in the entire text is the *process*. Conducting a successful portrait photo shoot, no matter the location, is based on a repeatable and reliable process that increases the quality of the images and creates a well-conducted experience for

▼ An example of a beautiful mid-key portrait taken in the studio.

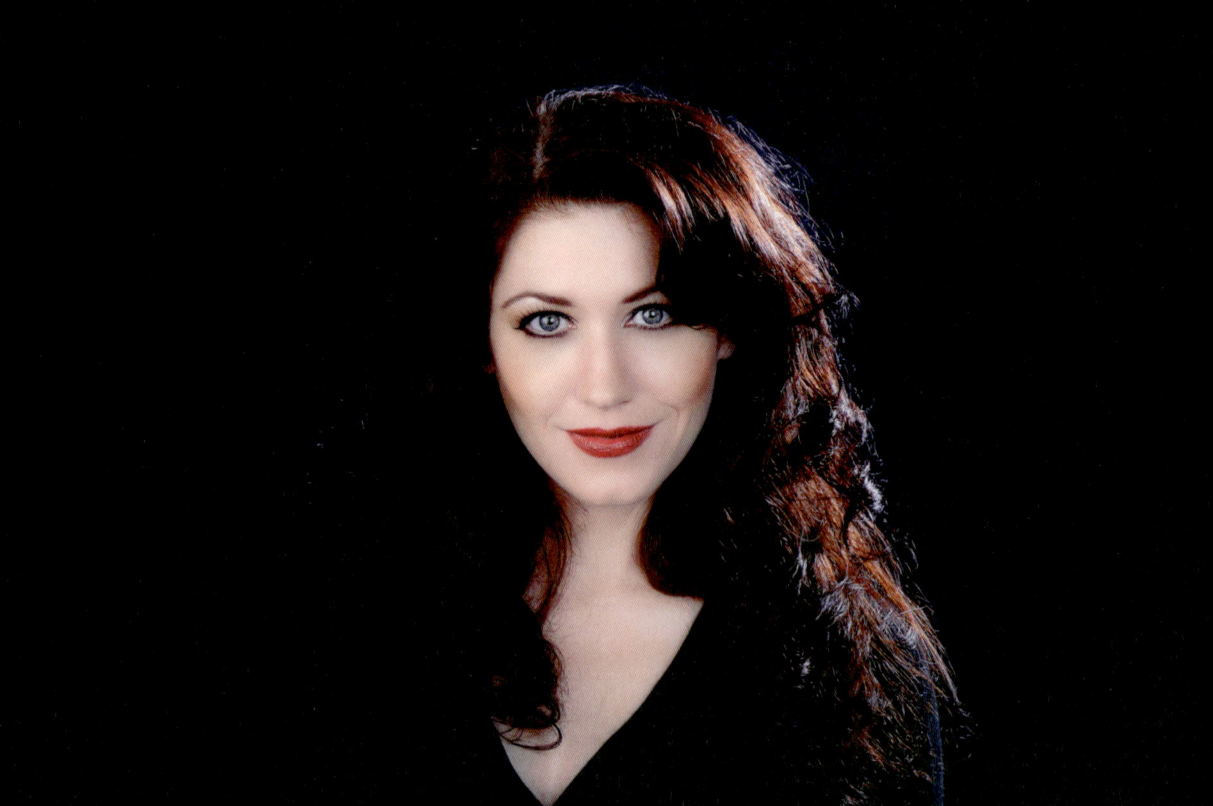

One-light-source portrait. A five-foot octabank with 300 watt/second strobe. The softbox in this portrait was less than one foot away from the subject and two feet from the backdrop. The falloff from the light source lit the backdrop sufficiently.

(left) An overcast day provides soft, even light on the subject, yielding excellent results.

(right) An example of excellent bokeh. Note the way the subject "pops" off of the page.

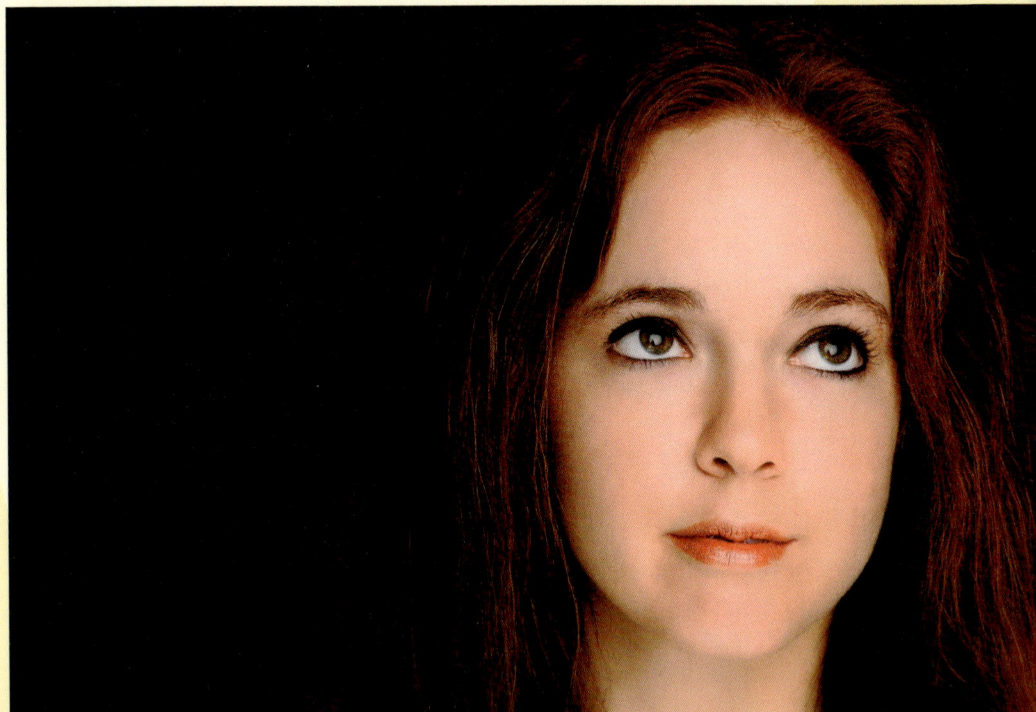

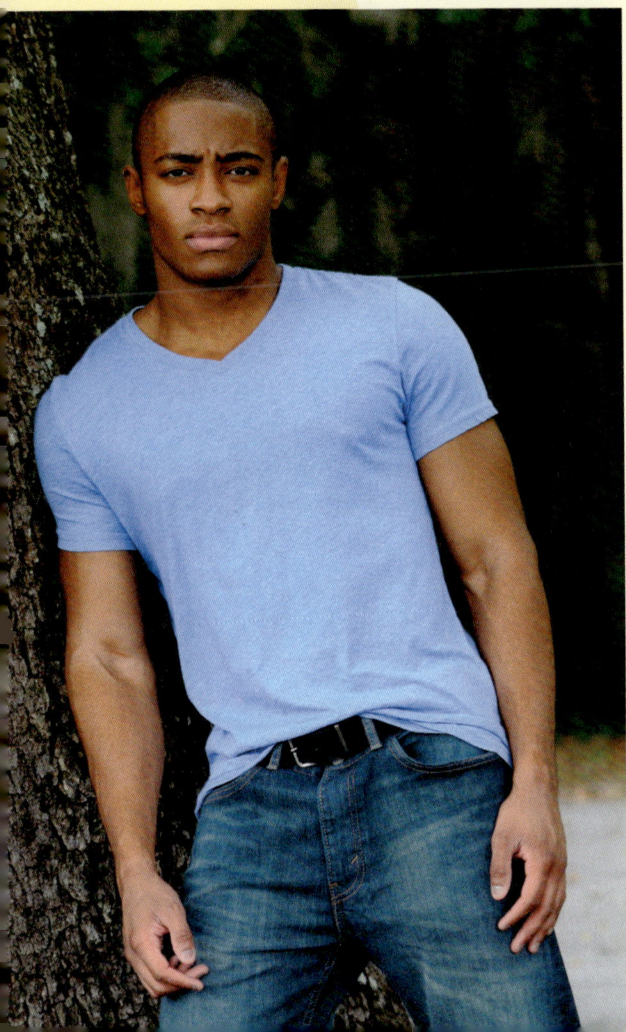

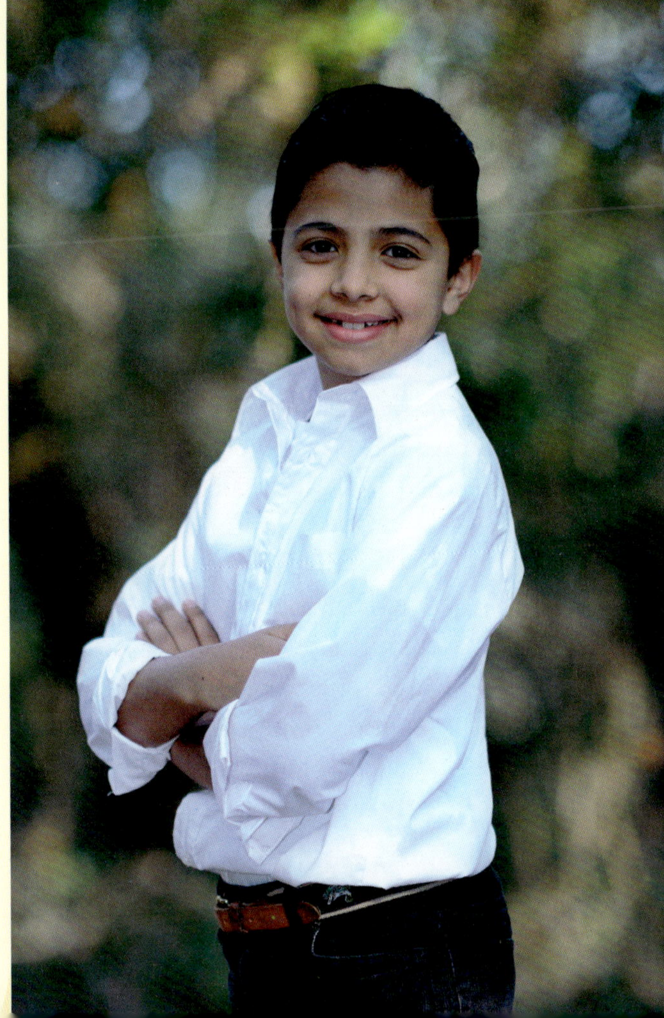

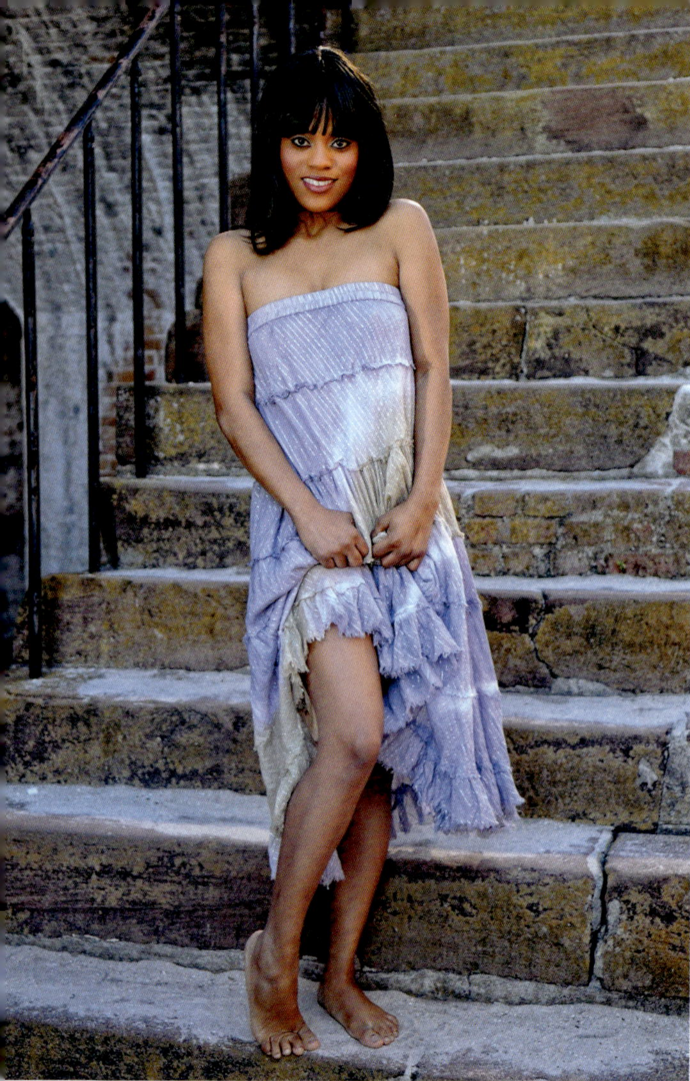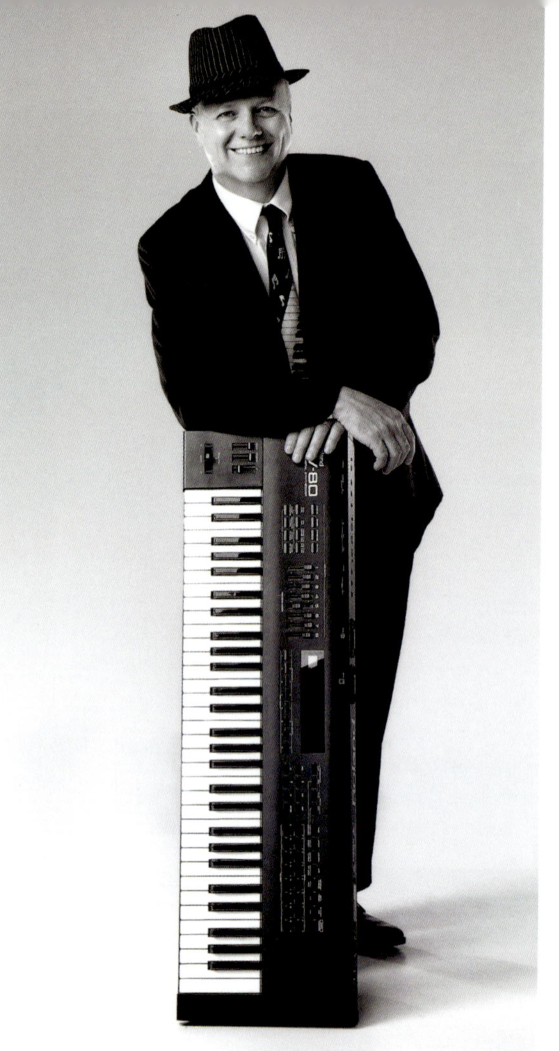

the photographer and subject. The unique and important issues of photographing people in the studio, outdoors, and indoors on-location are examined in detail with example photographs and descriptions of how the images were produced.

Frequently, I am asked by other photographers to demonstrate how to use a particular camera control or tackle a specific photographic problem. Sometimes the question concerns the setting of camera controls in a particular kind of situation such as bright sunlight or setting strobes in a studio environment. I am always glad to assist and provide advice on what I know works for me. This book contains many of those questions and answers. Technical jargon has been minimized. This book is not an attempt to impress the reader with complicated ideas or complex technical information. Quite the opposite—the information in these pages is presented as a straight-forward, one-on-one discussion on using proven portrait photography techniques to quickly make *huge* improvements in your image capture.

As you turn the pages of this book, you'll encounter Tech Tips. Don't be put off by the term "tech tip"—these sections, like the balance of the book, have been written to be easily understood and enjoyed. Each Tech Tip presents insights that support or build on information presented in the text. The major points covered in the book can be learned even if you decide to bypass the Tech Tip text.

It is my sincere hope that you will enjoy the content of this book and that the tips and techniques presented will help make a significant increase in your knowledge and skill and prepare you to be a better portrait photographer.

Obstacles to Good Photography

Learning to See the Light. The biggest obstacle to creating a great portrait is learning to see the light that surrounds your subject. I cannot emphasize this point enough. You're probably thinking, "C'mon Bill, we have heard that one before." Yes, I know. I remember feeling the same way when hearing such a statement. There was a time when while taking a portrait, I excitedly wanted to pose the subject, then show off and set up my state-of-the-art camera, then hurriedly get back to the shop to print the image. The first and most important step in the photographic process—seeing and evaluating the existing light—was sidestepped, and it showed in my work. I'm going to help you avoid making the same mistake. I'm going to talk with you about light, the various kinds and qualities of light that we encounter every day of our lives, and why you the photographer must train yourself to relax, take a deep breath, and see the light around you.

The biggest obstacle to creating a great portrait is learning to see the light that surrounds your subject.

In addition to learning to see the light, you must learn how to work with the sun, strobes, reflectors, and flash to illuminate the subject, ensuring that the light levels are not too high or too low. This brings us to our next concern . . .

Exposure. In order for an image to be effective, the exposure must be correct. Sounds obvious, right? Digital cameras are less forgiving than their negative film predecessors. When using film, you could take an exposure that was close to being correct, and the lab technician who processed your film was able to correct the exposure. With digital, if your portrait is overexposed, the subject's skin may lack detail. If the image is underexposed, the shadow areas may lack detail, and digital noise may result. Not to worry—in this book, you'll learn to avoid making exposure mistakes that can undermine your otherwise perfect portraits!

Posing. Posing rounds out the list. In my opinion, posing people for portraits is an art all in and of itself. Unless you are working with a professional model, you will be responsible for posing your subject, couple, or group. Many books offer excellent examples of posing—posing for weddings, high-school seniors, families, and glamour. I recommend that you purchase and read a few that appeal to you. But please understand that posing your client is not something that you can do from memorizing photographs. I know because I tried; it did not work. The reason is very simple: everyone and every situation is different. The people that you will

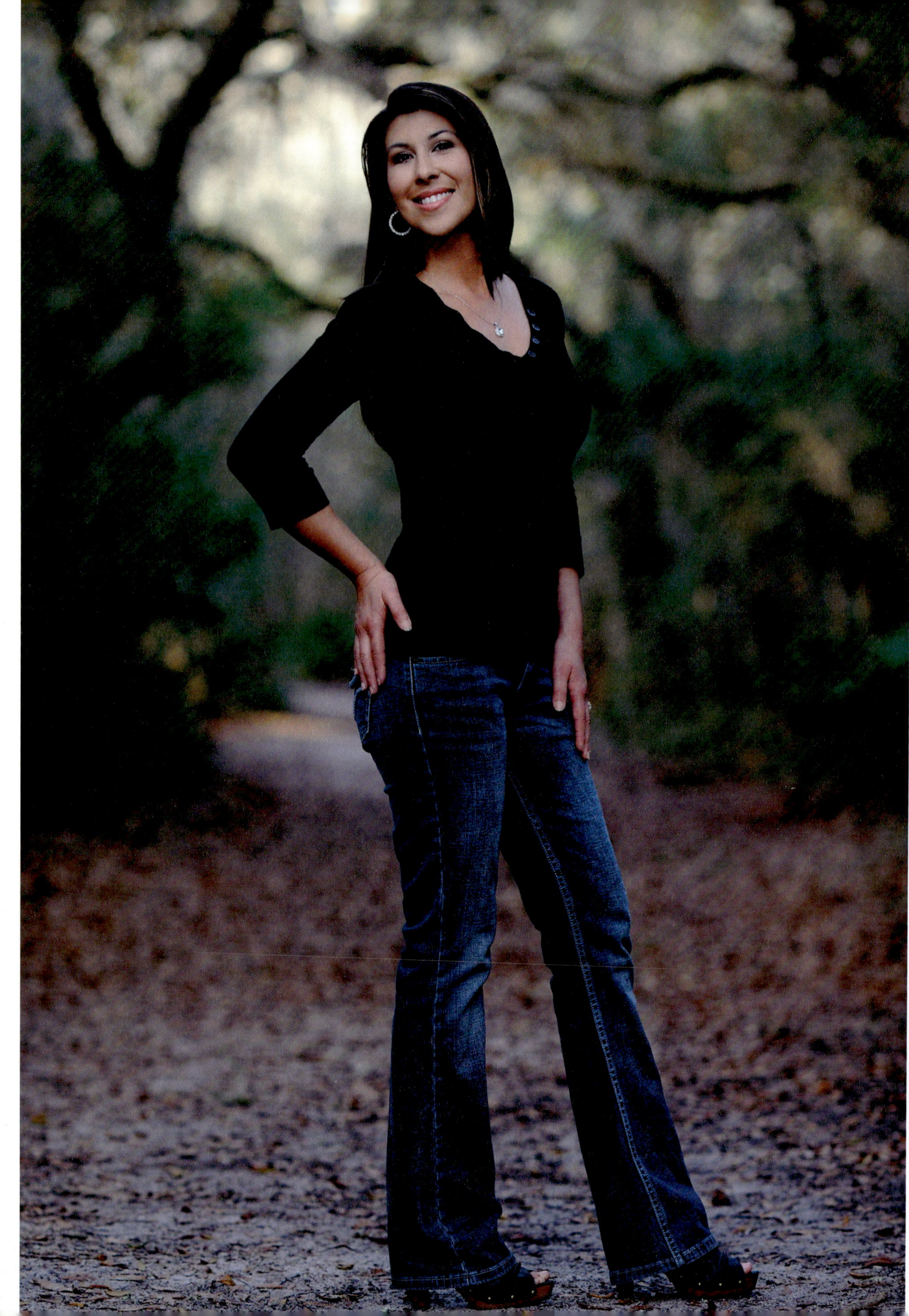

photograph have unique characteristics—face, size and shape, hair color, and their own unique personality. Additionally, there is an infinite number of combinations of place, placement, and pose. We'll go over some techniques for interacting with the folks you're photographing, determining what will make a good pose, and placing them within a setting to enhance the overall image.

I'll Fix It in Photoshop. Occasionally, I hear photographers say, "I'll fix the image in Photoshop." This way of approaching photography is a mistake. Adobe Photoshop is a phenomenal product and the people who developed it must be brilliant, but photography happens principally in the camera. Therefore, the goal must be to capture as perfect an image as possible at the moment of exposure. When capturing portraits, if you don't think that you achieved the proper exposure, composition, pose, or lighting, then make appropriate adjustments and continue to shoot until you have it right.

Disclaimer: Editing images to retouch skin blemishes and to sharpen and crop an image is a key to creating a salable portrait. However, editing an image should be a marginal task, not *the* task. If the image isn't correct to begin with, you cannot make it so in postproduction.

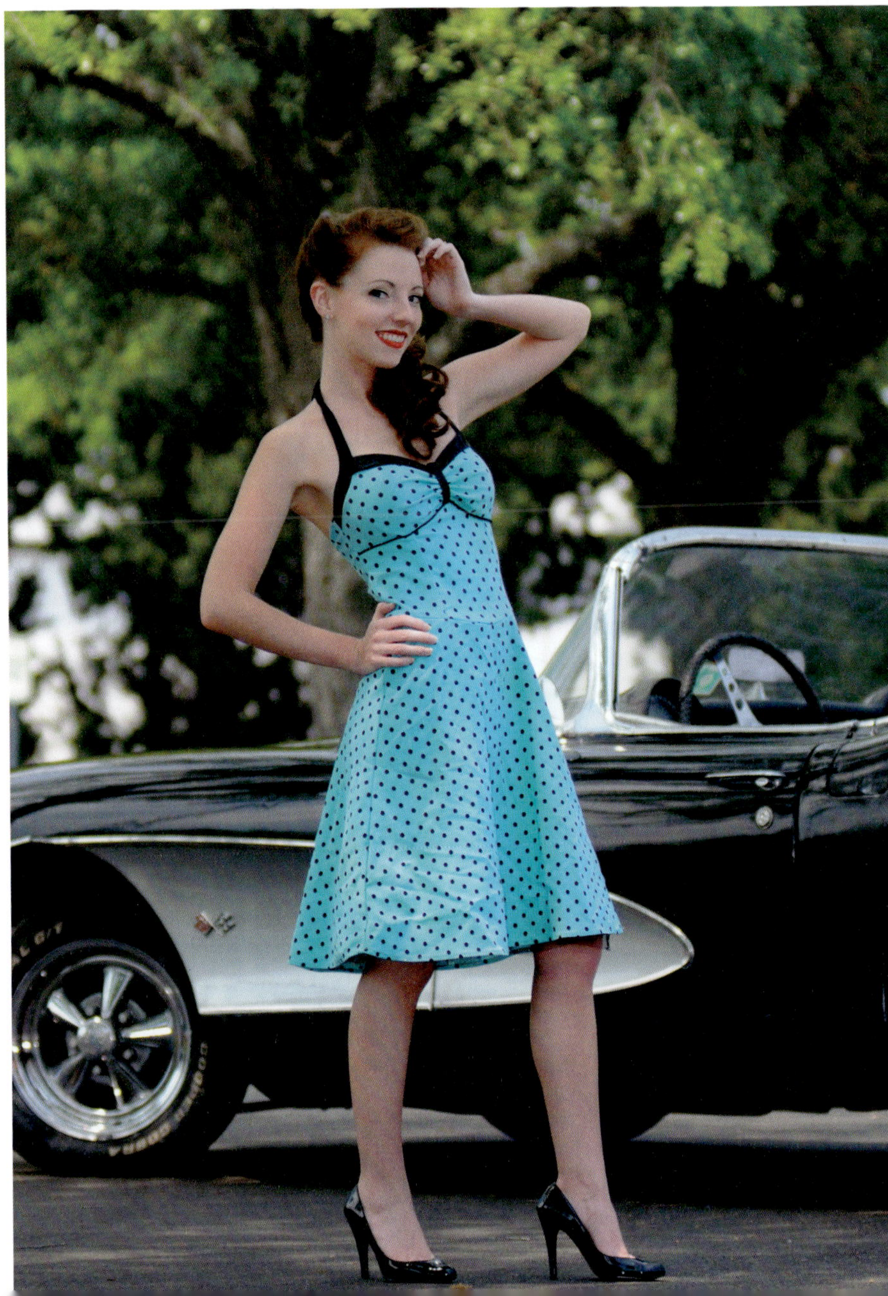

◄ In this portrait, the location set the context of the pose. Whatever the mood or personality of the subject, the pose helps to enhance and idealize the person being photographed.

► The background, prop, and use of bokeh set the model apart and creates and allows the subject to pop. It helps, too, that the model has a terrific sense of confidence and personality!

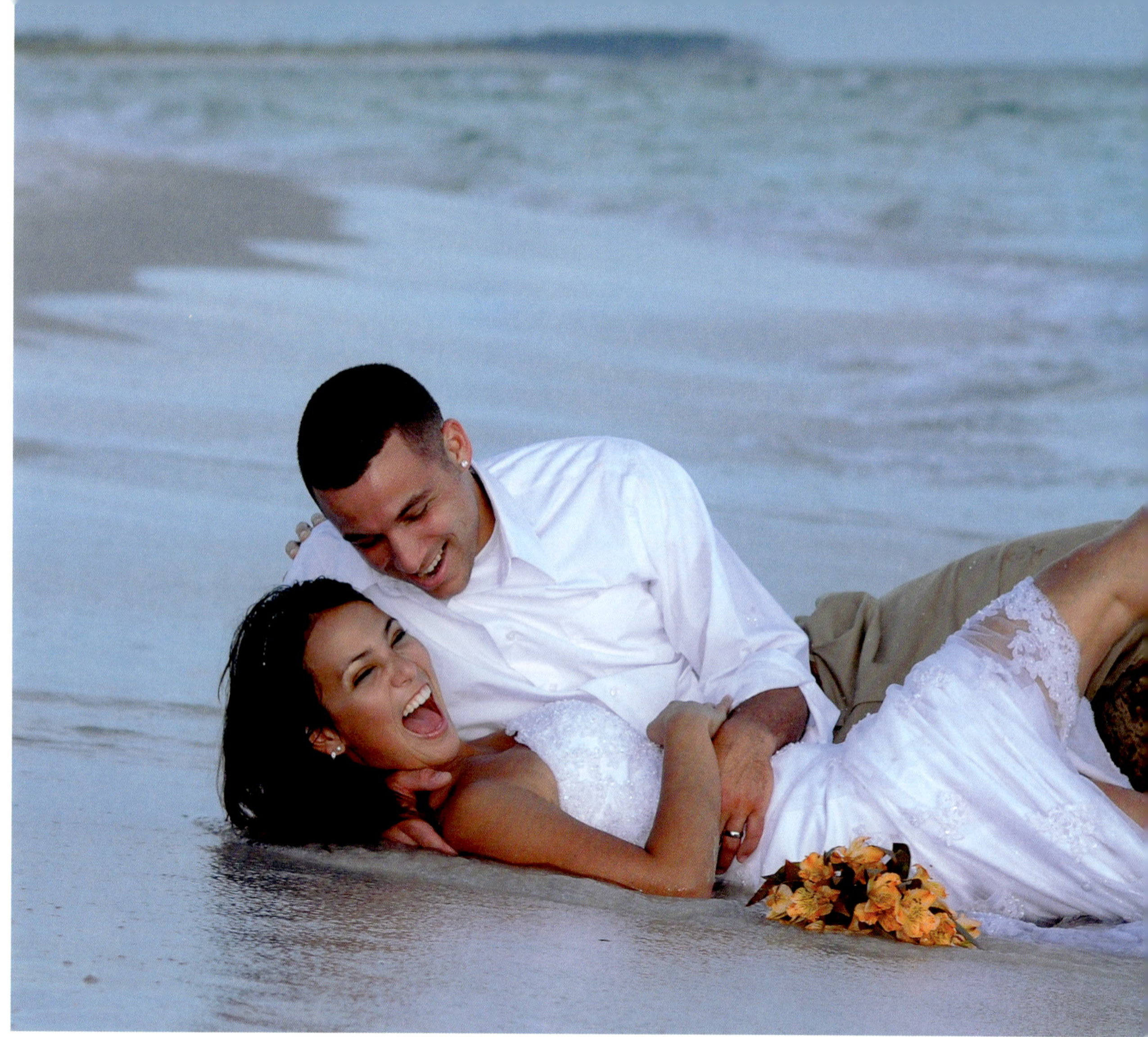

▲ (above left) In situations like this, you'd better have your camera settings spot-on. These kinds of opportunities don't repeat themselves.

▲ (above right) When photographing women, you will typically want to avoid poses that are straight-on to the camera. Here, the "rule" was broken, as the photograph was to be used in a clothing catalog.

Photography Is Art—But It Involves Technical Know-How

To me, photography is undoubtedly art; and for many, that is what makes it such a beautiful and enjoyable experience. As an art form, photography reflects a breathtaking range of works. We humans are very creative, and so there is a never-ending stream of examples of expression, design, and statements to be developed. With the advent of digital photography, and digital imaging via computers and software, we are lucky to be photographers in such an exciting time!

Before we get into all of the processes and techniques in this book, I want to state that what photography comes down to is what you,

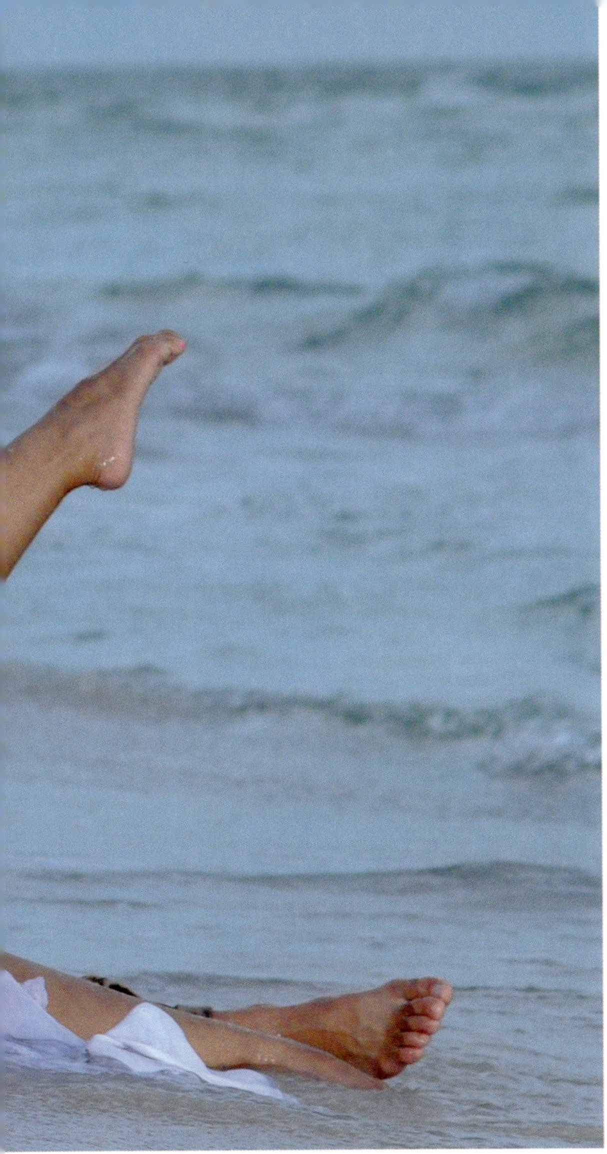

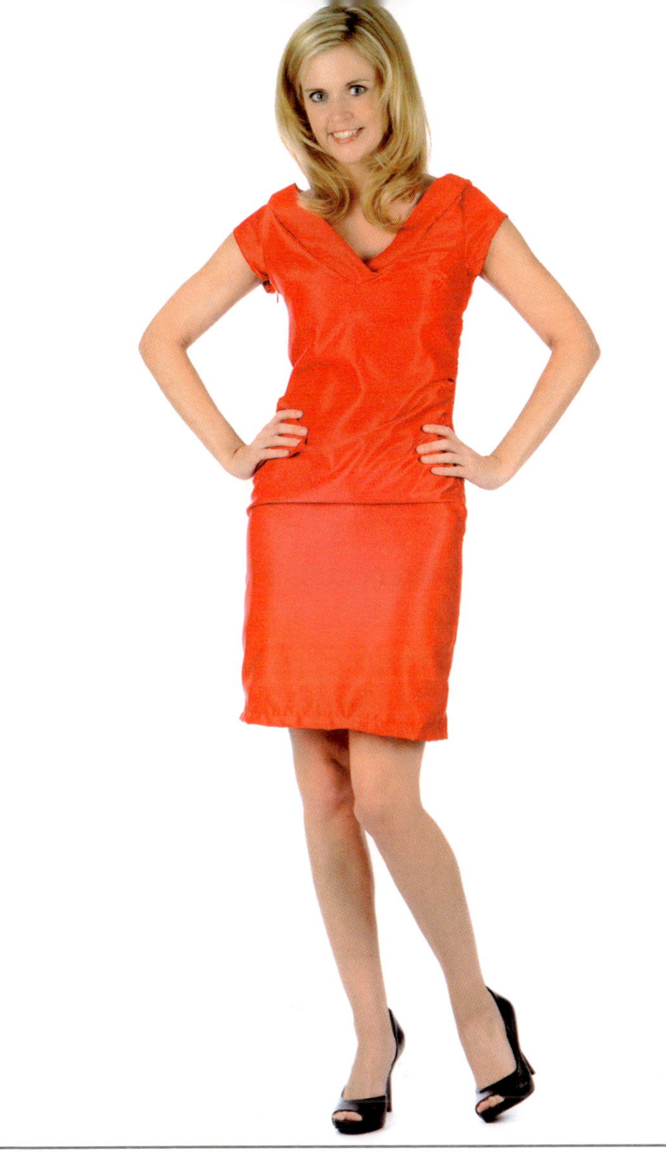

the photographer, prefer. Remember, we are having a conversation about what has worked for me. However, my hope is that what has worked for me will work for you too!

So, with the idea of art being subjective and very personal, let's now focus (no pun intended) on the actual photography. This book is not intended to be *overly* technical; we'll talk about the equipment, the processes, and the making of an image such that the mastery of the "technical stuff" will happen subliminally, make you a better photographer, and get you down the path of producing your own individual style of portrait photography.

1. Equipment

What Equipment Do I Need?

The range of photographic equipment that photographers can choose from is exciting. There are now thousands of manufacturers within the hundreds of product categories who are providing powerful high-quality products, most of which are financially within reach of most consumers. But with all of the choices, there may be hesitation or confusion as to what to acquire—and in what sequence. So, before we dive into the good stuff of examining the question of *how* to take professional portraits, let's first discuss what you should consider when you're building—one device at a time—your photographic kit.

This book relates to digital single-lens reflex cameras (DSLRs), not point-and-shoot or rangefinder cameras. Although point-and-shoot and rangefinder cameras can produce excellent photographs (and I like using them in certain types of situations) they do not offer the control that is necessary for portrait photography. This is simply my opinion. I will not suggest that you go out and buy the very best of everything, because it is a myth that the more expensive your stuff is, the better your images will be. In fact, one has nothing to do with the other. I'll share with you my experience and will show you how

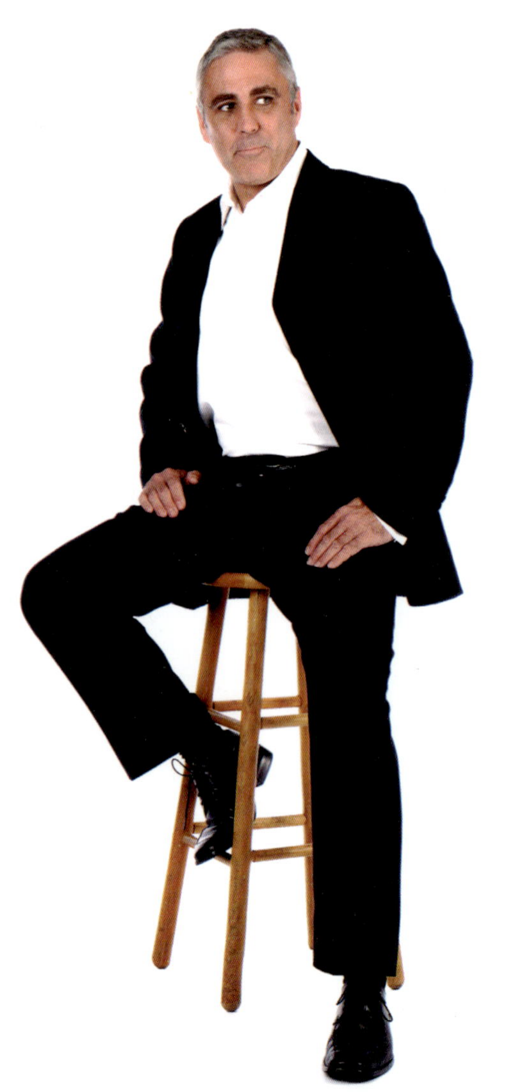

◄ This image is an example of a high-key portrait. Although the gent looked away from the camera, it is a successful portrait.

to play it smart, minimizing your costs while maximizing the quality of your photography.

The Basic Portrait Photography Kit

Let's talk about the basic set of equipment that you will need in order to produce portraits:

1. DSLR body
2. Lens
3. Flashgun
4. Loupe
5. Tripod

The above list represents a core set of components that will follow you as you progress as a photographer. For both outdoor and indoor work, you can produce exciting brilliant images with just these five components. For most of you, and for most of the time, you will be working alone, and probably won't be in the studio—the studio generally comes later. For now, I'd like to concentrate on the very core of what you need—and hopefully help you to make good decisions about where to spend your money. Think about it: wouldn't you rather have the flexibility of working independently, with everything you need in one hand (the loupe will be hanging around your neck), and save money? As you become better and better at seeing and controlling light, you will naturally need to acquire various pieces of equipment, and we'll discuss that equipment in the following sections. It is wise to learn the basics or fundamentals and then progress to more complex situations involving more equipment.

DSLR Body. Bodies are generally divided into three categories or grades: consumer, pro-sumer, and professional. The differences in the grade of these cameras can be seen in the

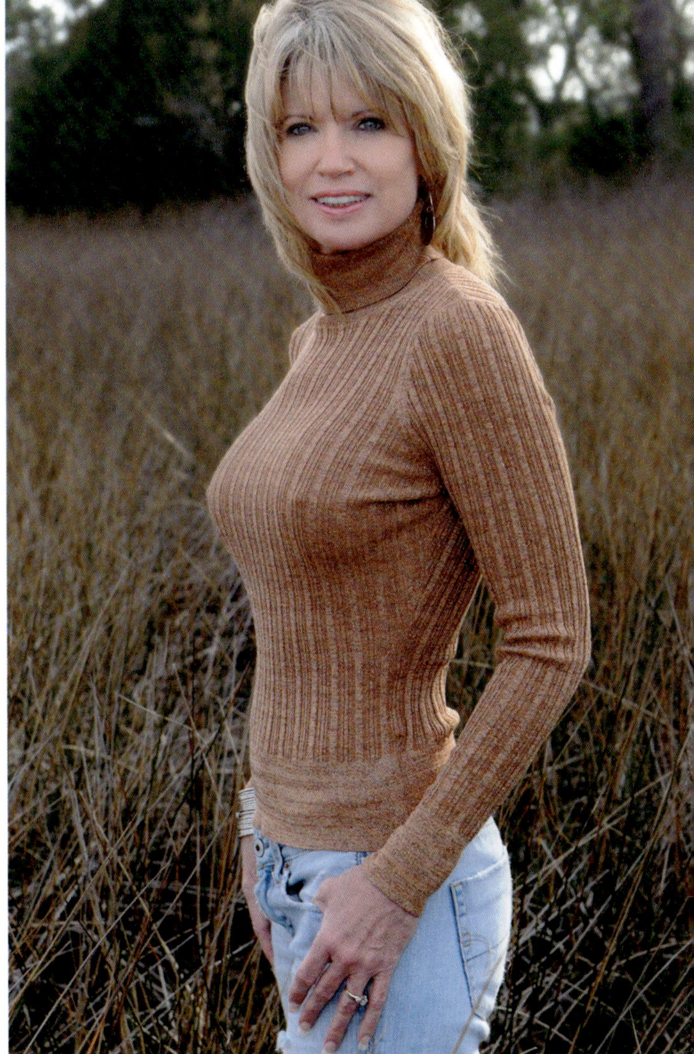

In this image, the setting sun provided rim lighting on the subject.

controls and build quality. By controls, I mean the manner in which you control exposure via the ISO, shutter speed, and aperture. At the consumer level, the camera can be set to make many decisions about exposure automatically; at the professional level, the camera *must* be set manually. In the middle is the pro-sumer level, which combines opportunities for automation and manual control. By build quality, I mean the materials that are used for the inner frame and exterior surface of the body, and how well it is sealed from the environment. The consumer-grade camera will be smaller, lighter, and will be moderately sealed to protect against dust and moisture penetration; the professional-grade camera will be large, heavier, made of high-grade metals and alloys, and tightly sealed to keep the most intrusive moisture and dust out of the inner workings.

One of two distinct sensor types is found in every DSLR body—the full-frame or the APS-C. The full-frame sensor is equivalent in size to a single frame of 35mm still photography film. Full-frame sensors have outstanding light-gathering performance; thus, they are excellent in low light conditions and absolutely fabulous for general photography. Full-frame sensors are typically found in professional-grade DSLRs. APS-C sensors are smaller than their full-frame sensor counterpart; the exact size of an APS-C sensor depends on the manufacturer and camera model. APS-C sensors offer a tremendous value when one considers the cost to performance ratio. When shooting with a DSLR body that incorporates an APS-C sensor, using a lens which was designed for a 35mm SLR or a full-frame DSLR will cause a cropping of the image circle that is formed on the sensor. This is not necessarily a bad thing. If you are using telephoto lenses, then you get about a 1.5x magnification of the focal length of the lens. However, this same magnification works against you when you are employing a wide angle lens as the "wideness" of the lens is narrowed.

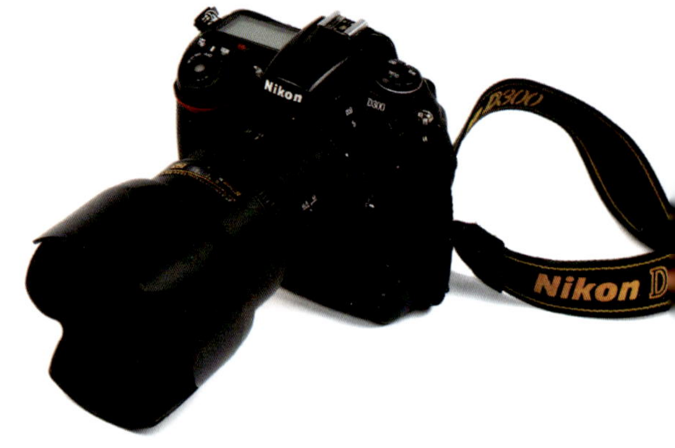

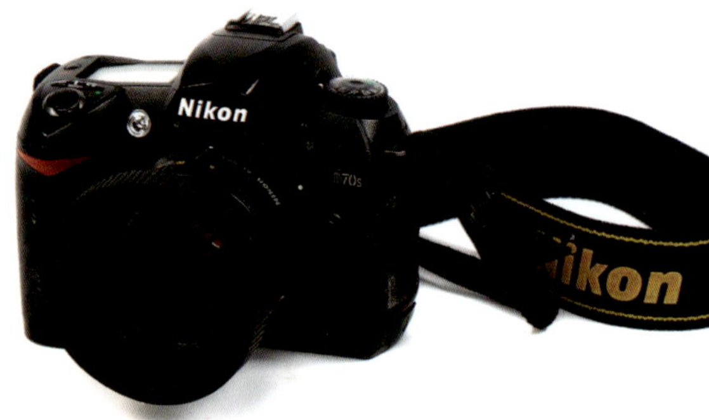

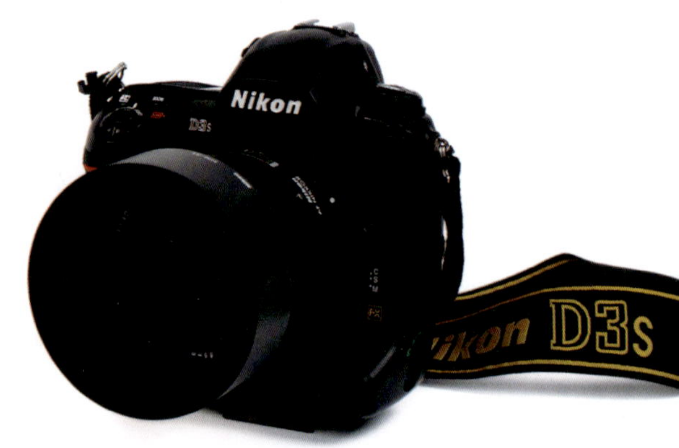

▲ The photos of Nikon DSLR bodies show a D300, D70, and D3s. The D70s purchased in 2006 continues to produce outstanding images and is well past the shutter cycle specification!

Finally, the number of shutter cycles that a body will perform increases when we go from consumer to professional. For instance, the Nikon D300 (pro-sumer) will actuate the shutter 150,000 times before needing servicing by the manufacturer, whereas the Nikon D3s (professional) is rated for 300,000 shutter actuations.

All of the major manufacturers are producing excellent products. I photograph with Nikon, but recommend that you do some research and shop around to determine for yourself which brand makes sense to you. Purchasing a new camera brings with it a warranty and "newness"—both good. But consider purchasing a better grade of camera than you could otherwise afford by purchasing a previously owned camera. There are several very good and reputable dealers in the United States that offer used equipment that has been inspected and given a condition score. This can be a smart way to maximize your dollar and move closer (or perhaps into) the professional category. Generally speaking, after a couple of weeks of employing a used camera, you'll forget that it was previously owned, and delight in the fact that you're holding a fantastic piece of equipment—at a fraction of what it cost when it was new.

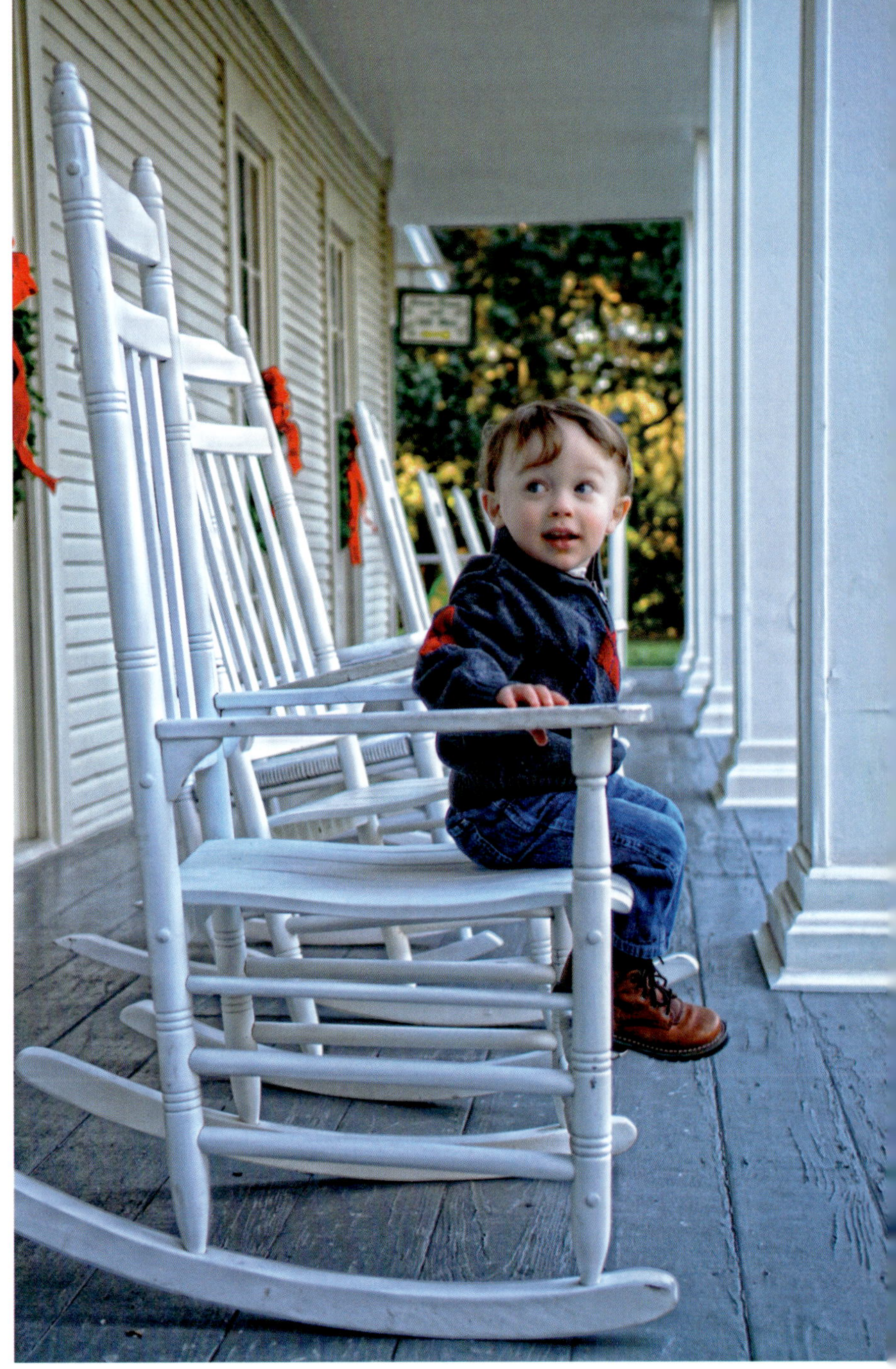

This tyke sat in the rocking chair for approximately two seconds. When photographing happy, vibrant children, the photographer must be alert!

 # Digital Sensors

It is important to understand the differences in sensor technology choices found in the DSLR. There are two major categories of sensor types: full frame and APS-C. A full-frame sensor is the size of a 35mm film gauge designed for still photography, whereas the APS-C sensor is considerably smaller and varies in dimension by manufacturer and model.

Both sensor types work very well and produce beautiful digital images. DSLR bodies which incorporate the APS-C sensor and the compatible lenses are considerably less expensive than their full-frame counterparts. Both sensor types have an aspect ratio of 3:2. All of the major DSLR manufacturers now offer APS-C and full-frame compatible lenses, so mating body/lens systems is pretty straightforward (the rules of interchangeability of lenses to bodies vary among manufacturers, so consult a company rep of the manufacturer you're considering). However, there is a technicality involved here that should be covered.

Digital sensors are comprised of a matrix of pixels that convert photonic energy into electrical current. From there, the current is evaluated by a microprocessor, which computes an image through the use of very elaborate hardware and software. Two major technologies employed in DSLRs are the Charged Coupled Device (CCD) and Complementary Metal Oxide Semi-Conductor (CMOS); both have unique designs and characteristics which are beyond the scope of this book. Which is better? That is up for debate. I happen to own bodies with both types of sensors and have yet to discover which type of sensor "outperforms" the other. Sensors are defined in terms of megapixels (MP), which is the product of the number of pixels arranged along the long and short sides of the sensor. It is common now to use a sensor that is 16 or 20 MP! The idea behind so many pixels is to increase resolution. However, resolution may be increased at the expense of noise and a reduction in the fidelity of the image. The absolute value of the MP is not necessarily the best measurement of the "goodness" of a sensor. The physical size of the sensor must also be considered. Why? Because the more pixels that are installed on a given square unit of surface, the smaller each pixel must be. Smaller pixels struggle to capture incoming photons. To overcome the struggle, engineers employ amplifiers to increase the strength of the electrical current produced by the pixel. This amplification can and usually does translate to noise or distortion in the resultant image. By comparison, fewer sensors placed on the same given unit of square surface means that each pixel is larger and has better light-gathering properties. Thus, amplification of the signal is less of an issue. Sure, the resolution will be lower, but noise will be reduced and the fidelity of the image will be better. Canon and Nikon have both produced full-frame sensors that are around the 12MP density. The performance of these sensors is remarkable.

The first popular DSLRs that were available a decade ago were equipped with APS-C sensor technology— again, smaller in size than a frame of 35mm film. The

▼ (top) Comparison of full-frame and crop APS-C sensor types.
▼ (bottom) Here is a photo of a typical digital sensor.

Film, Full Frame, & APS-C Sensor Size Comparison

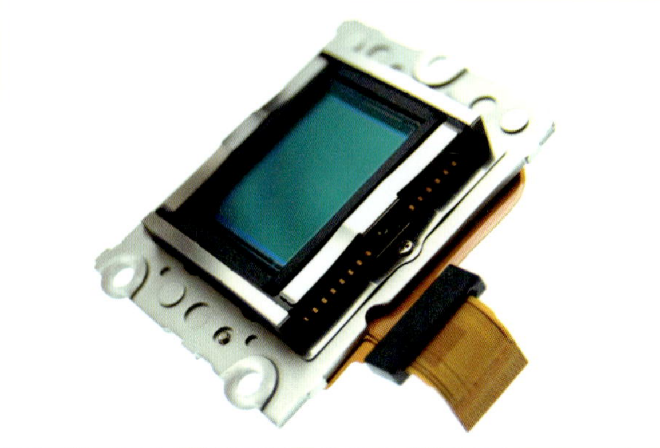

image circle formed from an attached lens on the APS-C sensor was larger than the area of the sensor. Thus, part of the image circle fell outside of the sensor and was cropped—lost from the image. This is known as a crop factor and is a function of the relative difference in the size of one frame of 35mm film compared to the size of the APS-C sensor. Mathematically, one way to calculate the ratio is to divide the diagonal formed by a frame of 35mm film to the diagonal formed by the APS-C sensor. For illustration purposes, let's assume that a given APS-C sensor is the same size as a frame of 35mm film. The ratio of diagonals would be 1:1 and thus, there would be no crop factor (obviously). Now let's assume that the APS-C sensor is half the size of the 35mm film. In this case, the ratio of diagonals would be would be 2:1 and so the crop factor would be 2. Since the size of an APS-C sensor varies among manufacturers (just a bit), the crop factor likewise varies. For Nikon APS-C bodies, the crop factor is 1.5; for Canon, it is 1.6.

Another way of thinking about crop factor is magnification referred to as focal length multiplier (FLM). I prefer to think in this way. For example, let's assume that we are using a Nikon APS-C body with an 85mm prime lens. We know that Nikon APS-C bodies have a crop factor or FLM of 1.5, so the effective focal length of the 85mm lens is 127.5mm. This would be the equivalent of using a Nikon full-frame body with a 127.5mm lens (if such a lens were made). Let's try Canon. Assuming a Canon APS-C body with an 85mm prime lens and Canon's published 1.6 crop factor or FLM, the effective focal length is 136mm.

Sensor sizes and lens technologies vary among manufacturers of DSLR cameras. Nikon has addressed this by creating the DX line of lenses. A DX lens coupled to a Nikon APS-C body produces an image circle that correctly covers the sensor. Whichever brand of camera or lens you are considering, I recommend that you take the time to do some research and ask questions of corresponding customer support departments.

The digital sensor by itself only measures the intensity or luminosity of light. To incur a color image, a Bayer filter is placed over the sensor; it filters the three additive primary colors of red, green, and blue (RGB). Think of the filter as a checkerboard with individual squares, most of which are green, and some red, and blue. Within the DSLR processing, each primary color is given a channel to process and compute a final color image. Through a mathematical calculation called interpolation, the intensity and color channel of each pixel is compared to the neighboring pixels, the result of which is a broad spectrum of color space and a color digital image.

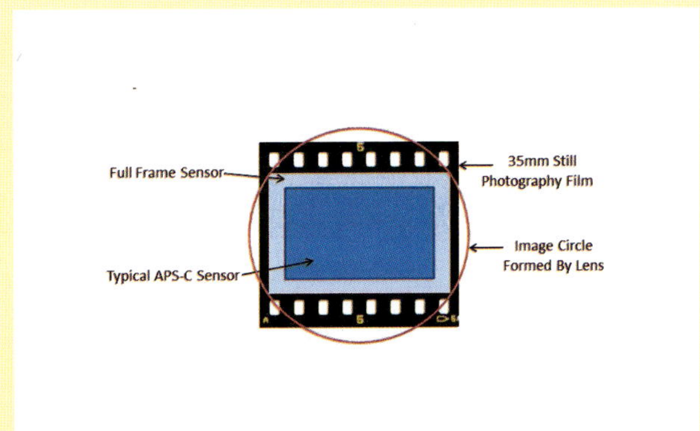

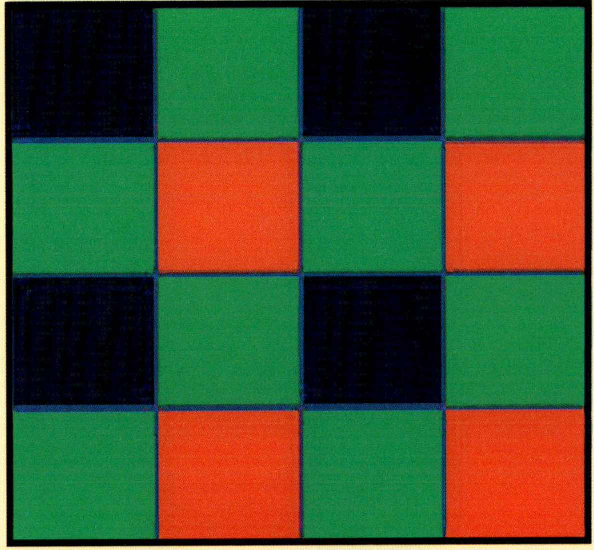

▲ (top) Lens-to-sensor crop factor.

▲ (bottom) This is an example of a Bayer filter.

As important as the selection of a good DSLR body is, the lens is the most important component in the camera bag.

Lens. As important as the selection of a good DSLR body is, the lens is the most important component in the camera bag. One high-quality lens—just one—is better than two or three average lenses. You may already know this detail about lenses. But if you don't, I guarantee that in time, after you shoot many portraits, you will come to discover that the lens becomes a critical component of creative and beautiful photography. Why? Because the quality of the lens governs how the light is treated as it is refracted (travels or is collimated) within the lens barrel on its way to striking the sensor.

Prime Lens. A prime lens has a fixed focal length, typically from 10mm to 500mm (and beyond). Primes are high performance and expensive. The good news is that prime lenses offer excellent performance as they are usually comprised of the best materials (such as the glass elements). You will find that when a prime lens is used for portraiture that the images are bright, detailed, and accurate. Vignetting, or dimness at all edges of the frame (away from the center), is rarely if ever noticed when using

▼ These are examples of prime lenses. I especially like the 85mm for its flexibility—it's a very good all-around performer.

➤ Here is an example of a three-quarter glamour pose with a close background. The red painted portion of the brick wall was selected to increase the vibrance. The young lady depicted is a professional model from Tampa, FL.

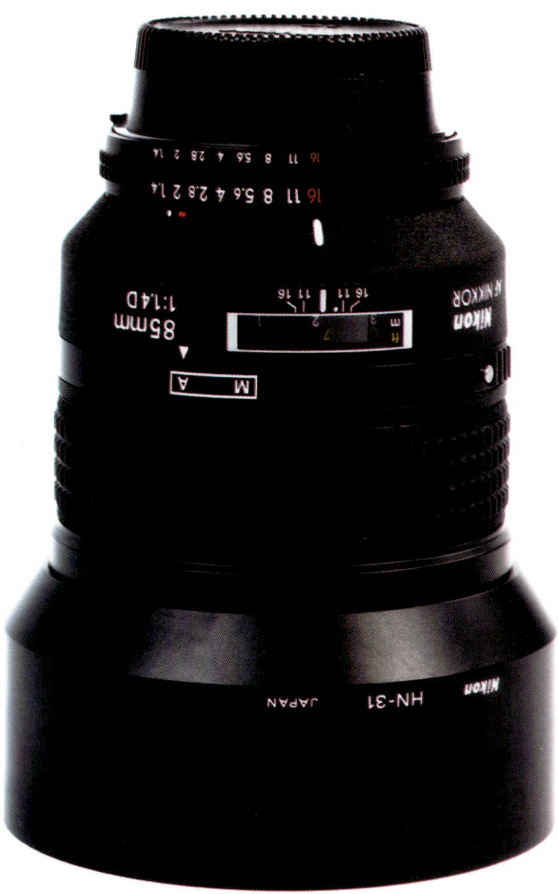

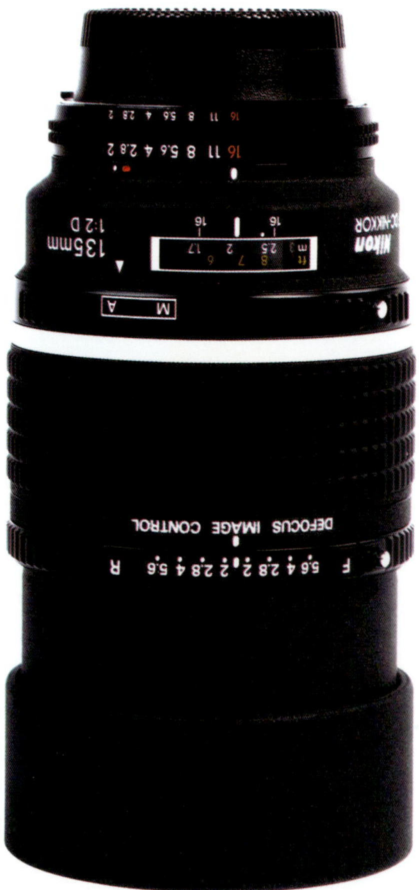

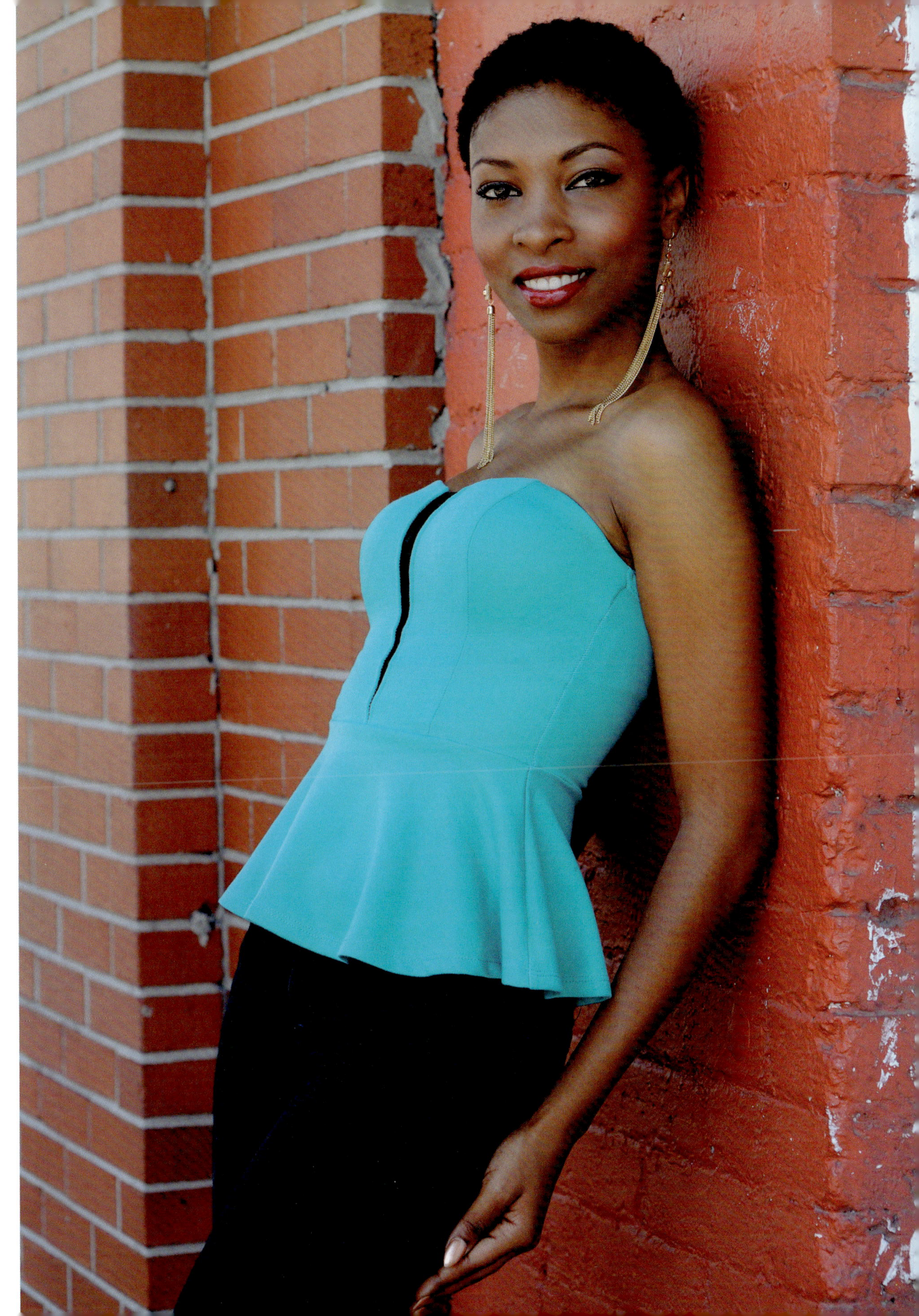

For portraiture, prime lenses such as a 50mm, 85mm, 105mm, and 135mm produce excellent results.

a prime lens, as it is when using lesser-quality lenses. Well-designed prime lenses offer extraordinarily wide maximum aperture settings. This is a good thing, as more light is permitted

to enter the lens, and creatively, the background of the image can easily be blurred. (See the Tech Tip on Aperture and F-Stops for more on this topic.) For portraiture, prime lenses such as a 50mm, 85mm, 105mm, and 135mm produce excellent results.

Zoom Lens. A zoom lens offers a variable focal length and thus provides a lot of convenience. Once you decide where you are going to position the camera, you can change the focal

TECH TIP Aperture and F-Stops

The amount of light that enters the lens is controlled by the aperture. The aperture is made up of a series of thin mechanical blades which form a circular opening as can be seen in the example. The opening can vary in diameter and is either set automatically by the camera or manually by you, the photographer. In either case, for a given lens, the f-stop (or f-number) indicates the relative size of the aperture.

The f-stop is calculated using the formula: f-stop = focal length/aperture diameter. Given an arbitrary focal length of a 100mm lens with an aperture diameter of 50mm, the f-stop would be 2. Given the same 100mm lens with the aperture diameter of 25mm, the f-stop would be 4. There is an inverse relationship between the size of the aperture and the f-stop. So, f/22 is a tiny aperture, whereas f/1.8 is a big aperture—regardless of the focal length of the lens. Note that in our example,

reducing the diameter of the aperture from 50mm to 25mm, the amount of light allowed to enter the lens is cut in half. Conversely, by increasing the diameter of the aperture from 25mm to 50mm, double the amount of light is allowed to enter the lens. The doubling or halving of the amount of light entering the lens is called a full stop. Below is an example range of full stops.

Moving from left to right, each increase in the f-stop halves the light. Moving right to left, each decrease in the f-stop doubles the light. This is tremendously convenient; dividing and multiplying by two is an easy mental function and translates easily when adjusting the camera to lighting conditions. As convenient as the full-stop scale is, most DSLRs provide even more power for the photographer, allowing users to make $\frac{1}{2}$ or $\frac{1}{3}$-stop adjustments.

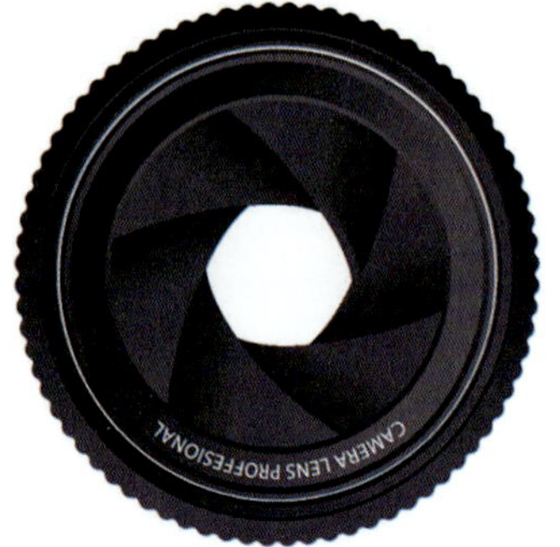

f Stop	1	1.4	2	2.8	4	5.6	8	11	16	22

◄ Typical aperture formed by flat blades.

▲ Each increase in f-stop (toward the right) results in a halving of the light, while each decrease in f-stop (toward the left) results in a doubling of the light.

length to frame the image rather than having to physically move your camera (as is the case with a prime lens). For portraiture, a popular telephoto zoom lens is the 70–200mm or 80–200mm, which most if not all of the camera and lens manufacturers produce. At focal lengths between 105mm and 135mm these lenses are very sharp, with excellent performance for the dollar. Due to the magnification of these lenses, any shake or instability will cause blur. Later, you will read about the need for a tripod, which arrests most of the vibration. To quell the blur, so to speak, manufacturers have incorporated vibration reduction (VR), a technology that compensates for the shake introduced when handholding the lens. Having VR on a lens is cool because it works, but it does increase the price of the lens. If you can afford it, then go for it. In the meantime, learn to attach the camera (and lens) to a tripod; you will see the difference a tripod makes when you view your *very* sharp images.

Wide zooms are useful when photographing a person in a panoramic setting, capturing wedding images, and for creative shooting. A typical focal length range for a wide zoom lens is 24–70mm or 17–55mm. When using these focal lengths, take care to keep the subject being photographed near the center of the frame to minimize distortion of their face and body.

Aperture. The aperture is an opening that allows light to enter the lens. A nearly circular hole is formed by a series of thin, flat blades. The aperture is an integral part of any modern lens and is all-important when controlling the amount of light that is permitted to enter the lens and the resulting depth of field (DOF). The term f-stop is used to denote the size of the aperture. The smaller the f-number or f-stop, the larger the aperture. The larger the f-number or f-stop, the smaller the lens opening. For example, f/2.8 is a larger diameter than f/16. Typically, higher-quality (and more expensive) lenses offer apertures of f/1.4 or f/1.8.

Flashgun. The flashgun, or flash, is a must-have piece of equipment. When in the studio, the flashgun is put away, but for all other situations I normally have a flashgun ready to go. As I will explain in detail in a later chapter, the flashgun functions as a fill light—and this is no small issue. In most cases, the absence of a flash will result in the portrait looking dark, smudgy, with little to no vibrancy or "pop." We will

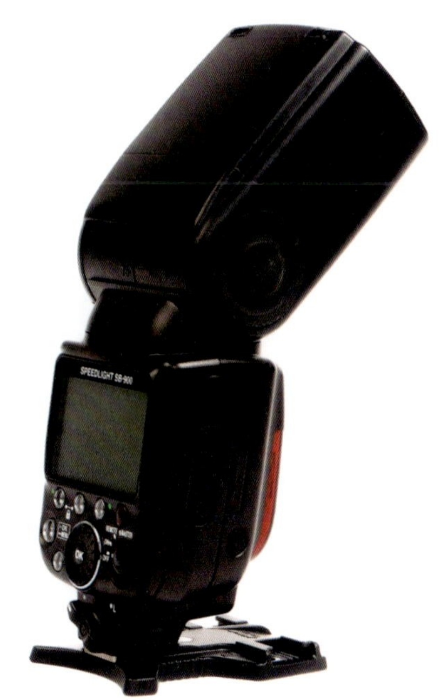

The Nikon SB-900.

Additional strobes will provide increased options in terms of lighting arrangements . . .

that you consider using a stand that will not allow whatever it is holding up to fall down. Over-engineer the stand if you must, but err on the side of safety. You absolutely do not want your equipment toppling over onto the client—or you, for that matter.

Advanced Studio Equipment

For those of you who want to be able to handle more complicated photographic studio assignments, additional equipment is necessary. First and foremost, additional strobes will provide increased options of lighting arrangements such as rimming your subject from the left and right. Rimming is lighting the edge of your subject. Having strobes on hand that vary in power from 300 watt/seconds to 1200 watt/seconds coupled to appropriate softboxes or umbrellas will result in dedicated setups from headshots to group or family themes and save you the time of moving equipment around. The number of strobes that you decide on should be a function of your budget and the dynamics of how you plan on using your studio. For example, in my studio I employ a 6-foot octabox with a 1200 watt/second strobe which serves both as a main light source and, when needed, a fill light to reduce or eliminate shadows.

Control over your strobes can become an issue. The time you consume moving from metering your subject to moving to set the strobe power can become tedious. Most of the major manufacturers of strobes offer computer solu-

tions to this problem. Using a computer (PC or Mac), with the brand software, you can control your strobes via wires or wirelessly. Thus, no matter the position of the strobe itself, you simply access your computer, select the strobe you want to set, and input the power level desired. One manufacturer has an app that will do all of this from an iPhone. There is no doubt that investing in this type of technology will save you time in the long run.

There are many sizes and shapes of softboxes. In terms of advancing your studio, consider adding a narrow rectangular box ranging in size from 12x30 inches to 14x50 inches. Such a softbox can be used as a strip light above your subject to produce highlights on the hair or set vertically on the floor and behind your subject at an angle to add rim light. Due to the vertically narrow pattern of light that this softbox produces, it is ideal for creative black & white work. When used as a single illuminator, the larger dimension of this softbox is excellent for creating a sense of mystery and interest.

Tethering your camera by an electronic wire or wirelessly via radio frequency to a computer is another high-tech means of conducting a photo shoot in the studio. Instead of reviewing the photos on your camera's LCD, you do so via a personal computer and display. There are many applications that will allow you to do this, from Adobe Lightroom, to Nikon, and others. This is a very cool way for you and your client to see their portraits in near real-time (it does take a few seconds for the images to arrive at the computer).

➤ For this image, a reflector was used to the left of the model. An on-camera flashgun was used to fill in the shadows, while the reflector illuminated the left side of her face.

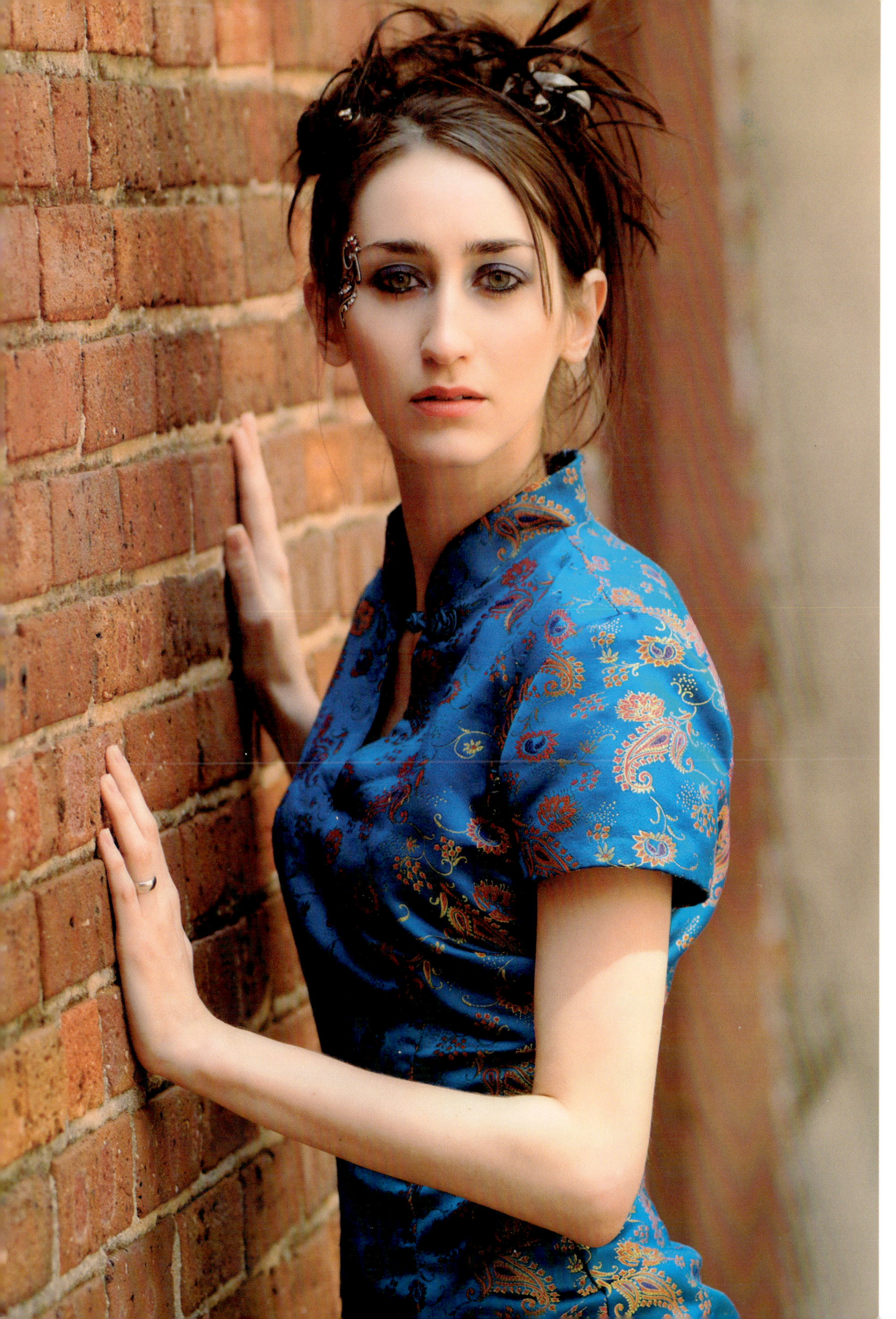

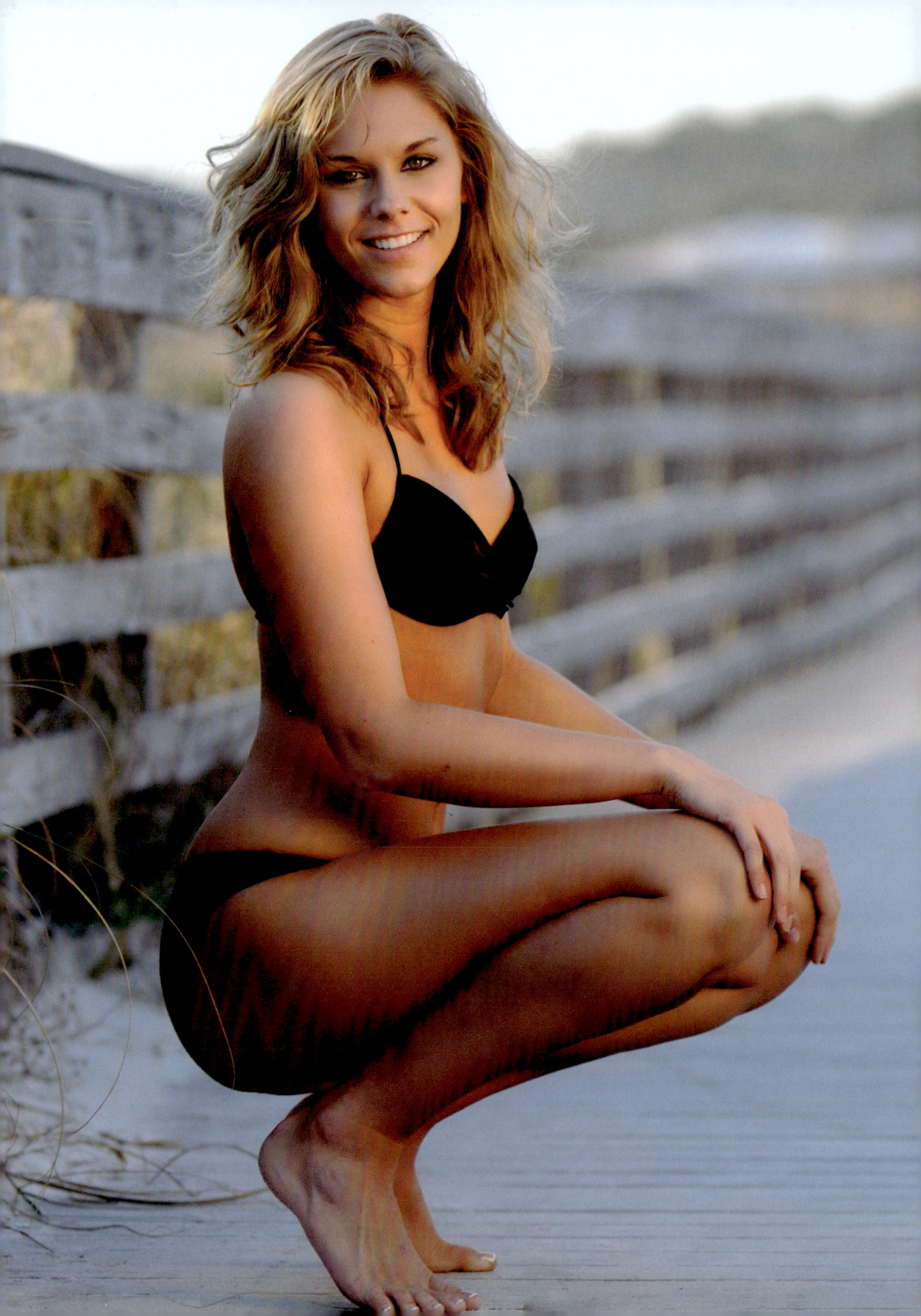

2. Photographing People

Idealize the Subject

The final image of a person should reflect an ideal version of both the physical qualities as well as personality. By ideal, I mean that the image is a superlative—the best-possible rendition of the person; that by a great margin, their appearance in the photograph is much better than it is in everyday life. Although this might seem to be an obvious goal for the portrait photographer, it is one that is often missing. People are not coming to you to get what they quite easily can do with their own camera—a decent image. They are employing you because they believe that you can produce something

Bokeh and a diminishing line combined to create interest in this portrait.

This well-known saxophonist was captured during a concert. Note the rim light provided by the spotlight downstage.

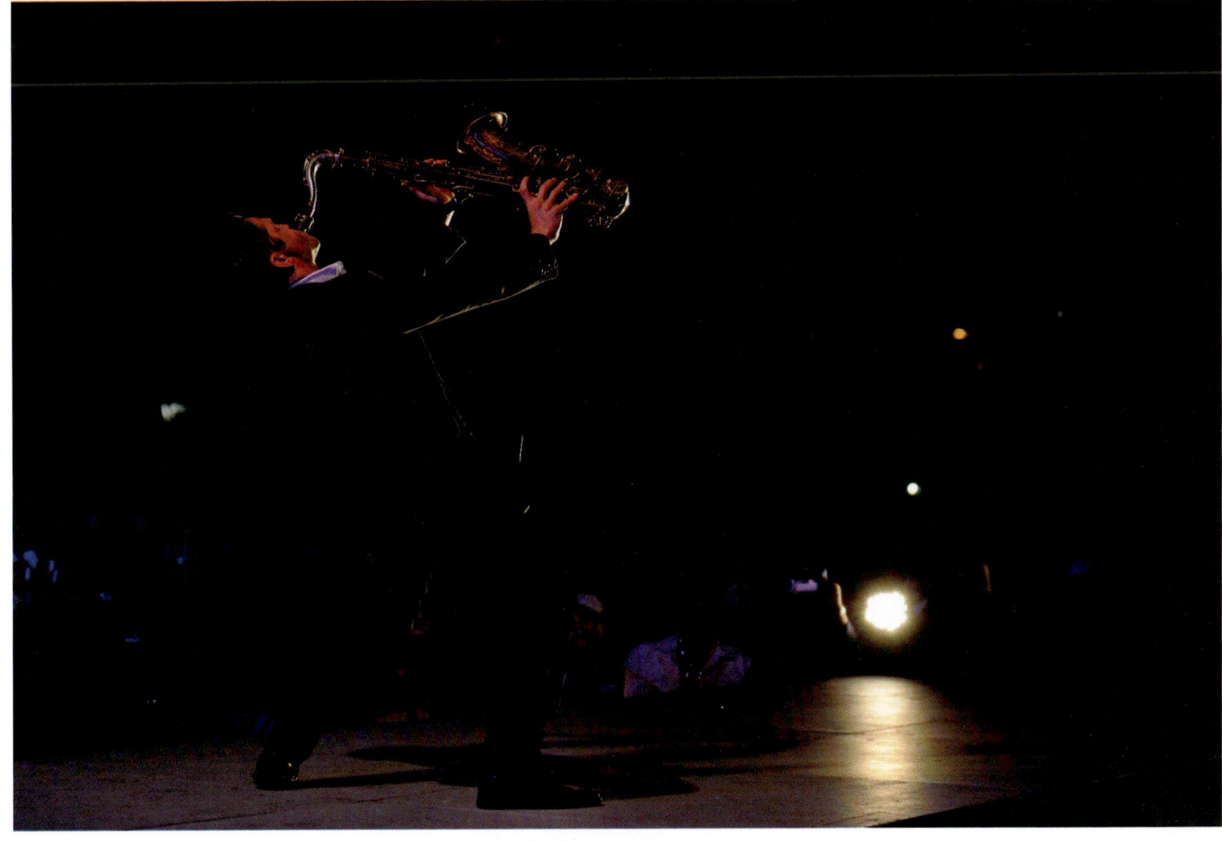

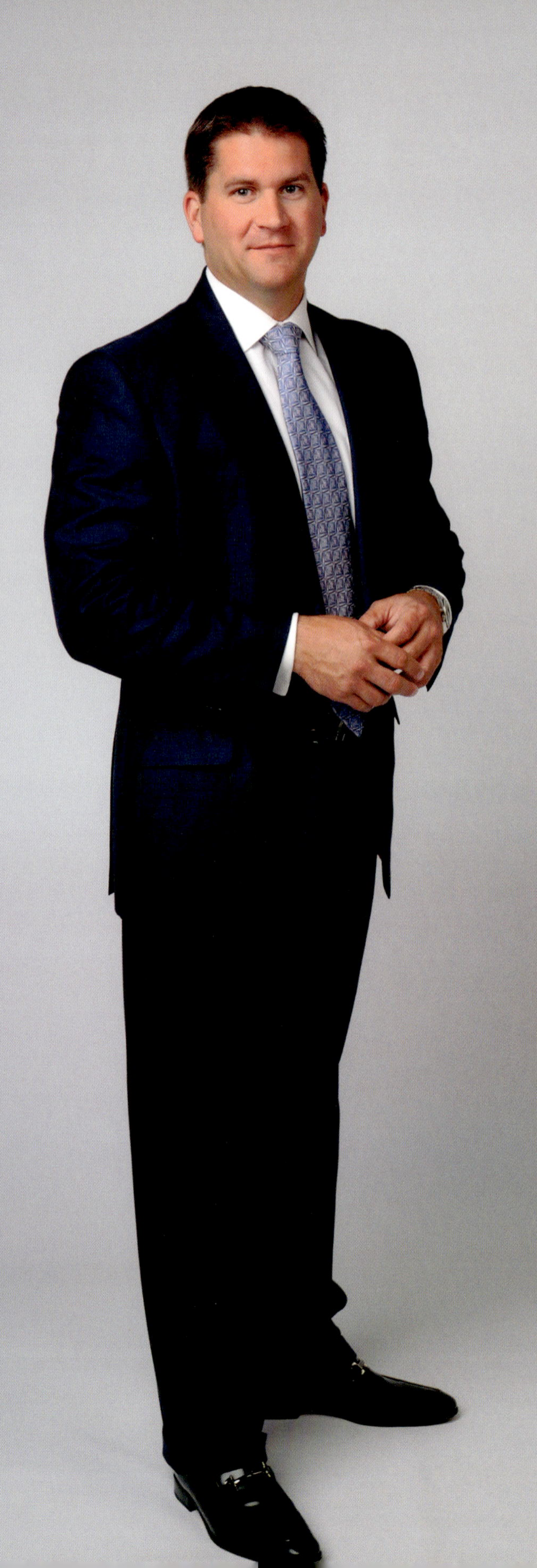

truly unique, outstanding, and that makes them, their loved ones, business partners, or friends look really great. This next section will outline key factors in producing beautiful and involving images of people.

What You "See" Is What You Get

Fundamental to producing a professional result is visualizing the final image in your mind. By visualizing the final image, I mean that you mentally "see" specifically the setting, wardrobe, pose, expression, and lighting as though you were looking at the photograph itself. By virtue of the fact that you are interested in photography, you own a brain that is predisposed to visual processing, imagination, and artistic creativity. So, I'm suggesting that you use it to your advantage. Instead of just pointing the camera and clicking away to see what you get, why not decide first what it is that you want to create, and then work toward that goal? I can attest that you will feel a tremendous sense of gratification when you remove the guesswork and create an image that was thoughtfully planned. The really great portrait photographers do what I've just described inherently, quickly, and with ease. I continually strive to develop and hone this skill.

People will arrive in front of your camera in various combinations of age, gender, body structure, hair color, eye color, and so on. Unless you are working for a high-end fashion magazine, the majority of your work will entail photographing everyday people. Most of the time they will have very little knowledge about posing, coordinating wardrobe, makeup, and

There is a timeless elegance in keeping the pose as straightforward and simple as possible.

setting—nor should they, that is your job. Upon initially meeting the person or persons you are going to photograph, commence with the mental process of taking into account their physical nature. Ask yourself, what are the positive attributes of this person that can and should be emphasized? What is it that should be diminished or even hidden? In the context of indoor or outdoor settings, what selections of wardrobe and makeup will enhance their appearance? How should the person be posed to maximize their physique? Continue this type of evaluation with the seriousness of a physician diagnosing a patient.

Posing: Keep It Simple

There is a timeless elegance in keeping the pose as straightforward and simple as possible. Look to the masters such as Rembrandt or Renoir, and you might agree. After all, their work is not easily forgotten and has stood a great test of time. It is easy to get caught up in whatever the current trend might be, and so be it. But I'm making the suggestion that if you stick to a fundamental approach to posing, you will increase the artistic and emotional depth and quality of your photography. I've broken it down to five categories: women, men, children and families, groups, and glamour/fashion. Some basic rules of thumb can be applied in each case that will serve you to produce images with a lasting quality.

Posing Women. Women are photographed at an angle to the camera. Do this as a matter of habit. As you develop your skill of posing women, you can bring the camera around for an orthogonal perspective, but I do so rarely. The female form is accentuated by creating S shapes. This can be accomplished in all portraiture perspectives: full length, three-quarter, or upper body/head shot (discussed in the glamour/fashion section). The bending of the neck, arms, lower back, and knees (in various combinations) will result in an ethereal, feminine posture which normally results in a "better" portrait.

Think about it, the opposite of what I am suggesting would be to stand straight and tall, facing the camera; that doesn't work. The head should be tilted slightly forward or back, and not straight up and down. Combined, your perspective and her pose should take into account that the end of the nose does not break the line formed by the cheek. With older women, slightly lifting the chin provides a more flattering, younger appearance. The shoulders should be lowered without tension, with the shoulder closer to the camera slightly lower than the other. Whether the subject is standing or sitting, the arms and legs should never be straight but should have natural bends. The legs specifically should be "scissored" so that the feet are offset. The hands should bend naturally at the wrist, with fingers in a natural position (no fists or a claw-like presentation). When it makes sense, the hands can come together with palms facing, one placed on top of the other, and sometimes the fingers can be interlinked. I usually ask the subject to sit up as much as possible; at the moment it might feel slightly unnatural, but it improves the look of the final photograph. It is a good idea to avoid extreme angles of the head and eyes. In the case of the head, do not have the woman turn her head to the point that her chin is approaching her shoulder; similarly, do not have her turn her eyes so that she is looking out of the corner of her eye socket. Both of these mistakes will ruin what might otherwise be a great image. If one eye appears larger than the other, pose the subject so that his or her smaller eye is closer to the lens. The majority of the time, the subject should smile. If the portrait is to be used professionally (e.g., a senator, doctor, military member), forgo the smile.

Posing Men. Men can be photographed either straight-on or at an angle—it is your choice. However, with the

male form, we are not interested in forming an S shape. Whether casual, or formal, when photographing a man, the pose should accentuate strength, confidence, happiness—that the guy in the photograph is a winner, someone you would like. The man's head should be turned to look straight into the camera regardless of photographing from an angle or straight-on; doing so will result in achieving a masculine and

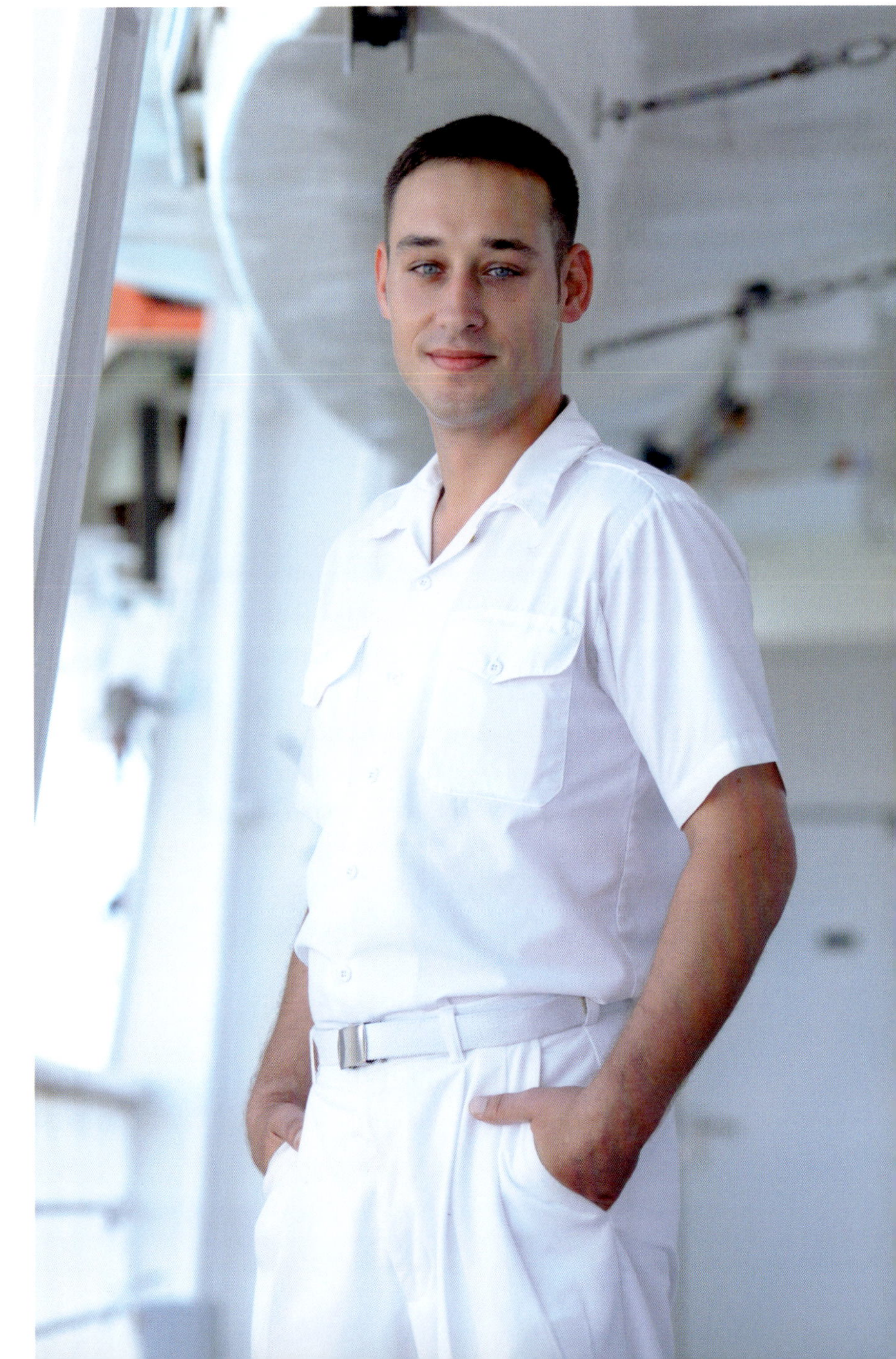

▶ The soft sunlight found on the shadow side of his ship provided excellent results for this handsome merchant mariner.

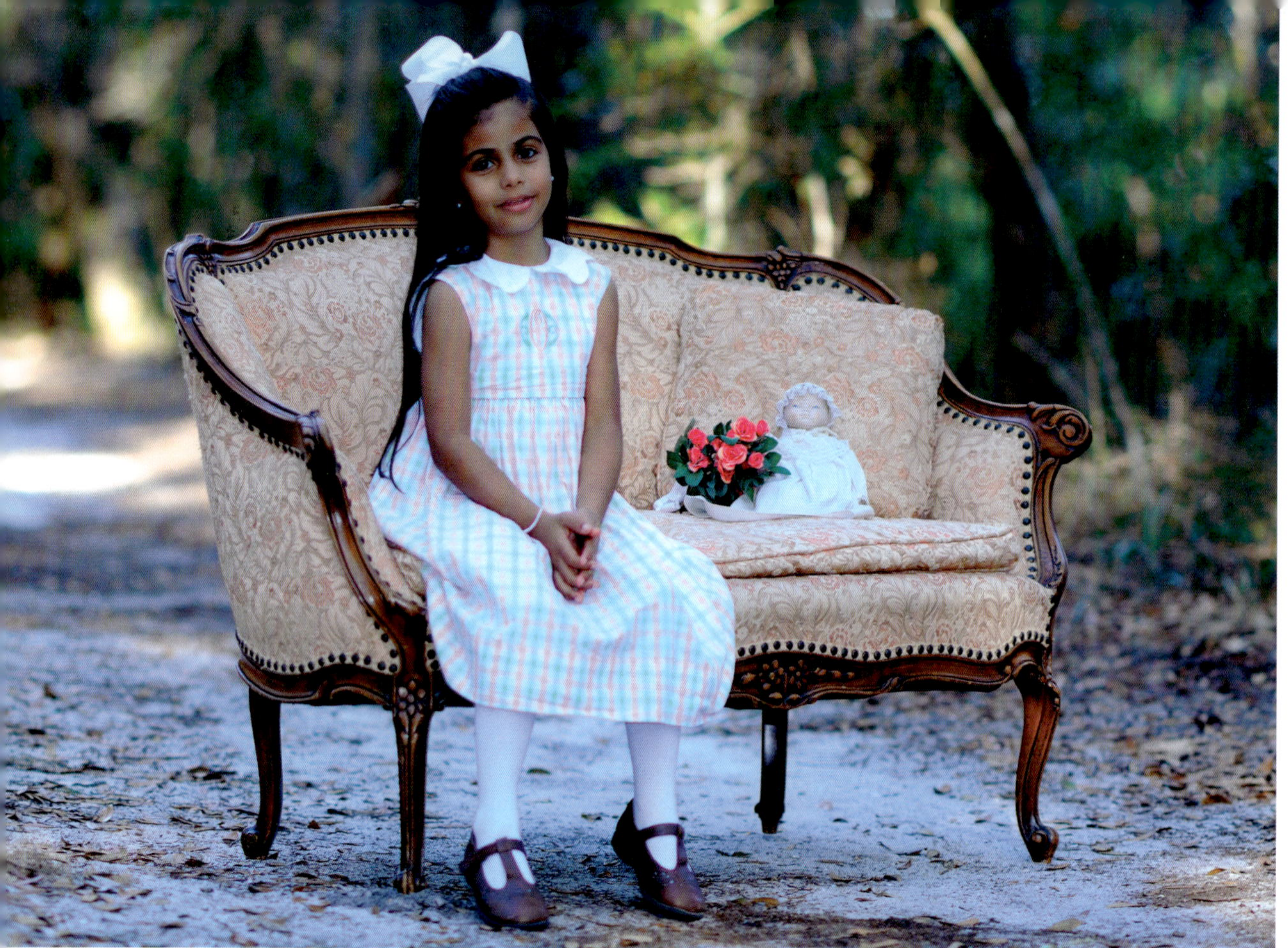

confident look. One hand in a pocket, or arms folded, or hands clasped together will work in almost every pose whether seated or standing. The shoulders should be blocked so that they are even with one another; if the perspective is at an angle, the shoulder closer to the camera should be slightly lowered. Whether sitting or standing, the individual should project confidence by sitting up or standing straight and tall. Generally, I do not tilt a man's head unless he is being posed with a female such as his spouse—personally, I just don't like that look. Again, I will argue that a smile should not be wasted. Get your gent to smile—even a slight grin will often take the image up a notch.

Posing Children and Families. My wife and I raised three boys, and throughout those years,

With an extraordinary shallow depth of field and soft afternoon sunlight, this portrait captured her personality.

This beautiful family is captured on a Florida beach as the sun is just above the horizon (camera right). The horizon was intentionally blurred to minimize the effect of "cutting" the subjects.

I took thousands of photographs of the "three amigos." What I learned from photographing my own children is this: when photographing kids, you are rarely if ever in charge! Most of the time, kids are aware that photography is taking place, but their attention span is much shorter than that of an adult, and in most cases, they care only so much about what is going on. So, you must be prepared and ready to get that terrific image (for Mom and Dad) very early on in the photo session—and I do mean early.

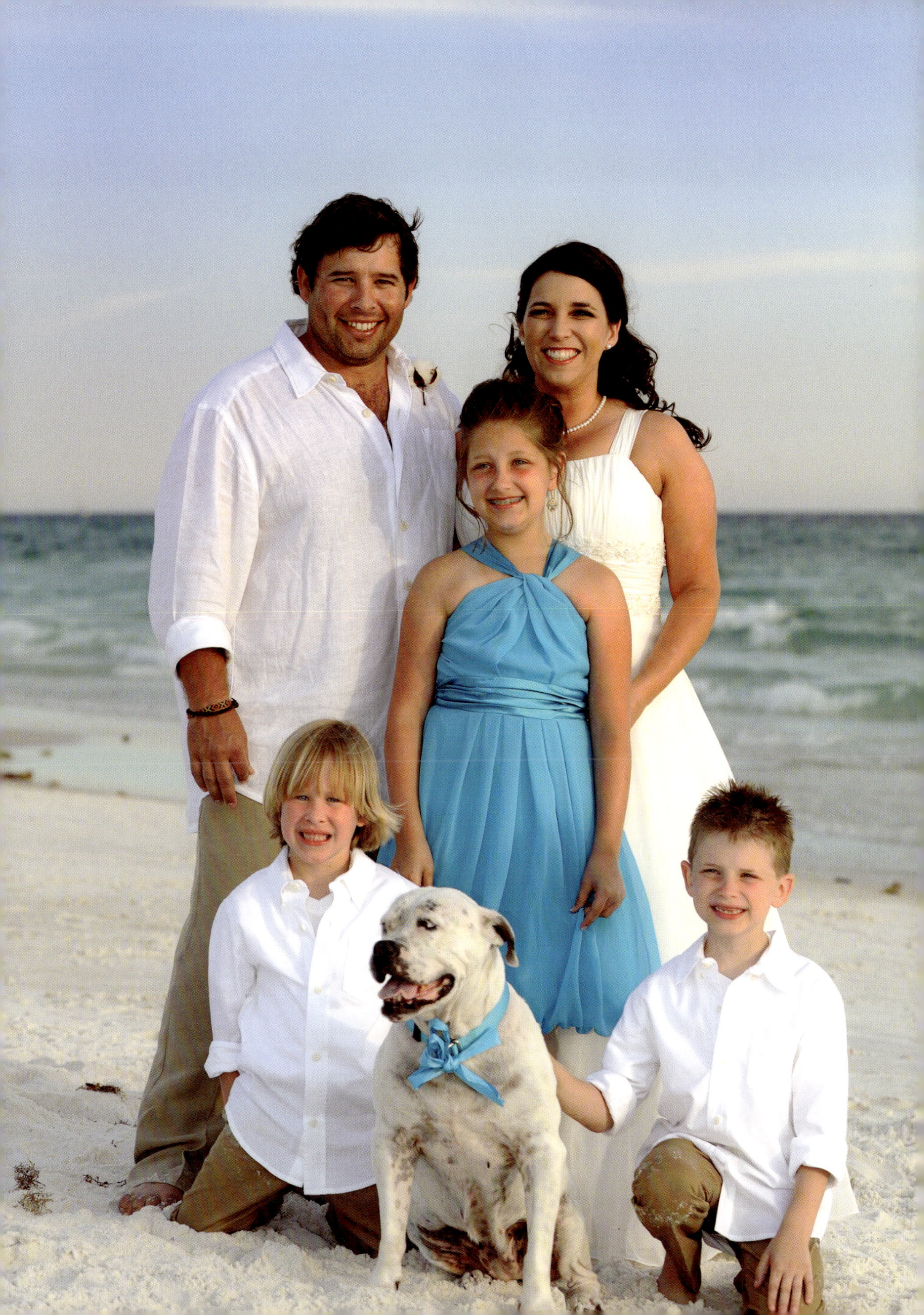

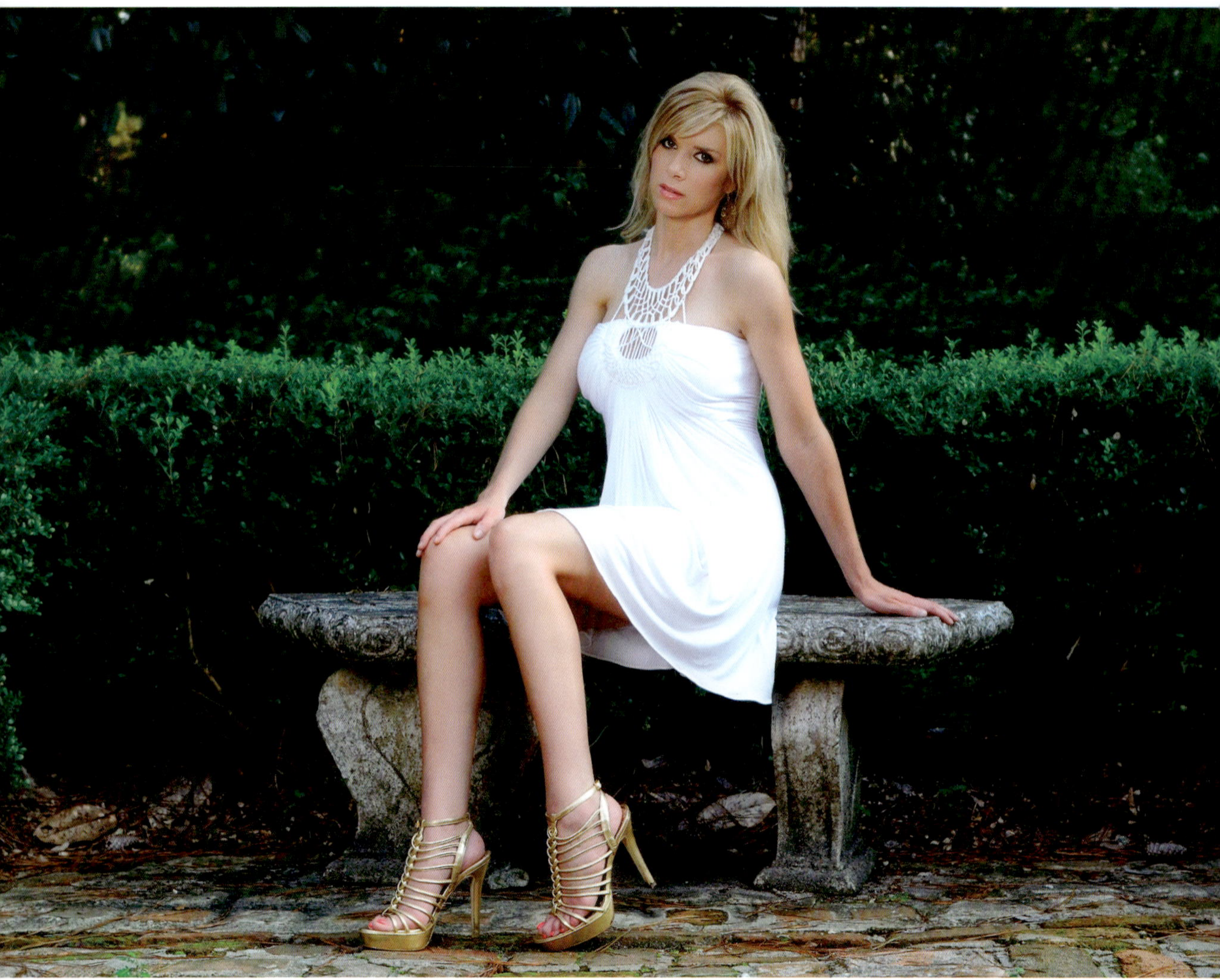

Posing a child is straightforward: whether sitting or standing, allow the child to do their own thing. Yes. Let them jump, sit, move around, even clamor. Crank up your "patience meter" and take a few more frames than you normally would. Children will surprise you with a smile, a laugh, an endearing look to one of their parents—so capture that moment.

With families, the pose should resemble a triangle. This is easier to achieve when there is an odd number of people in your frame. But as a general rule of thumb, anchor the image with adults, surrounded by the children. There are hundreds of combinations of parents kneeling or standing with children flanking or standing just behind.

Have all members dressed in monochromatic or patterned attire, but try not to mix the two; otherwise, those wearing the patterned clothes will get all of the attention in the image. Create

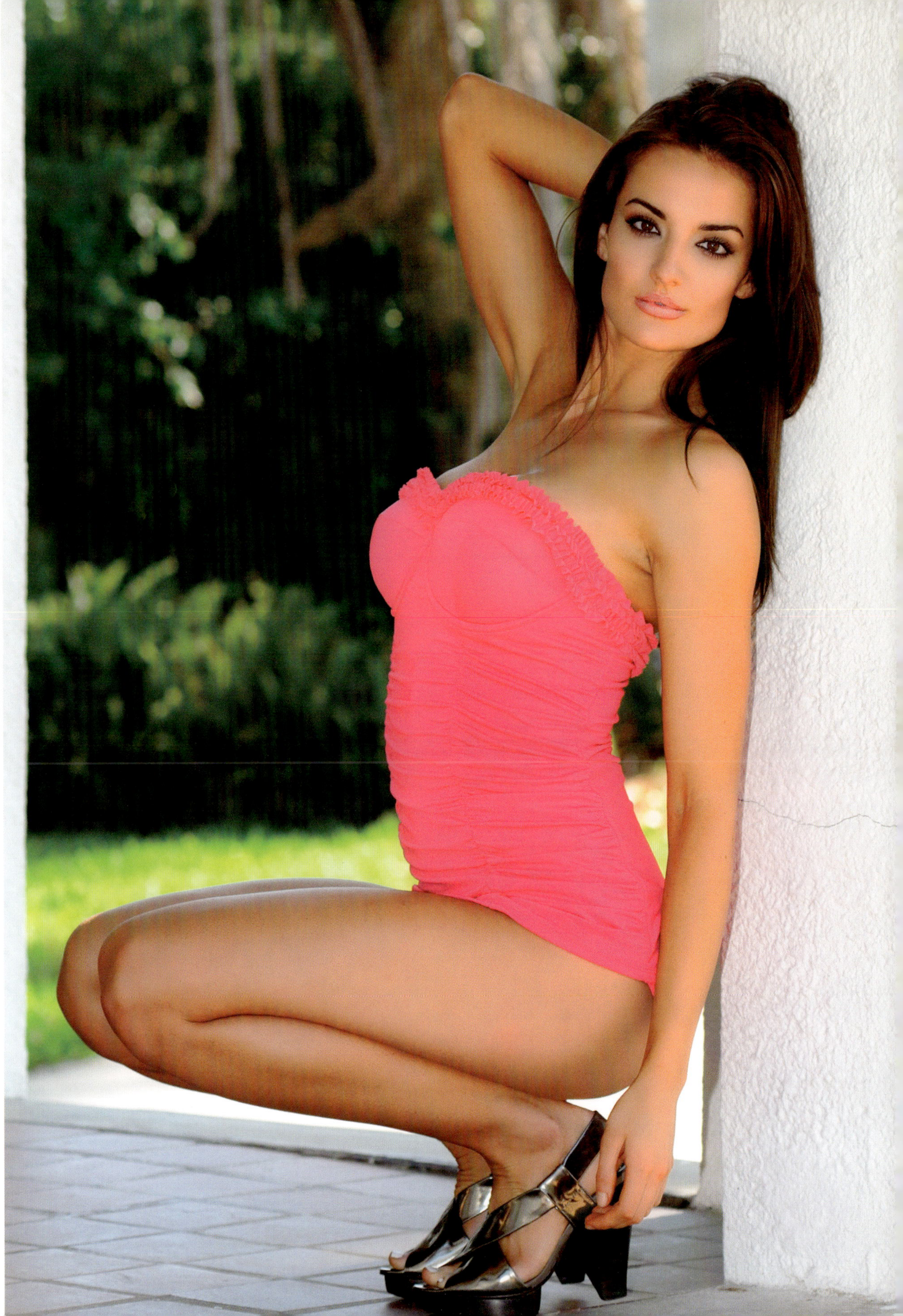

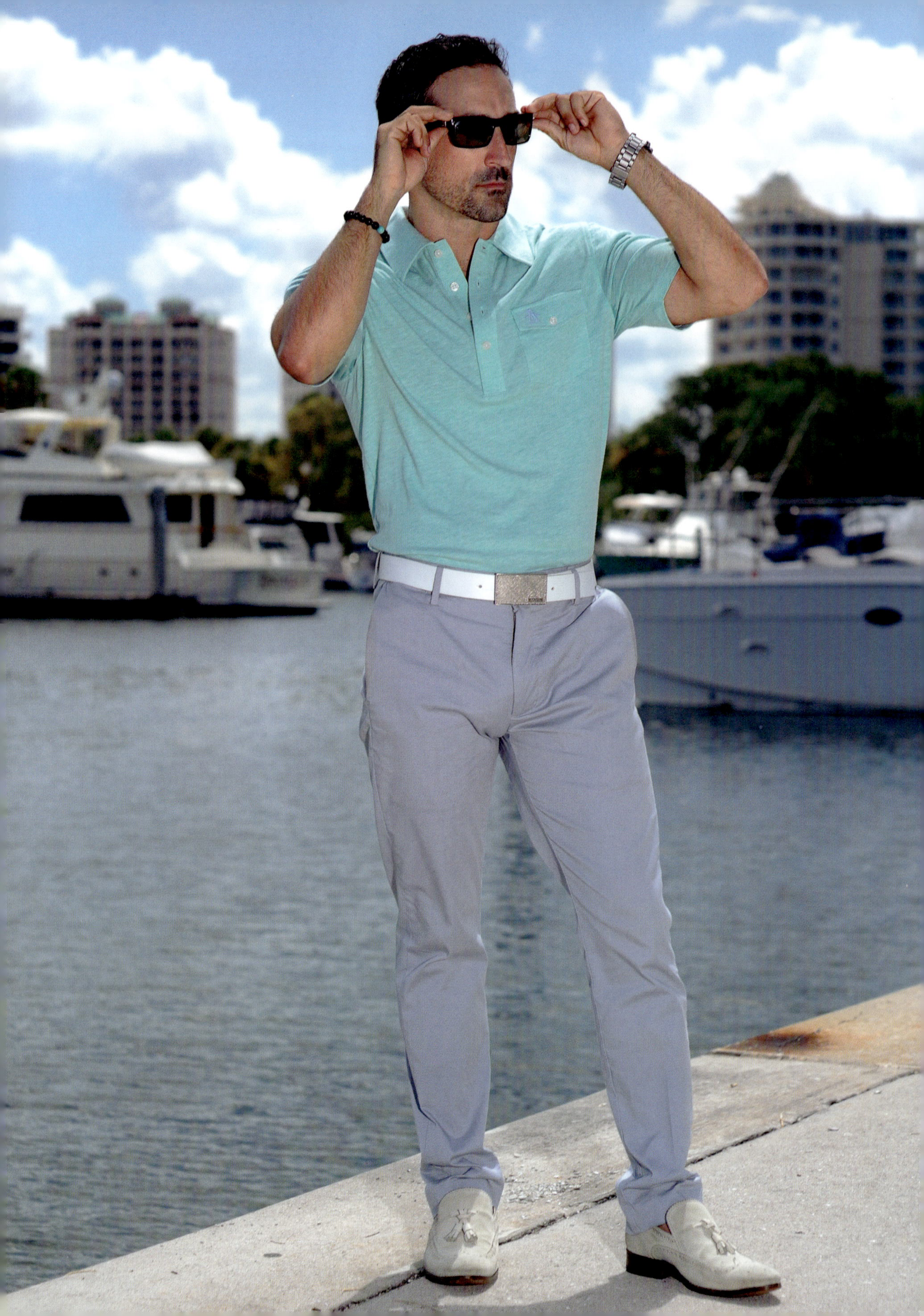

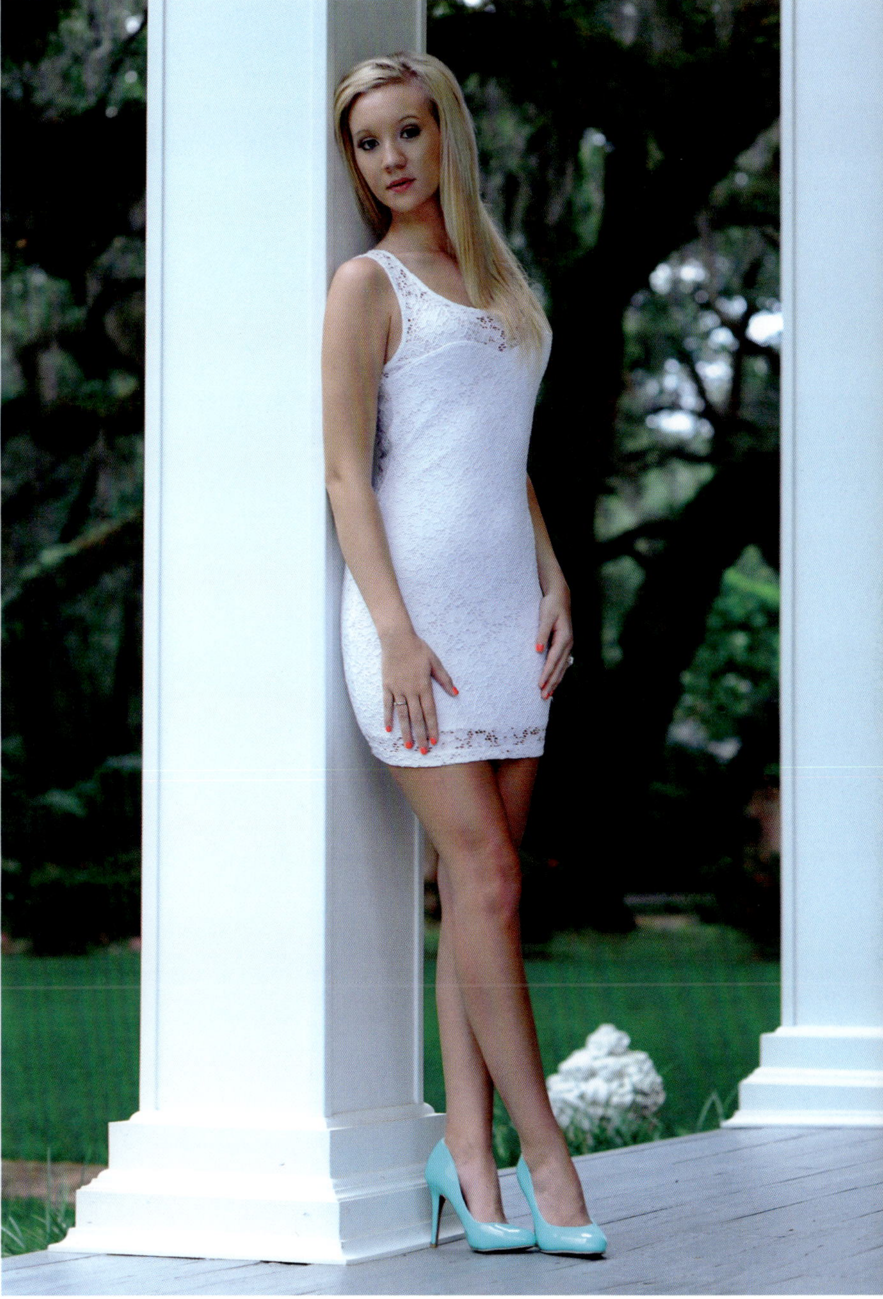

a cohesive look between the parents and their children. This comes with experience.

Glamour and Fashion

Depending on who you talk to, glamour photography has a wide range of meanings in contemporary media. So right up front, I want to define glamour photography as it pertains to my business and my approach: glamour photography involves the intentional accentuation and exaggeration of the physical beauty and emotional state of a person, regardless of gender. Glamour photography does not involve nudity; nude photography is its own category. Glamour photography is absolutely and only about the person in the image. Some might disagree with me, and that's okay. But if you draw the line on glamour as I have, you can provide the public and commercial sector with a worthwhile service that continues to be in high demand.

When posing a person for a glamour image, there are three basic perspectives that one should understand: full length, three-quar-

ters, and upper body/headshot. Full length is just that, a head-to-toe image of a person; three-quarters is just above the knee, while upper body/headshot ranges from the waist to just below the bust/chest line. Recall the fundamentals of posing a female or male and combine

There is a timeless elegance in keeping the pose as straightforward and simple as possible.

them with these three perspectives. In a glamour image, the person being photographed is always looking straight into the lens.

Fashion photography is far less about the person in the image and more about the clothing, shoes, or jewelry with which they are adorned. The subject being photographed will almost always look away from the lens, indicating indifference. This increases the focus of attention on the adornment(s) and away from the person.

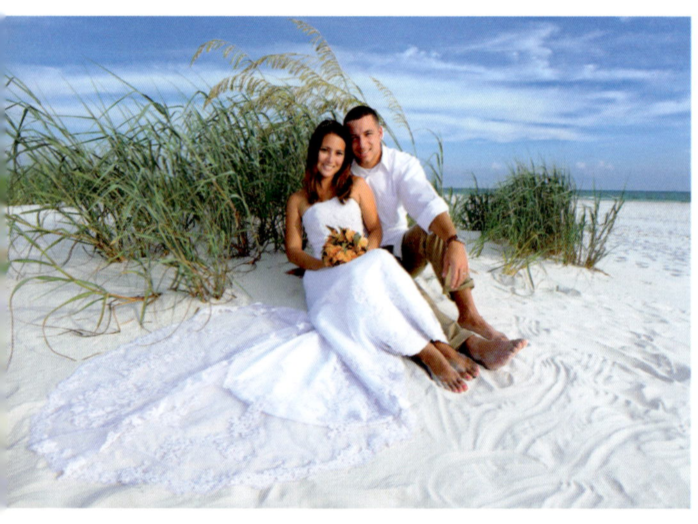

◄ With the setting sun low on the horizon, its light was soft enough to serve as the main light source. Fill light was added with an on-camera flashgun.

▼ The diagonal lines in the background and the pose of the subjects add a nice, dynamic feel to this portrait of a bride and her young brother.

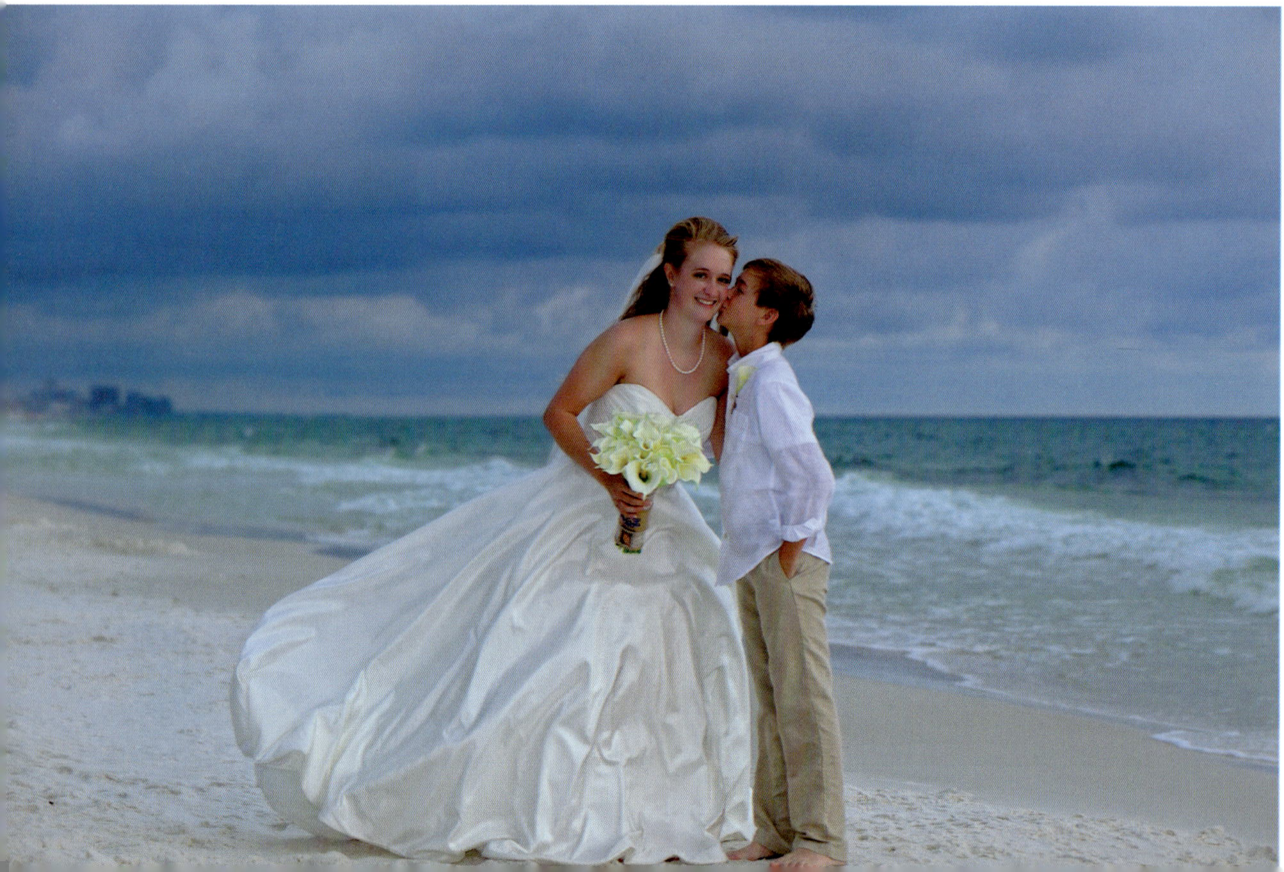

3. A Simple Process

You just might be thinking, "Bill, if you reduce portrait photography to a process, you are taking the creativity, art, inspiration, and fun out of the equation." My response is that by applying a simple process, the exact opposite happens: the creativity, art, and the inspiration actually increase!

Most of us would agree that photography is a combination of technical and artistic components that come together as a documented

Here is an example of a portrait involving excellent bokeh and high contrast background which results in three-dimensionality and "pop."

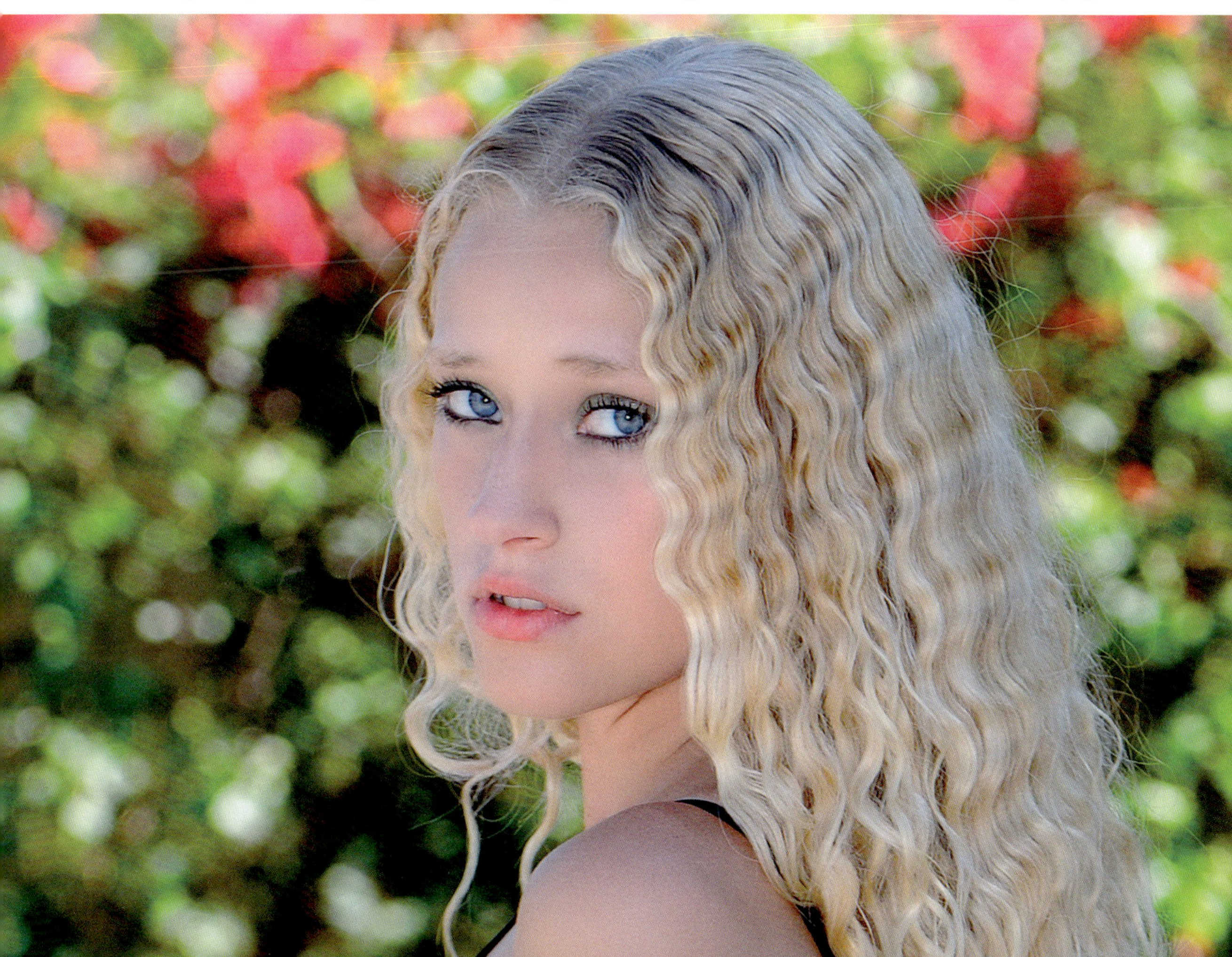

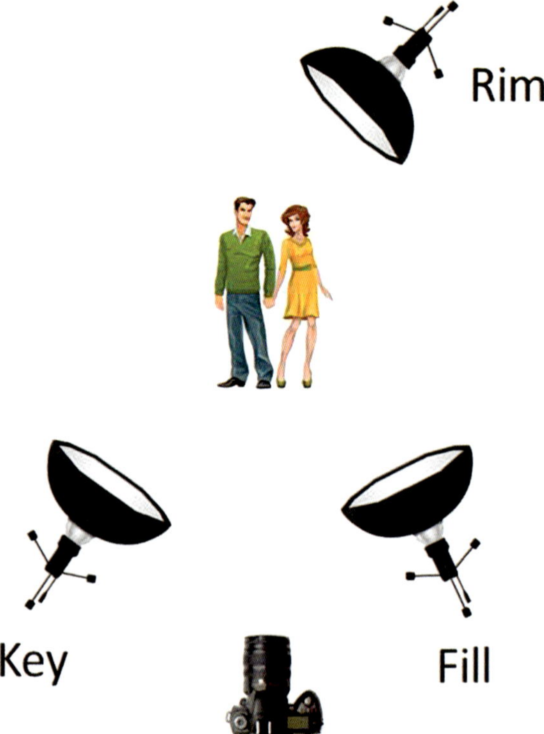

image. On the technical side, photography involves: optics, mechanisms like shutters and apertures, photons (light), proper focus and exposure of those photons to a sensor or film, computers, and the printing or virtual representation of the final image, and more. Artistically, photography involves the human condition, emotions and feelings, composition, beauty, attitude, and various statements of expression. The technical side of photography can be taught, repeated, and mastered because it is based on physics, while the artistic side is a continuous domain of the imagination and freedom of expression. I wouldn't dare to attempt to teach art principally because I am not an artist and therefore not qualified; to me, art is very personal and subjective. But, if you master the technical aspects of photography to the point where executing the creation of a photograph becomes inherent and in some ways even

subconscious, then you have more time and mental energy available to devote to the artistic side. The simple process that we are going to discuss in this chapter is designed to increase your ability to produce high-quality images quickly and with relative ease. The problem of creating a photograph is reduced to six logical steps. Once the six steps are complete, nothing remains but to take as many excellent photographs as you wish.

Since the following terms will be used throughout the rest of the book, some definitions are in order. Bear in mind that the three types of light sources—the key (also called the "main" light), fill, and rim lights are common to the studio, outdoors, and indoor locations.

Key Light

The key light is the primary illuminator and places light on the face, torso, or entire body of your subject (depending on the composition). In most cases, the person being photographed will be facing or looking into the key light. Examples of key lights are a strobe, strobe with softbox or umbrella, the sun, and in rare cases, an on-board flash that is bounced off of a surface such as a ceiling. It is easy to think of the key light when referencing a studio environment. However, the key light is equally important outdoors and in non-studio indoor locations.

Fill Light

The fill light is used to reduce contrast and thus eliminates shadows. Used properly, the fill light has a softening effect that smooths the appearance of the skin and generally improves the quality of the photograph. Examples of fill lights are strobes, strobes in softboxes, on-board flash, and reflectors. You may be thinking, "Wait a second Bill, the examples that you give for the fill light are practically the same as the key light?" Yes, that is correct, and we'll soon discuss the inter-changeability of these sources, depending on the type and quality of light.

Rim Light

The rim light is a source of light that is usually higher in luminosity than the key and certainly the fill. The rim light or "kicker" as it is some-times called, places a high-contrast rim of light on at least one edge of the body of your subject. The rim light is highly directional and is situated to some angle behind and aimed at the person being photographed. Rim lighting is not an ab-solute must, but when used properly, it provides a nice three-dimensional effect by separating the person from the background. Examples of rim lights are strobe, strobe and softbox, the sun, and remote flash.

If you start with poor light, you put yourself at a disadvantage with little chance of producing a beautiful result.

The following process is common to pro-ducing portrait photography no matter where you happen to be creating the image. Whether you are in a fully equipped studio or on a sunny beach, this process works equally well. The rules of good portraiture remain the same regardless of the setting. My hope is that after a period of time using this simple approach, it becomes sec-ond nature to you; at that point, only a fraction of your mental energy will be dedicated to "set-ting up the shot," and an abundance of your energy will be driven toward creative spontaneity!

Step 1: Carefully Evaluate Light Sources

As most of us go through our daily lives, we are not particularly aware of the light that sur-rounds us. Whether it is bright sunshine, office light, or the twilight hour, we do not have a

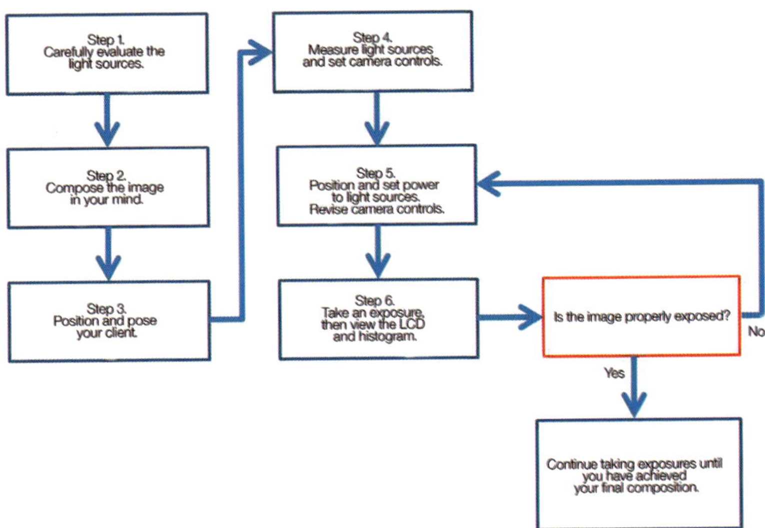

➤ This diagram depicts the six steps to successful portraiture.

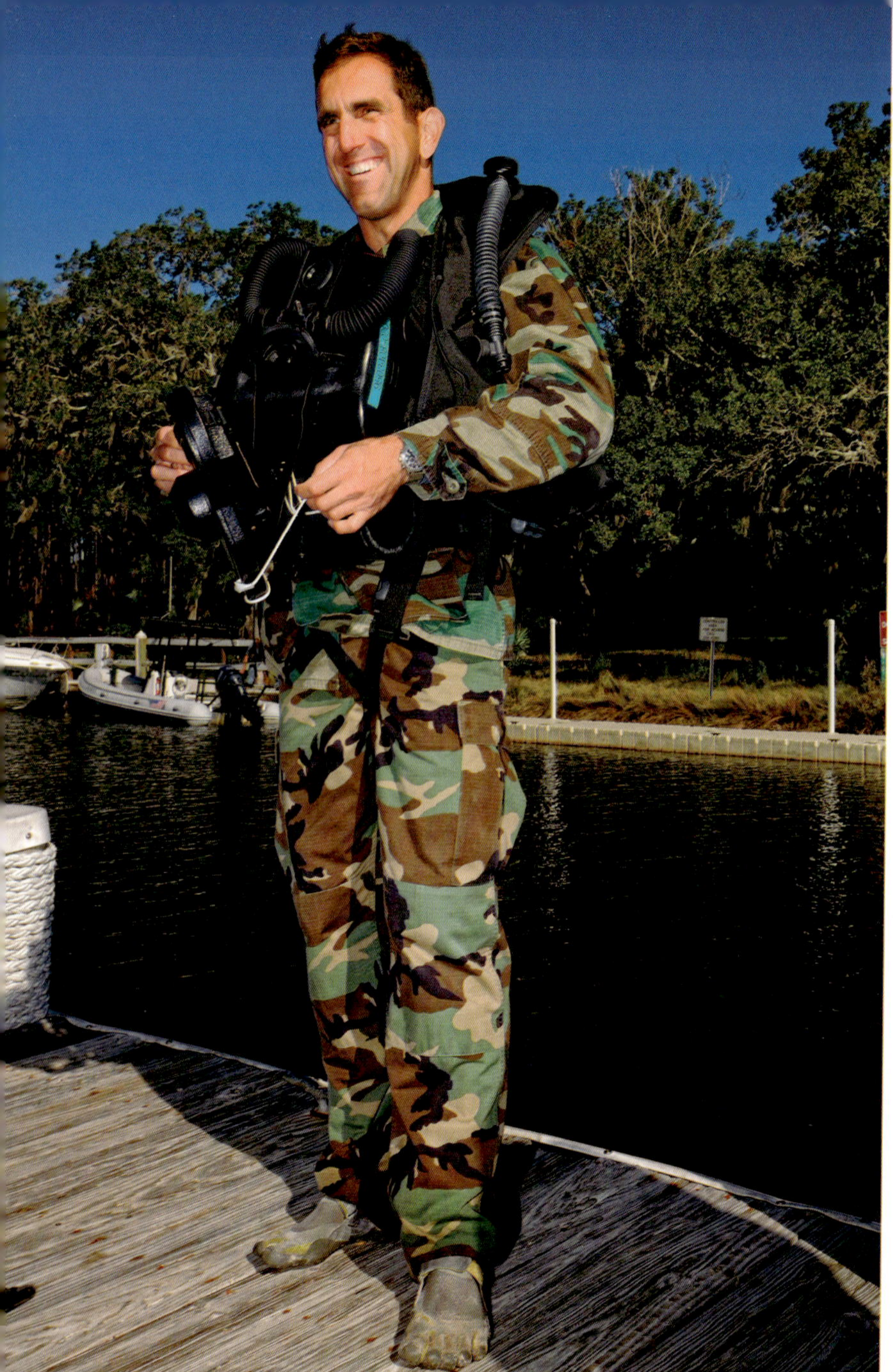

result. The evaluation of light involves both the selection of a primary light source and the analysis (or feedback) of how the light is affecting the look of your subject. By primary light source, I'm talking about your key (main) light. There are other light sources such as the fill, and we'll get to that. The key light comes in many forms, such as a softbox, the sun, or a flashgun mounted on your camera bounced off of the ceiling. It does not matter if you are working in a studio, your living room, or the great outdoors; this first step holds true.

Analysis. Analyzing the light source is in large part making a decision to discriminate against poor light and utilize the good light that you have available. What constitutes good light? It is soft or flat light that helps people to look their best in a photograph. I generally agree with this assertion. However, what constitutes good light has a lot to do with the objective of the final image. Thus, good light can be the hard,

reason to analyze the light conditions in which we find ourselves. However, as a photographer, you must evaluate light in order to produce professional results; if you start with poor light, you put yourself at a great disadvantage with very little chance of producing a beautiful

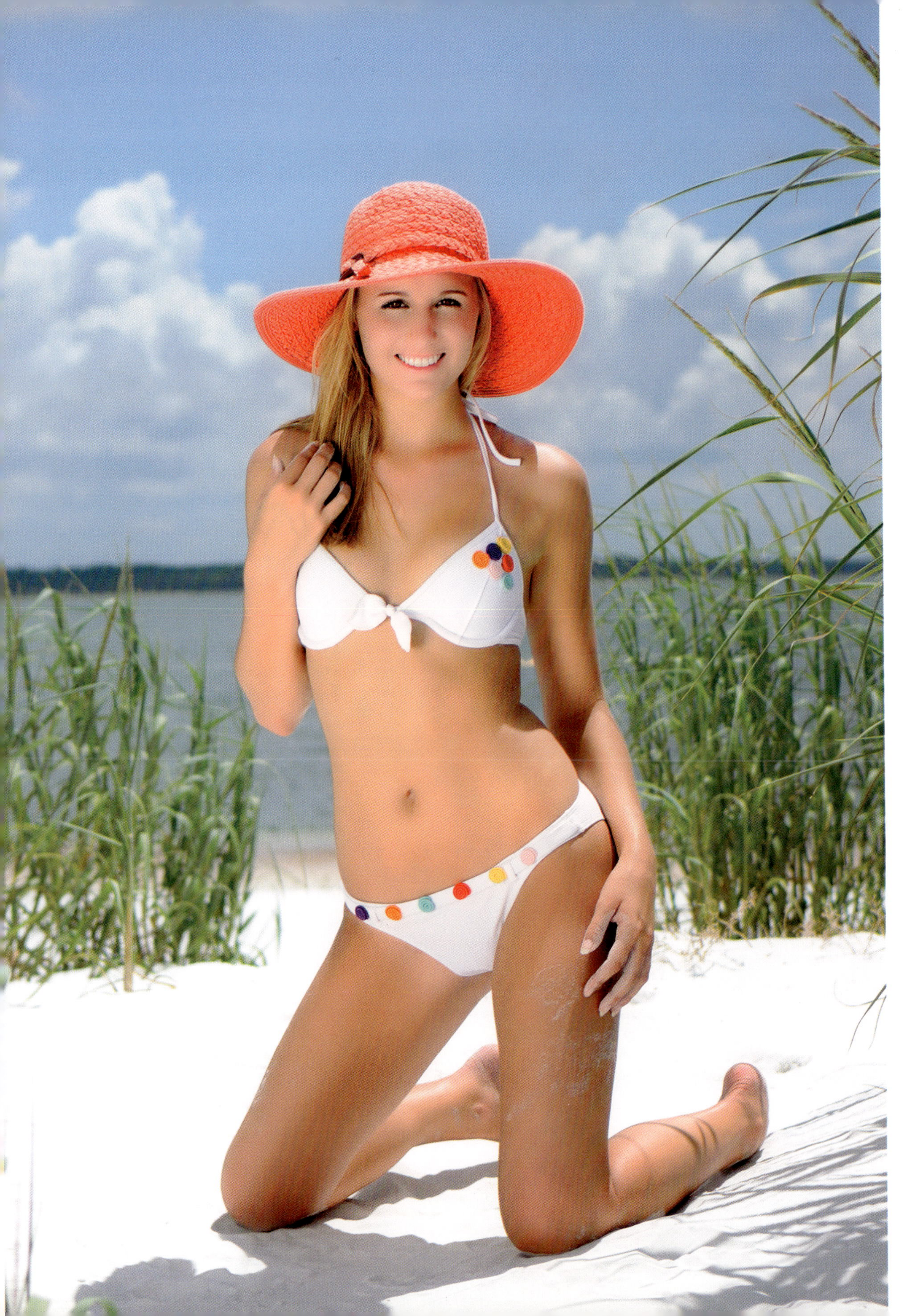

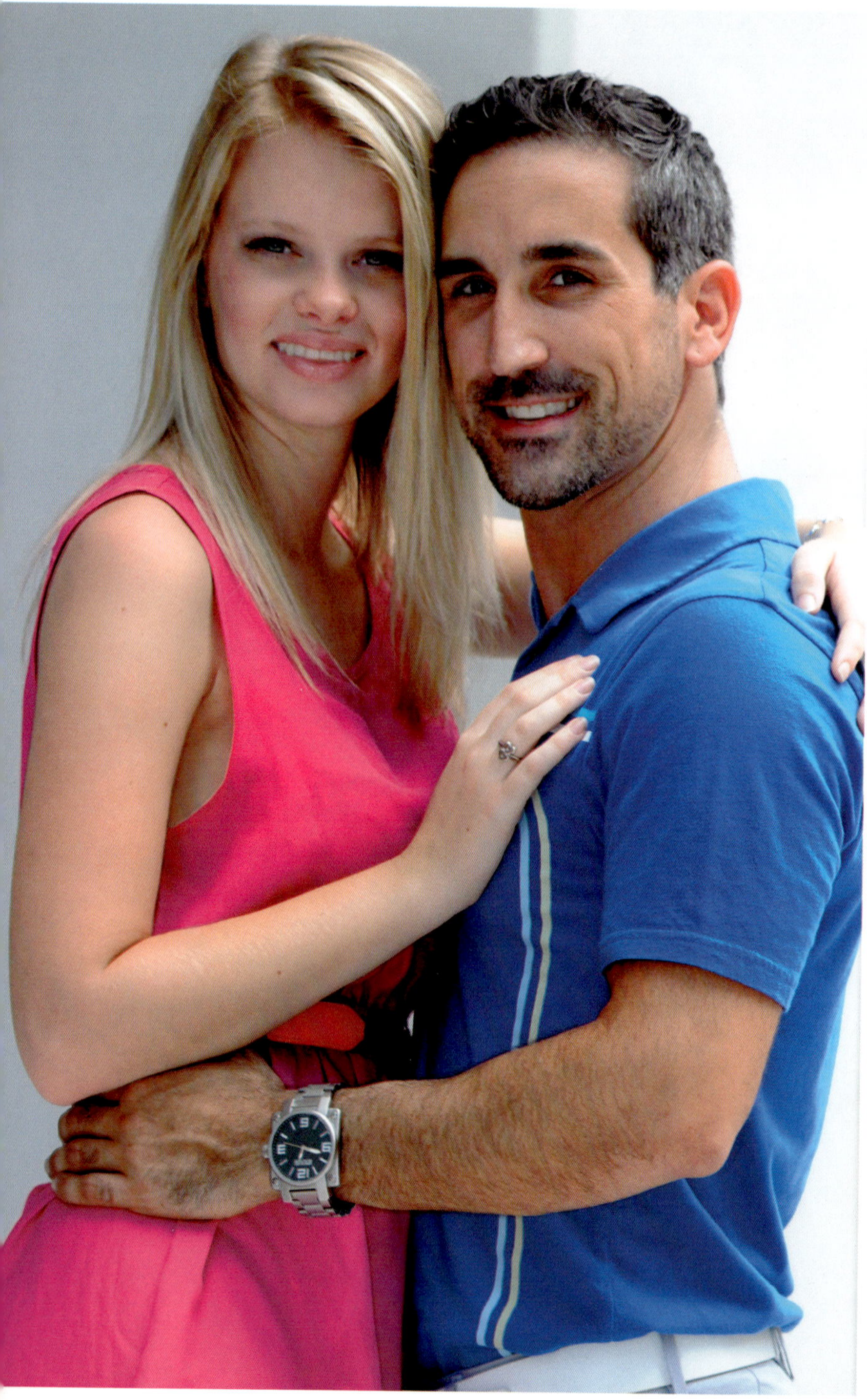

sense as the photographer. Contrast is the difference between the bright and the dark portions of a scene; for portrait photographers, it is the difference between the highlight (illuminated) and shadow (nonilluminated or less illuminated) sides of the human face and body. Does good light exist somewhere between high contrast and low contrast? Yes. However, by making the conscious decision to distinguish between high- and low-contrast light, we are being deliberate and avoiding the guessing game.

With practice, you will develop a manner in which you will analyze, evaluate, and make judgments about the way in which a light source is interacting with the person being photographed. Sometimes, waiting for the sun to drop in the sky increases the quality of the light (softer, warmer), and even then, it may be necessary to move the subject when pos-

specular, high-contrast light from the sun or the soft, low-contrast wraparound light from a softbox—it depends on your goal and creative

ing to get the light to illuminate their face in an optimum manner. When in the studio, you will start to move softboxes and umbrellas at

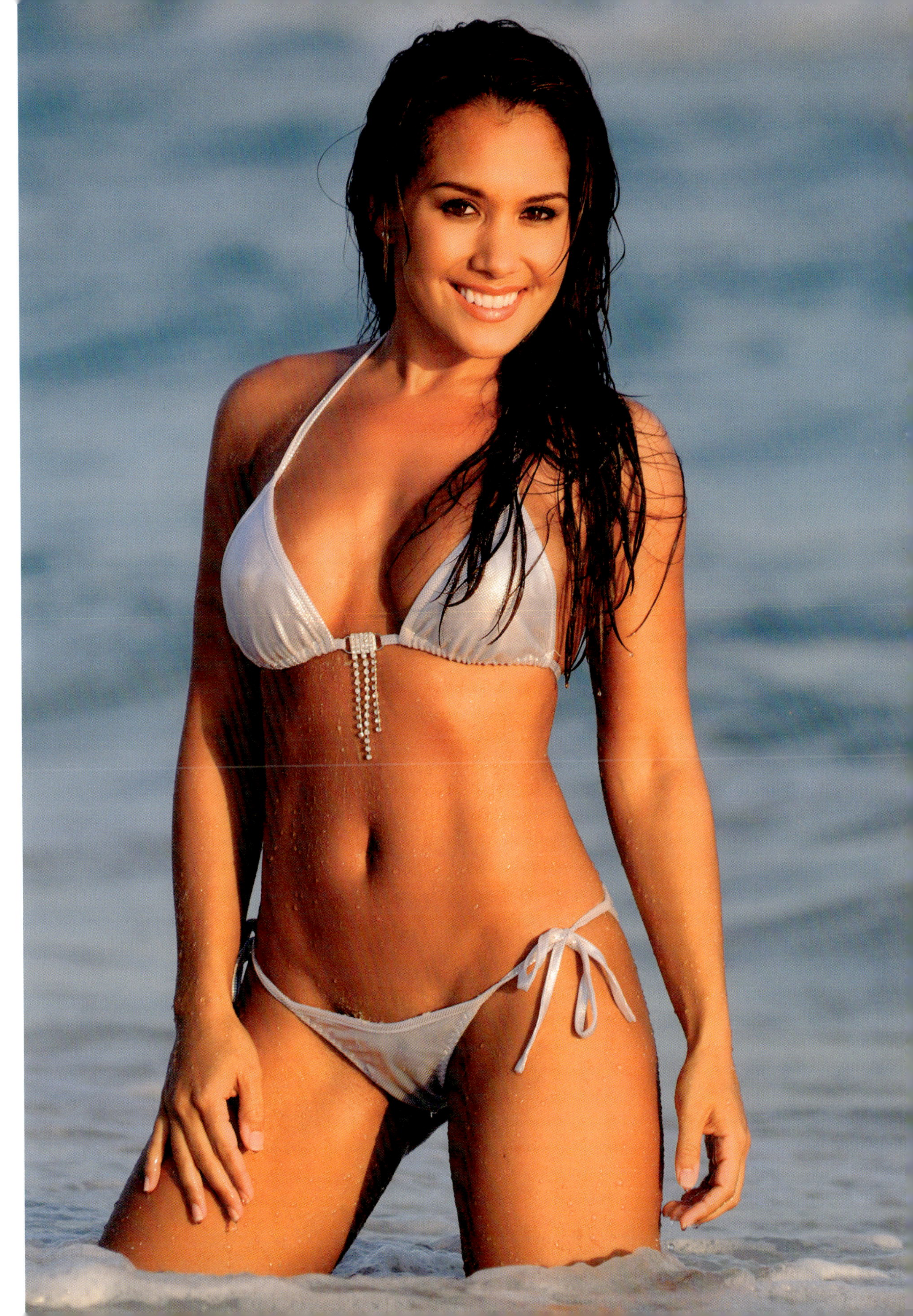

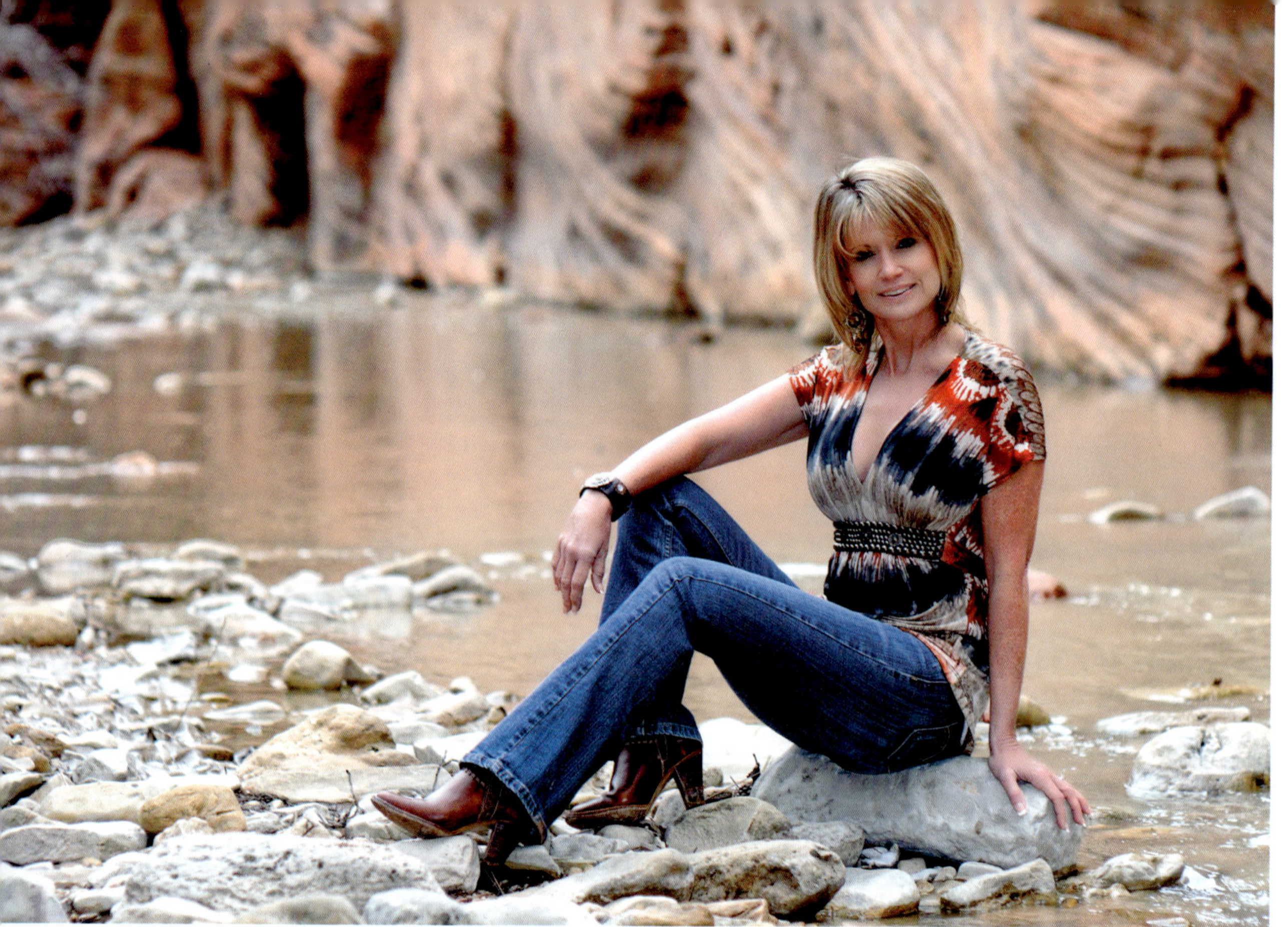

angles to the face of the subject ("feathering" the light) because you will see the difference that incremental adjustments can make to the quality of the image.

Selection. As portrait photographers, we concentrate on how a given light source is illuminating the person being photographed. It is the relationship between the light and the skin, eyes, hair, and clothes that we are concerned about. Again, it does not matter whether we are using a strobe in the studio or the sun in the outdoors, the goal is the same—to ensure the best-possible use of light on the subject.

Good light has a quality of being *evenly* distributed across the person being photo-graphed—especially the face and exposed skin. The result of even light is consistent, stable contrast of your subject; the skin tone will look consistent, and the photograph will be pleasing to the eye. Examples of light sources that offer even light are a properly positioned 24x36-inch softbox, the sunlight on a cloudy day, the shade that appears from a large overhanging roof or truss on a building, and the sunlight that comes through a skylight in a building.

If the light source is not even, then the problem arises of having both dark and bright areas on the subject which degrades the quality of the photograph. Examples of uneven light are the sunlight light that penetrates branches of a tree, light that bounces off of interior and exterior walls of a building, and improperly positioned strobes, softboxes, or umbrellas either singularly or as a grouping. The result of uneven light is inconsistent contrast on the skin, hair, and clothing.

Although it is not the final word, the chart below serves to categorize optional light sources. By cross referencing the photographic domain with the intended look of the final image (high or low contrast) an appropriate choice of light source is made; it represents a starting point.

The image on the right illustrates my point. The analysis and selection of the sunlight at midday rendered a beautiful image of this young couple. In this instance, the midday sun in the cloudless sky served as the key light. The contrast was high, the light perfectly even. The result is an image with an abundance of density that flatters the couple.

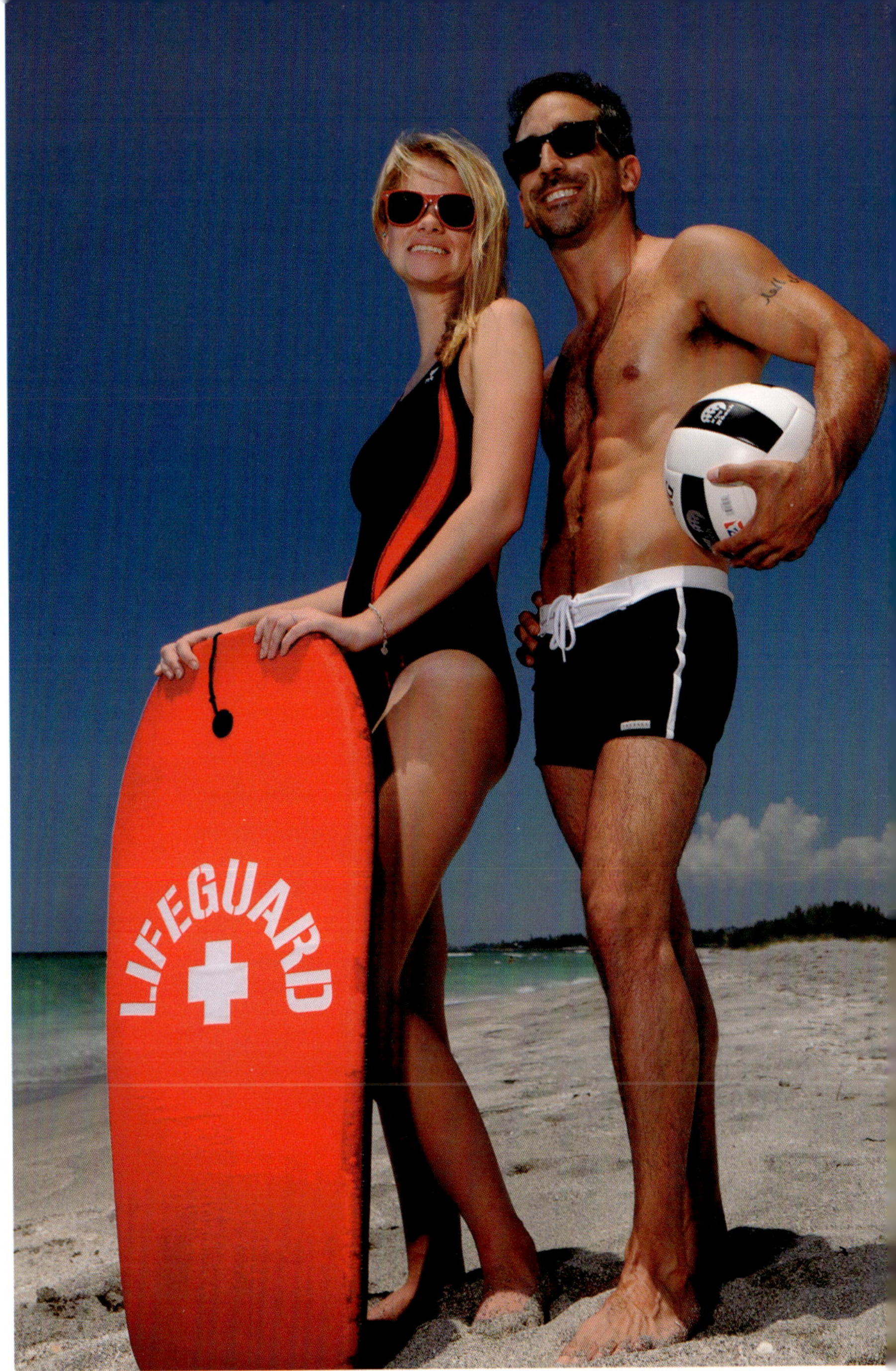

➤ (top) Taken at the brightest time of day, this is an example of a high-contrast portrait.

➤ (bottom) A simple cross-reference for selecting a light source appropriate to your domain and intended theme and look of the final image.

	High Contrast	Low Contrast
Studio	Bare Strobe Strobe + Softbox - Front Panel	Strobe + Softbox Strobe + Umbrella Strobe + Scrim
Indoor	Bare Strobe Strobe + Softbox - Front Panel Flash Gun	Strobe + Softbox Strobe + Umbrella Strobe + Scrim Strobe + White Ceiling Flashgun + White Ceiling Sunlight + Window
Outdoor Beach	Direct Sunlight	Shade Scrim Cloudy Day

Step 2: Compose the Image in Your Mind

Successful portraiture involves having a preconceived image that you, the photographer, visualize prior to exposing the frame. To the best of your ability, you should develop the skill of conjuring the finished work in your mind. Within your mental framework, photographing the person and the creation of the image is underway. Perform some analysis by asking (and challenging) yourself: Is this an outdoor image? If so, is it a field, a brook, a street? What time of day is the image to be shot? What will be the position and intensity of the sun? What wardrobe will integrate well within the image? If this is a studio project, what backdrops, seating, props, and lighting will constitute the image? If your client asks you to photograph his family at their residence, what architectural aspects, furniture, and available light will add impact to the photograph? Asking yourself questions such

Successful portraiture involves having a preconceived image that you visualize prior to exposing the frame.

as these is the most fundamental step in creating the mental picture of the final photograph; the answers will become the foundation for the rest of the process.

Composing the final photograph in your mind builds on step 1. For example, you have taken the time to evaluate possible sources of light. You've made the decision to use the

▼ Careful selection of the background, direction of the sun, and wardrobe led to this beautiful image.

➤ This is a great example of a low-key studio portrait. The mood exhibited in the photograph is due to the facial expression and contrast.

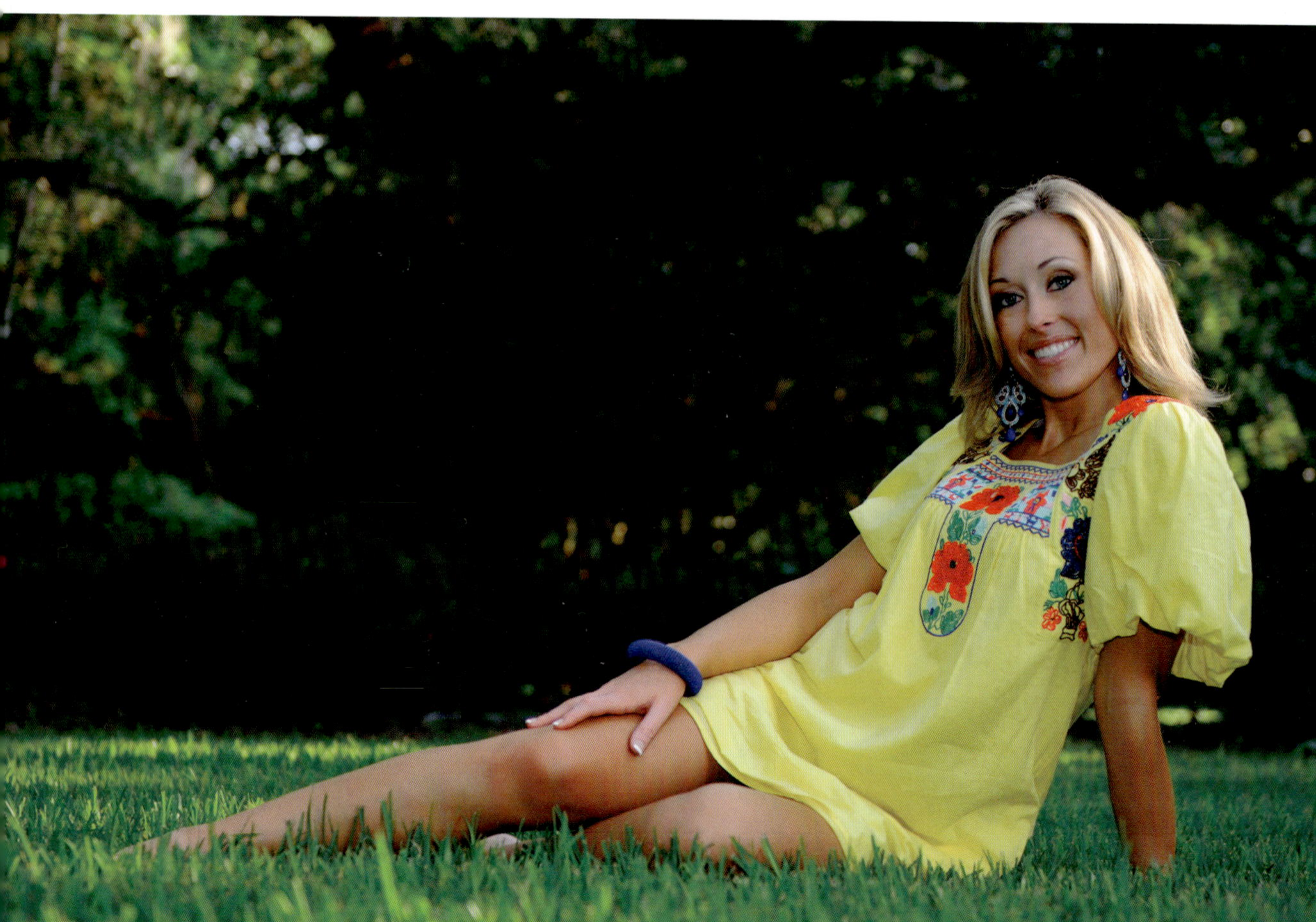

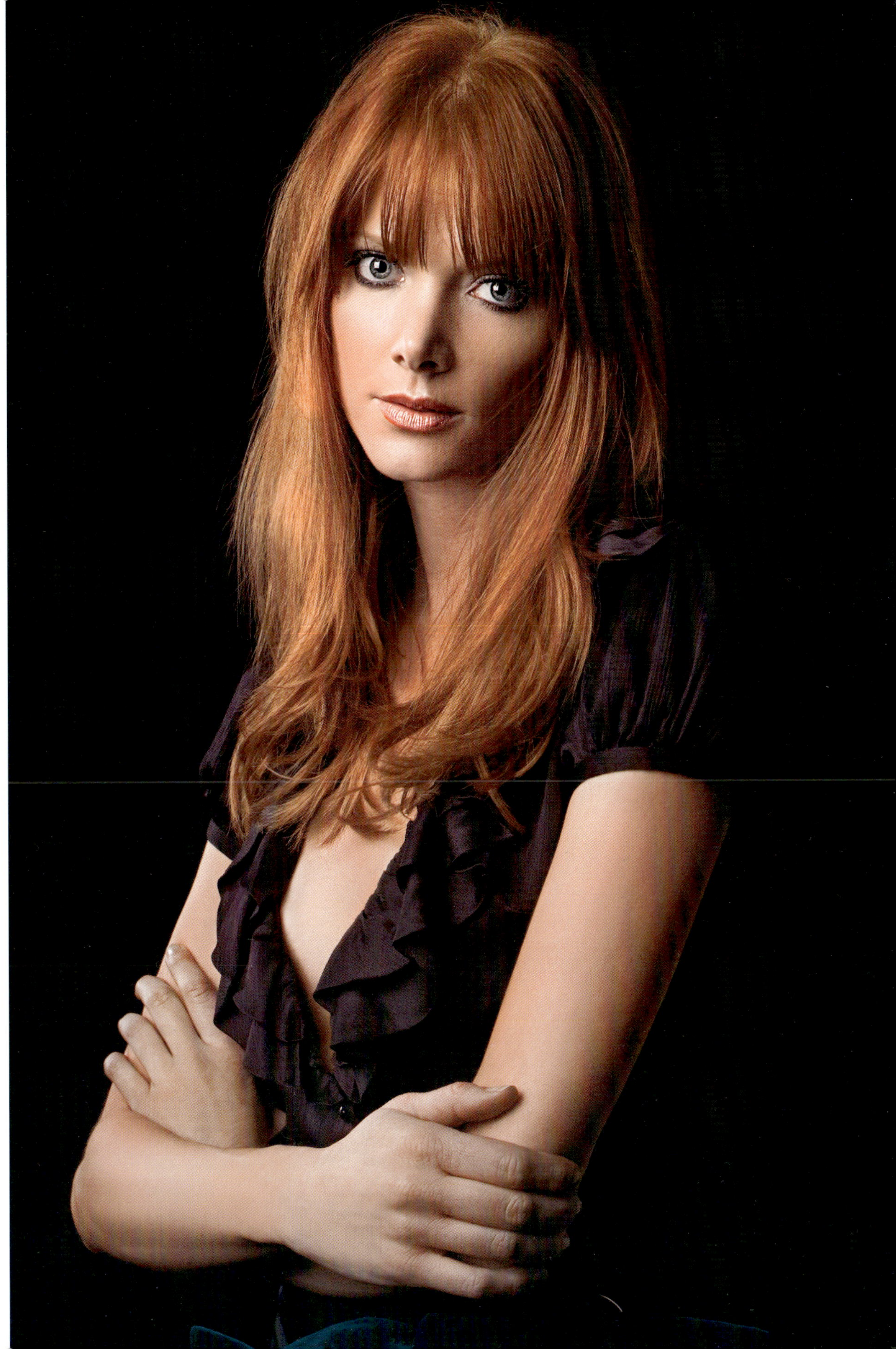

Photographers tend to become fixated on the person and forget about the greater context of the image. Ensure that the background is consistent in both luminosity and texture. Luminosity goes to brightness. The background may be slightly more or less bright than the subject being photographed, it all depends on your taste and the lighting conditions. But avoid having extremes within your frame such as dark spots approaching black or white spots. Such artifacts will cause the viewer to turn his attention to them and not the person. Texture goes to the real objects that make up the background. The background could be a brick wall, or a forest, both of which are comprised of textures. Keep this consistent and avoid abrupt inconsistent objects.

shade from a tree. You have found a spot under the tree where the light is both even and low contrast. Now it is just a matter of composing the person or people to be photographed. Since the example given is outdoor and not in the studio, there is an important point to be made. Take the time to examine the background.

For example, I will often remark at how well a photograph was taken of, say, a family in a park, only to notice a telephone pole in the background jutting out of the head of the father. A simple repositioning of the camera would have eliminated this. You may be thinking, "But Bill, we can just Photoshop that telephone pole out later!" My answer to that is "Yes, you can. Have fun doing that."

The rule of thirds suggests that you avoid centering your subject in the frame. Think of the frame as a 3x3 matrix and attempt to place your subject at the point where two lines inter-sect (indicated by a blue triangle in the diagram on the right).

➤ Placing the main point of focus of the portrait (usually the face and, more specifically, the eyes) at a point of intersecting lines creates a dynamic, visually compelling image.

▼ This image, illuminated with a 5-foot octabox, successfully depicts a ballerina stretching prior to her dance.

Try to avoid having an obvious symmetry in either the vertical or horizontal axis. For example, if there is a horizon in the frame, push it up or down but do not let it fall in the exact middle.

Step 3: Position and Pose Your Client

You are closing the gap between what you see in your mind as the final image and the steps

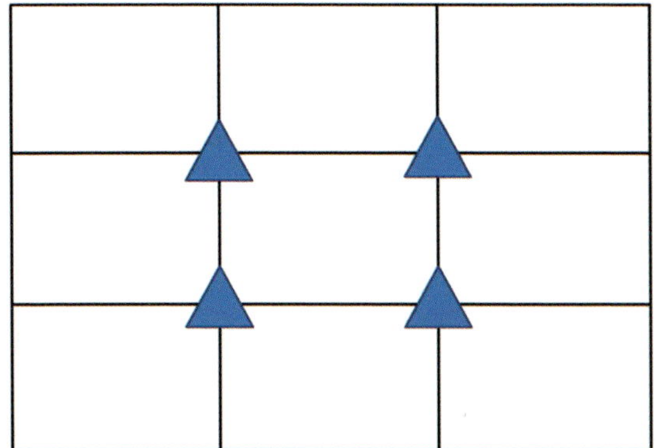

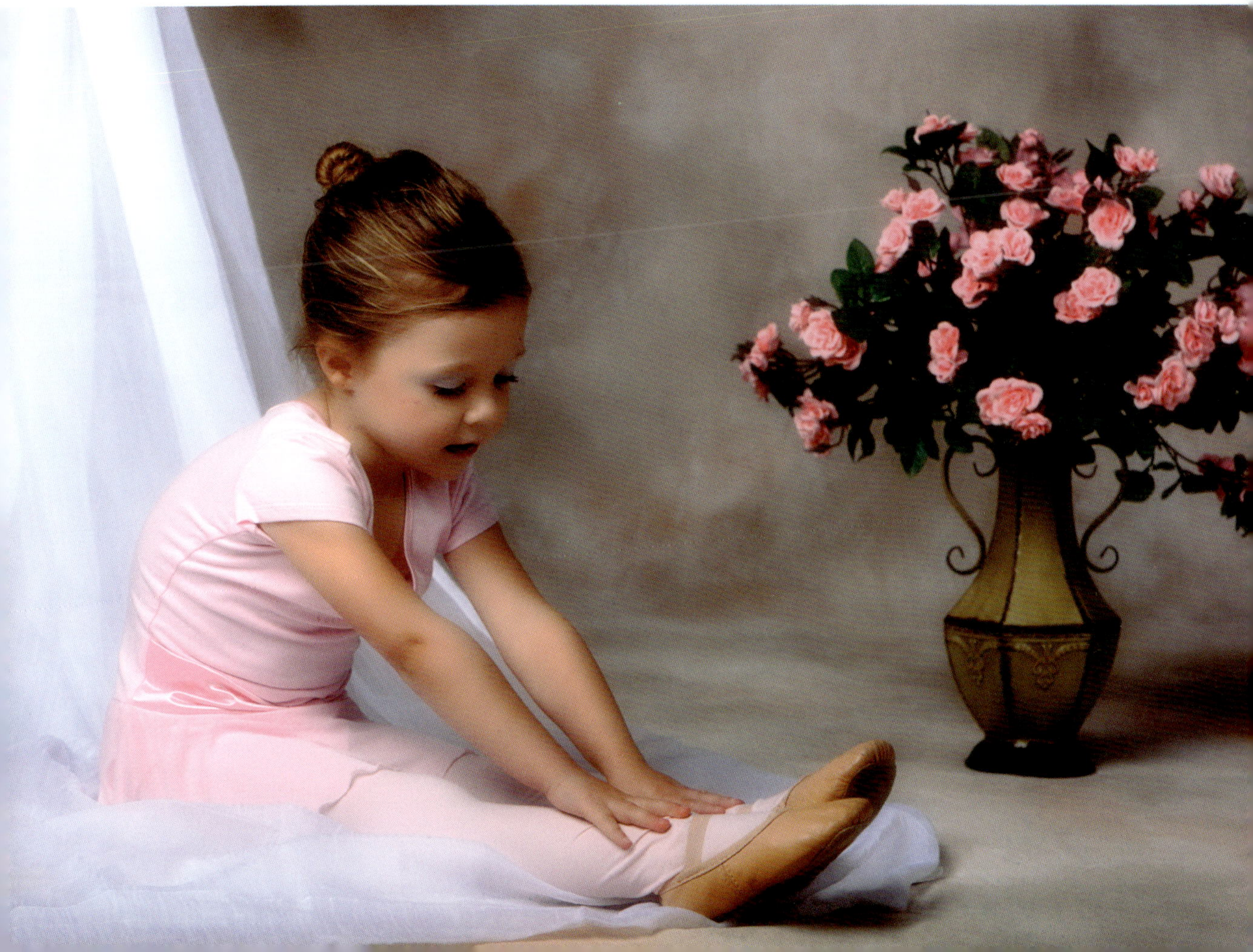

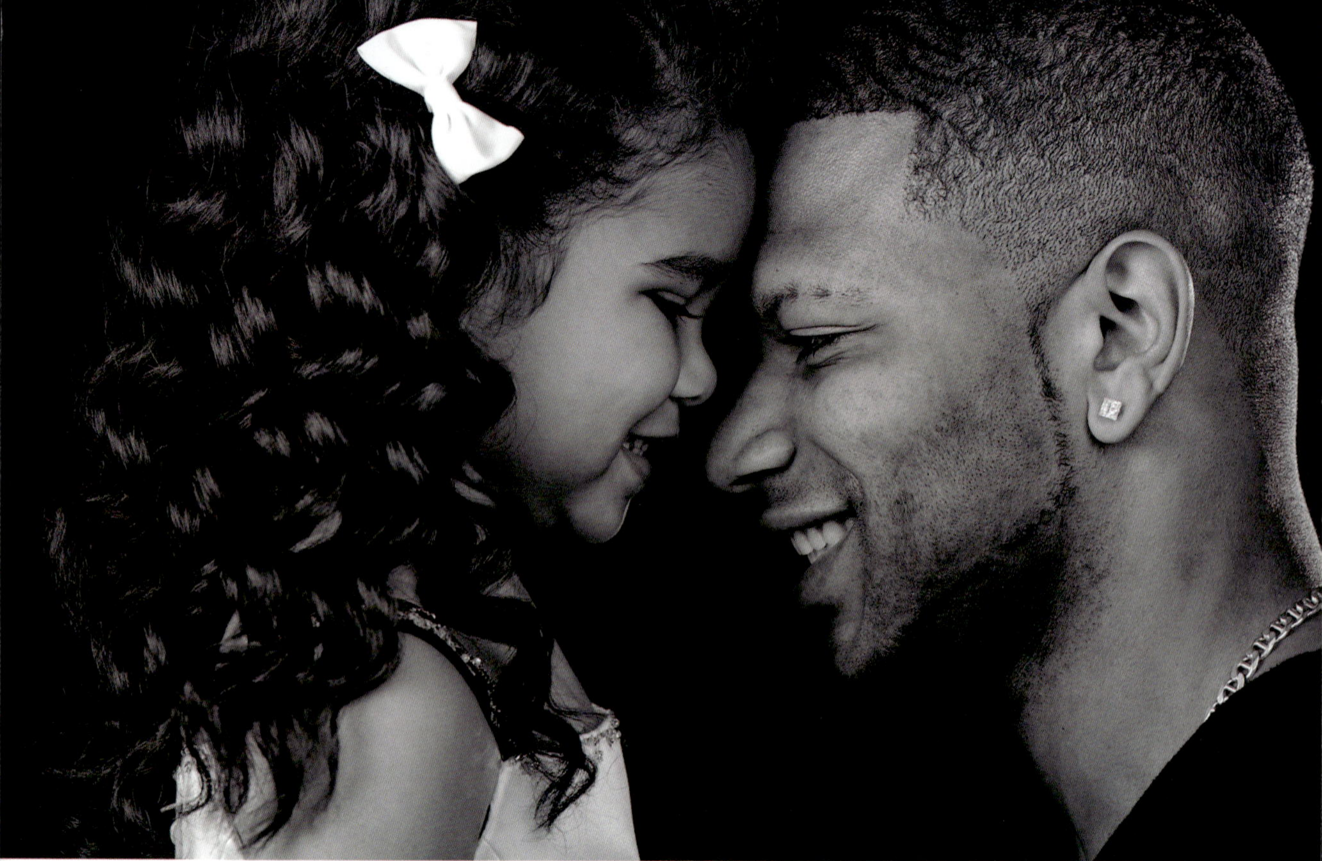

By letting this father and daughter interact without direction, this remarkable portrait was obtained.

that lead to exposing a frame and producing the image. The person being photographed is now positioned. Regardless of whether you are working outdoors, indoors, or in the studio, the fundamentals of lighting your client hold true. Place the person in front of the key light (e.g., the sun or a strobe) and let it serve as the primary source of light.

Recall from chapter 2, "Photographing People," where we discussed the elements of posing. We discussed perspective and angles formed between the person and the camera; how men and women differ in the manner in which the body is formed and stationed. Now is the time to execute posing. The important point to make

here is that the pose must "fit" the positioning of light sources and camera.

Step 4: Measure Light Sources and Set Camera Controls

Measuring light and setting the camera controls happens together—so the next step involves measuring the key light and inputting your exposure settings on your camera to allow the right amount of light to strike the image sensor and make an ideal exposure. The key light— whether natural (the sun) or artificial (e.g., a strobe) is *always* the primary source of light; the exposure is always based on the key light's strength, and any other light sources are

 # White Balance

"White balance" is a term that relates to the accuracy of colors within an image. For portrait photography, it is vitally important that your camera's white balance is correct so that the people in your photographs look correct. By correct, I mean that the color of their skin, hair, and eyes depict the actual color; of course, all other colors in the screen should also be correct. When white balance is wrong, the colors are off by either shifting to slightly orange or slightly blue. The reason for this shift is a discrepancy between the color temperature of the source light and the white-balance setting of the camera. When steps are taken to calibrate the camera for the white balance, the resultant colors in an image are considered correct. Color temperature is measured on the Kelvin scale and is denoted as K. For example, direct mid-day sunlight is approximately 5700K and casts a bluish light, whereas an incandescent light bulb is approximately 3000K and casts a reddish-orange light. If the camera is not calibrated to conform to the Kelvin temperature of the light source, then colors are rendered incorrectly in the image and the photograph will look reddish or bluish.

The following are simple techniques that can be employed to achieve proper white balance. However, they all depend on one common setting on the DSLR—that the camera is set to RAW mode. By setting the camera to RAW mode, you give yourself the opportunity to make final white balance corrections in post processing (editing) in such software applications as Lightroom, Photoshop, and Nik NX2. The following techniques assume that the camera is set to RAW mode. For more on camera RAW, see the Tech Tip: RAW Mode.

Preset White Balance. The pre-set white balance setting appear as icons of various light sources, from the incandescent and fluorescent bulbs, to sunshine, and cloudy. These will work, and if you're in a hurry, they will get you close. On most DSLRs, there is a K setting that provides the ability to dial in the Kelvin temperature as a value. This is the way that I set white balance when working outdoors. For example, when shooting in the mid-day sun, I set the white balance to 5600K; as the day progresses closer to sunset, I dial the temperature down to match the changes in the sunlight (it gets redder as the day goes on). When I conduct post-processing, I can

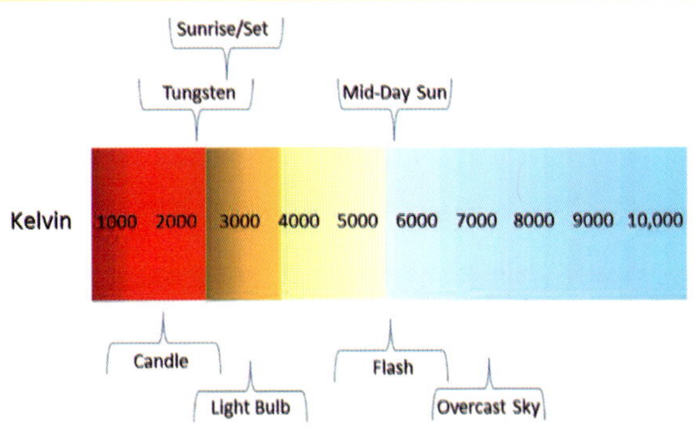

▲ This is a typical Kelvin scale reference, organized by the type of light source.

make fine adjustments to the white balance—but this assumes that the DSLR was set to RAW mode.

Auto White Balance. Auto white balance allows the camera itself to set the temperature exposure by exposure. If the scene that you're working in has a single type of light source (e.g., the setting sun), then this can work well. If there are two or more types of light sources (e.g., fluorescent and tungsten), then it will be difficult for the camera to achieve correct color.

Manual White Balance DSLR. The white balance of the DSLR can be set by photographing (close to the lens) a white or 18 percent gray card while holding a button on the camera that "tells" the DSLR to set the white balance accordingly. Refer to your camera's manual. For subsequent exposures taken within that scene, the white balance will be correct; remember to reset the white balance when moving on to another scene or shoot.

Manual White Balance Software. Start by using a preset white balance, place an 18 percent gray card in the scene, and take one proper exposure. Now shoot as you normally would. When you conduct post-processing, editing software such as Lightroom has a function that allows you to indicate the 18 percent grey card within the image. Once you indicate the 18 percent gray card, the software sets the proper white balance. You can adjust all of the other images that were taken in that scene with this white balance setting.

When the white balance setting on your camera matches the color temperature of the light sources in the scene, you will see a definite difference in the quality of your images. The people in your photographs will simply look better—and we have already established how important an ingredient that is to portrait photography.

positioned and powered based on the key light.

There are two ways to measure light to ensure that you select the camera settings that will result in a proper exposure: you can use a light

meter or the trial-and-error method.

Light Meter. In order to determine our ideal exposure settings for the scene we wish to photograph, we must meausre the key light. To do this, we begin by entering our shooting ISO into the meter. Typically, ISO 100 is used for bright, sunny days and studio work. ISO 400 is used for cloudy days and low-light situations. ISO 800 is used when there is very little available light.

With the ISO set on the light meter, you can enter one of the remaining settings and have the meter determine the third (missing) setting. I always input the shutter speed that I want to use and have the light meter calculate the aperture. *(Note:* The shutter speed setting determines the brightness of the background; the aperture setting controls

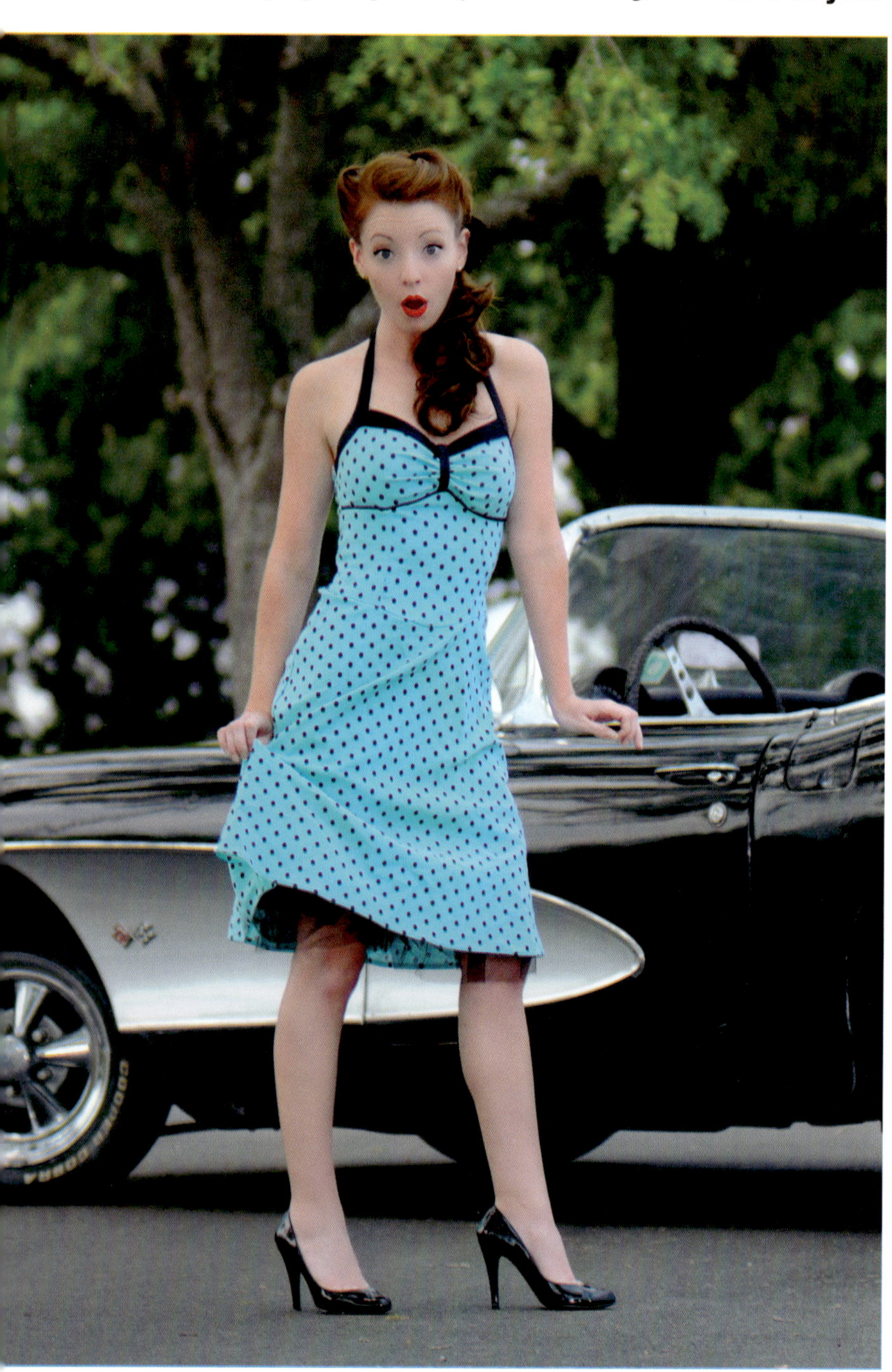

◄ As with the similar photo taken during this project, the young lady added her own dynamic in both posing and facial expression.

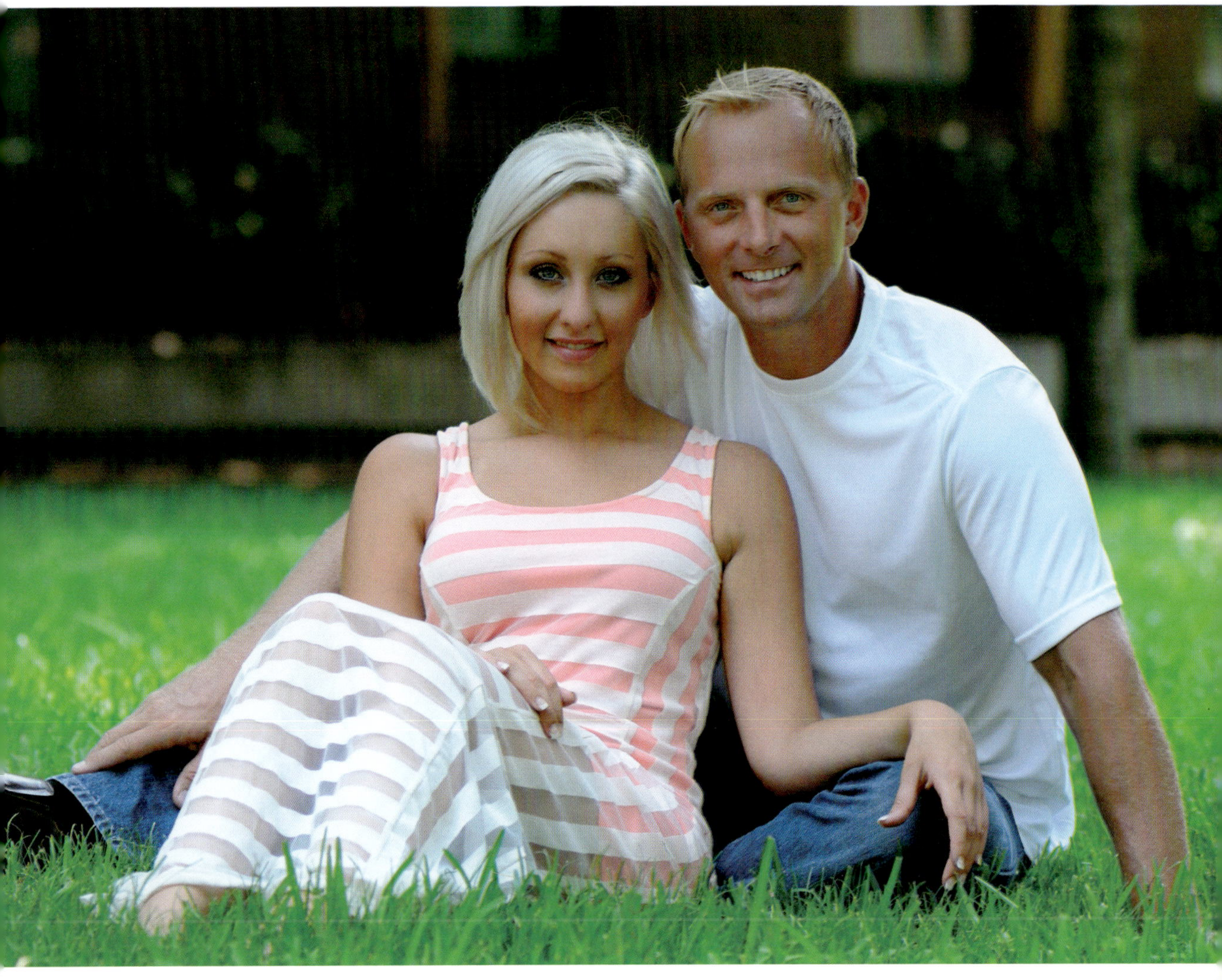

the brightness of the subject.) If you prefet to choose an aperture and have the light meter calculate a shutter speed, no problem—but realize when using a flashgun or strobe, the shutter speed cannot exceed the sync speed of your camera ($^1/_{200}$ or $^1/_{250}$, depending on the manufacturer).

When working in the studio or in another indoor location, the light meter will be set to incident mode since the light that falls on the subject from the key light is direct (incident) light. When working outdoors, the light meter will be set to ambient mode, as the light illuminating the subject from the key light (the sun) is all around the subject.

Once the metter has calculated the third exposure setting, simply set your camera using the recommended exposure settings. At this point, your camera will be aligned with the light source for proper exposure. Proceed to step 5.

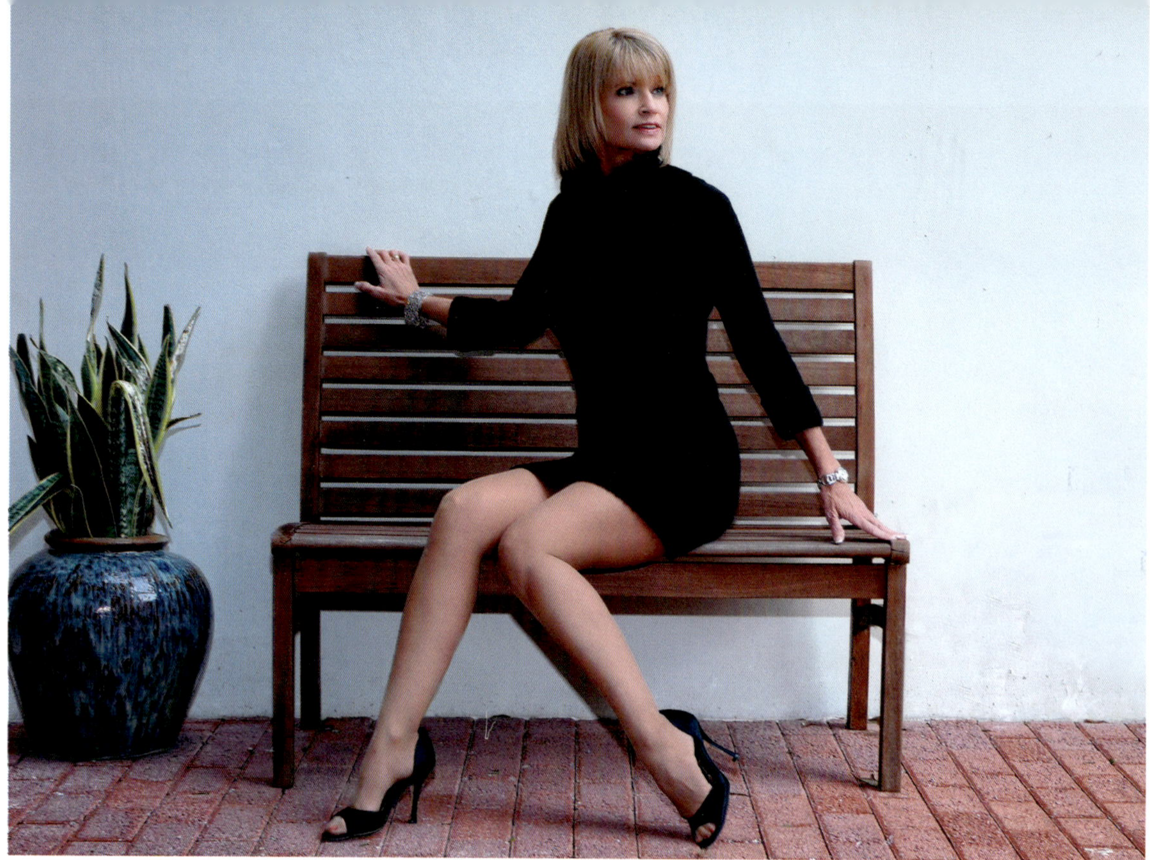

Trial-and-Error Method. If you don't have a light meter handy, you can perform the previous step using a trial-and-error method (it works quite well!).

First, set your ISO. Next, you'll need to set your shutter speed. Take your time and think about the light source. If it is a bright, sunny day, a shutter speed of $^1/_{200}$ is a good starting point; if it is a gray sky or you're shooting in the shade, then start with a shutter speed of $^1/_{100}$. The shutter speed is responsible for the brightness of the background of your portrait—outdoors, indoors, and studio alike. Practice using variations of the shutter speed with the same portrait scene and you will see the difference in how the background changes as a result. Also understand that motion is arrested with faster shutter speeds—an important factor when photographing children. Finally, select an aperture. Recall that lower f-stop settings (e.g., f/2.8) produce more bokeh but let in more light, while higher f-stop settings (e.g., f/22) produce less bokeh and let in less light. Practice and experience will result in your ability to make very good initial setting selections. With the ISO, shutter speed, and aperture set, you are ready to proceed to step 5.

Step 5: Position and Set Power to Light Sources

The next step involves augmenting the key light such that shadows are softened or eliminated as and the light adds some "pop" to the image. The fill light is brought in to illuminate the shadow side of the face (and body).

Whether in the studio or outdoors, the fill light can be a reflector, an off-camera strobe, or an on-camera flashgun (used very precisely).

ISO

ISO is an acronym for International Standards Organization. What is important to you, the photographer, is that the ISO setting on your camera controls the light-sensitivity of the digital sensor. Most DSLRs have an ISO range that begins with 100 and continues to 6400 and for some professional bodies, beyond 12000.

The lower the ISO number, the less sensitive the sensor; the higher the ISO number the more sensitive the sensor. For example, on a bright, sunny day we would set the ISO to 100. On a cloudy day, the ISO is set to 400; in dim situations, the ISO is set to 800 and higher. Increasing the ISO by a factor of two doubles the sensitivity; each decrease halves the sensitivity. For example, ISO 400 is twice as sensitive as ISO 200, which is twice as sensitive as ISO 100. This doubling and halving comes in handy when assessing the lighting for a given environment.

In the DSLR, ISO translates to the amount of amplification that is performed on the electric current (signal) exiting the individual sensor pixel or photosite once exposed to light. On a bright, sunny day, so much light energy is present that the signal exiting the photosite is strong and there is little to no need to amplify. However, in a dimly lit scene, there is less light energy. In this scenario, the exiting signal requires amplification in order to be useful for processing and image creation. The drawback is that when the signal is amplified, distortion is introduced, which in turn distorts (creates noise in) the image; this is called the signal-to-noise ratio. The greater the ISO, the greater the signal-to-noise ratio. Engineers try to keep this ratio as low as possible by employing sophisticated electronic processing in the DSLR.

As a photographer, be aware of this trade-off. Keep the ISO setting as low as possible. Gather light by opening the aperture or using slower shutter speeds if the scenario permits. It is easy to increase ISO to overcome low light conditions, but use this setting with care in order to maintain the highest-quality images.

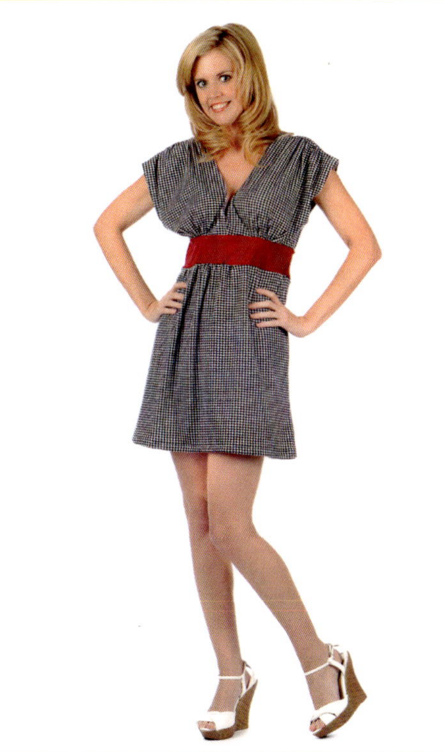

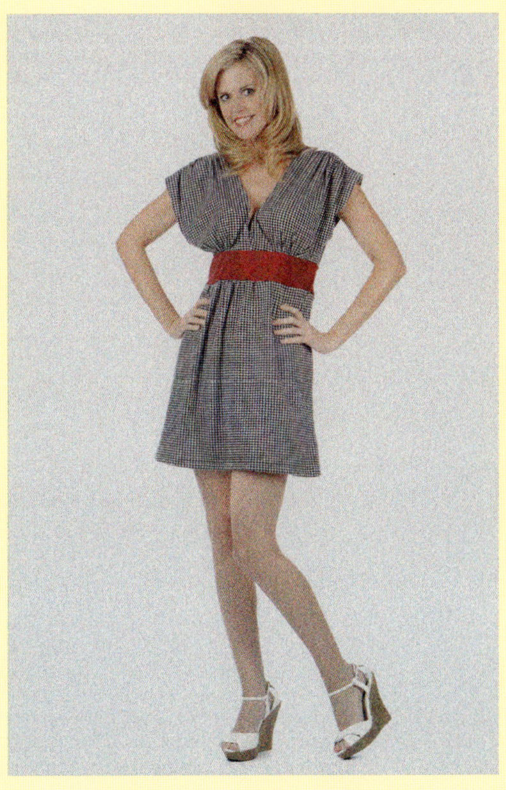

➤ Noise was introduced in the bottom photo due to the use of a high ISO setting.

The rim light can be the sun or a strobe used to illuminate the edge of your subject.

The position and power setting of the fill source depends on the key light; recall the key is the primary illuminator and all other light sources follow. The rim light can be the sun or a strobe used to illuminate the edge of your subject. A rim light is necessarily stronger than the key and the fill; otherwise, it would not be visible. I try to use rim lighting as much as possible because it adds pop, vibrancy, three-dimensionality, and interest to the image.

Step 6: Take an Exposure, then View the LCD and Histogram

The final step is to take an exposure. You will now examine the image that is rendered to your LCD and the histogram. There are a variety of modes that are offered by DSLR manufacturers whereby you can view the image and histogram combined with exposure data or singularly. Use the mode that best suits you. I view the image and histogram separately because I zoom in on the image when I do the inspection. The objective of this step is to critically analyze the image (subjective) and the histogram (objective) in combination to determine if the exposure is correct. *Important note:* If you refer to the flow diagram of the six-step process, you will notice that the act of viewing the image and histogram is performed to verify the exposure; once you are comfortable that you have a correct exposure, there is no longer a need to view the LCD; your only task at this point is to take as many exposures as you feel are necessary.

The LCD: Seeing Is Believing. Using your loupe and LCD, carefully examine the image of the photograph just produced. Zoom in and pan around, concentrating on the person in the frame. The principle issue here is getting a perfect exposure. You must divide the evaluation of exposure up into two domains: the first is the person being photographed, the second is the background. Let's begin with the background.

Examine the background and look for proper exposure. If the sky is a part of the scene, is it blue, or is it white? If it is white, your image is overexposed, and you will need to increase the shutter speed. If the background is dark and muddy with little detail, then decrease the shutter speed. Verify what you see in the image by examining the histogram. If you determine that a change to the shutter speed is necessary, then repeat step 5 by making the change to the shutter speed.

Once the background is correctly exposed, the analysis shifts to the person in the frame and the aperture setting. Starting with the face, determine if the skin appears to have detail and normal tone. Examine the eyes of the person; do they look natural, and bright? Are there any blown-out areas where what you are seeing is white? If the skin looks plastic, the image is overexposed, so stop down the aperture to cut the amount of light allowed into the lens (i.e., use a smaller aperture/higher f/stop setting) and take another shot; if the skin is dark and the person lacks detail and vividness, the image is underexposed, so open up the aperture (choose

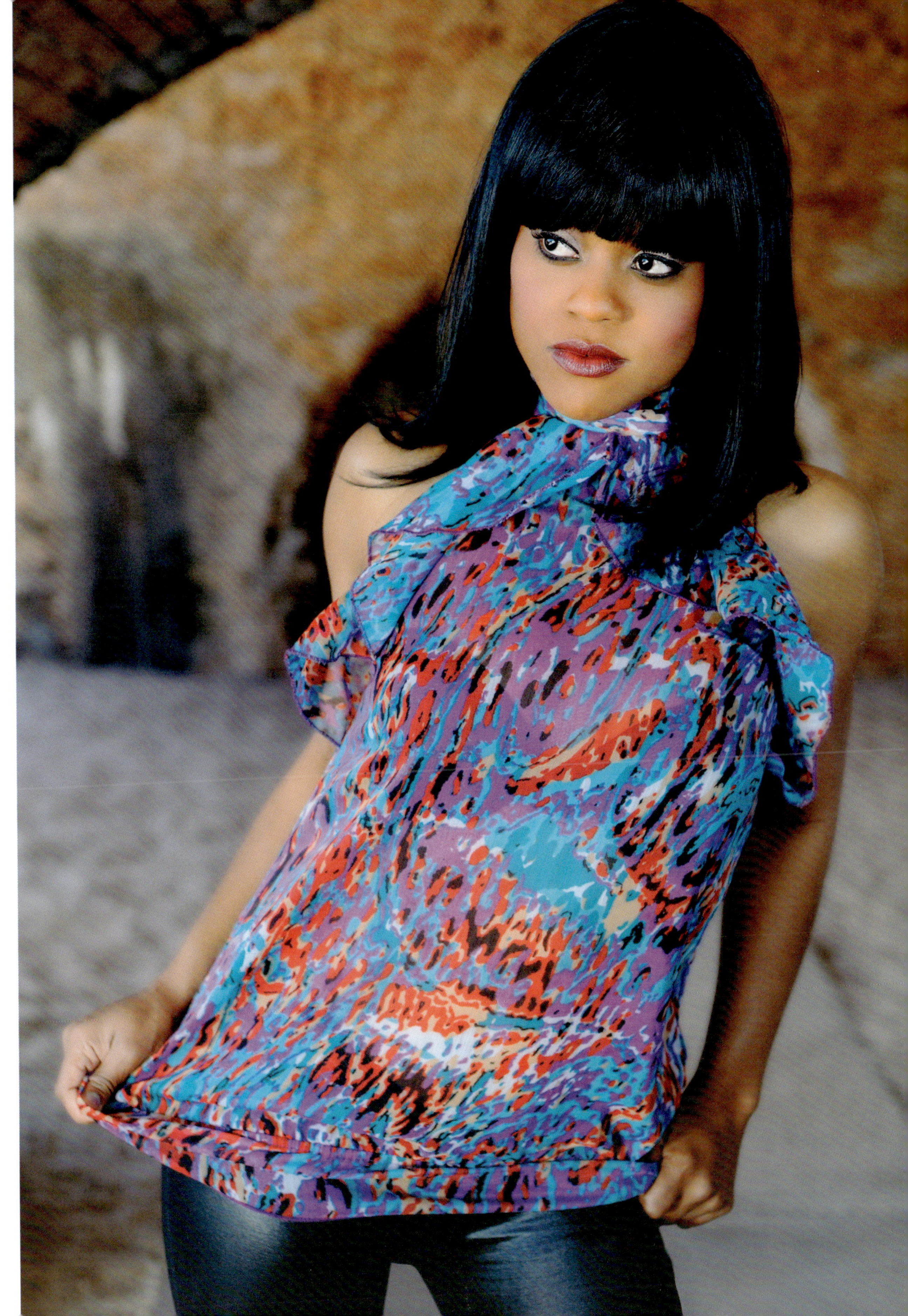

 # Histogram

The histogram is a graph of the pixel count of tones in an image ranging from black to white. What would a correct exposure look like in the histogram? Assuming that the scene you are photographing is not predominantly white or predominantly black, the histogram should look similar to a hill, with the bottom slopes of the hill ending neatly in the left and right corner of the histogram.

If the histogram is predominantly to the left, then the image is underexposed (too little light). If the histogram is predominantly to the right, then the photo is overexposed (too much light). Important information about the image has been lost in both cases. By examining the histogram against the image, you can determine if you have the correct exposure. This is where your judgment comes into effect. If the background is too bright, then adjust your shutter by increasing the shutter speed; if it is too dark, then decrease the shutter speed. If the person being photographed has blown-out skin and your histogram indicates that the image is overexposed, then stop down (choose a smaller-size aperture). If the person is too dark, then open up (choose a larger-size aperture). The goal is to achieve an exposure setting that has the histogram completely contained inside of the left and right boundary as close to the bottom corners as possible.

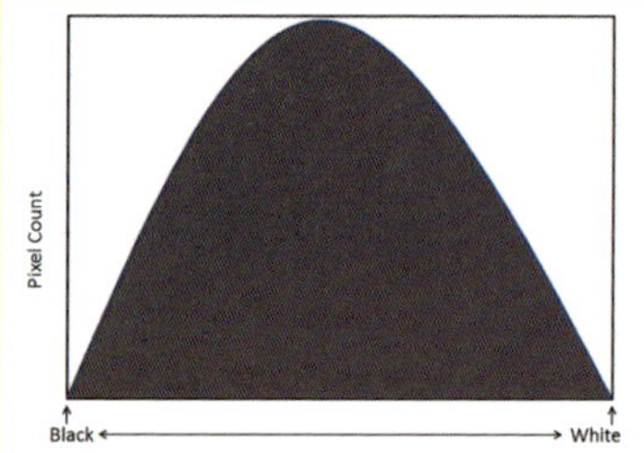

▲ An ideal exposure.

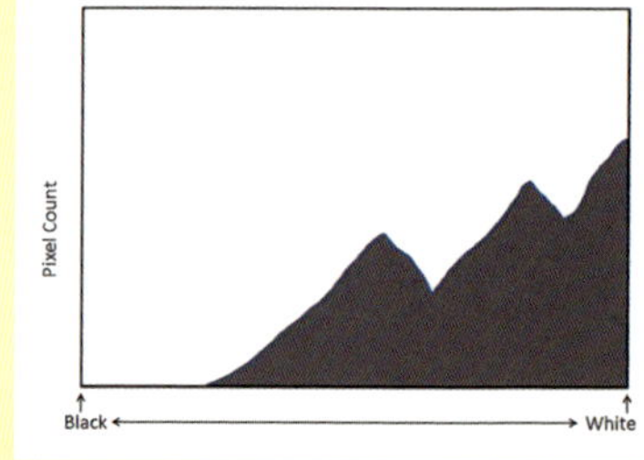

▲ Overexposure.

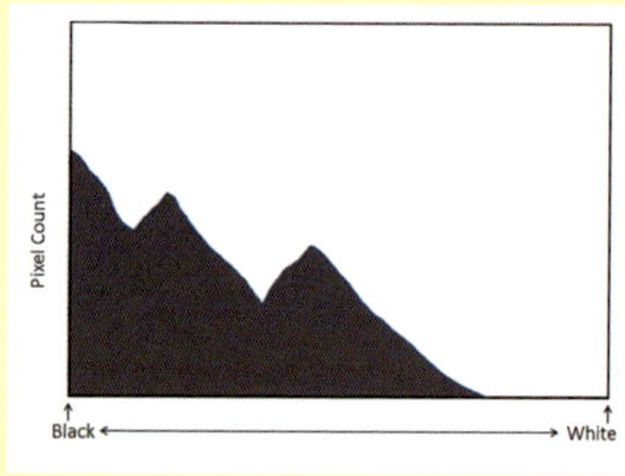

▲ Underexposure.

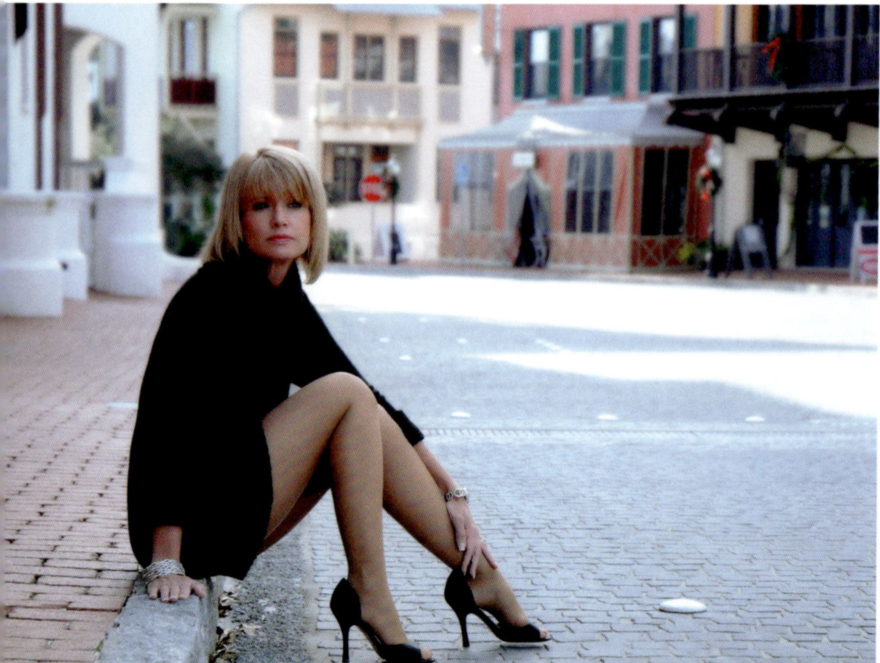

◄ Due in large part to the pose, this portrait has a romantic feel.

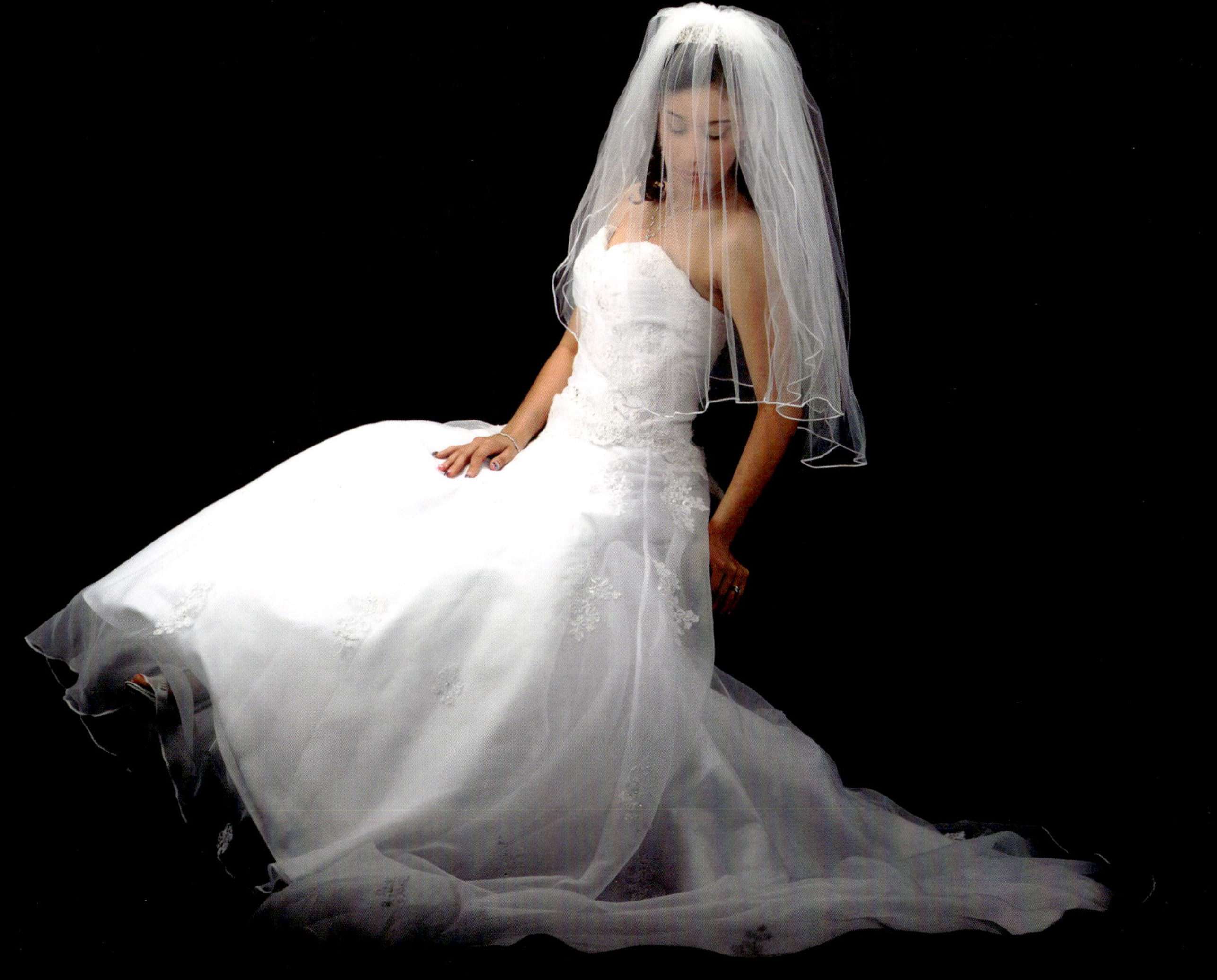

a wider aperture or smaller f/stop number) to allow more light in, and take the photograph again.

The Histogram: Seeing Is Verifying. The histogram is a graph of the pixel count of tones in an image, ranging from black to white. By looking at the histogram, you can quickly determine the "correctness" of a digital exposure. The histogram objectifies the exposure of an image and provides a factual means of verifying the "correctness" of a given exposure.

What would a correct exposure look like in the histogram? Assuming that you are photographing a scene with an average tonal range (one without a predominance of black or white tones), the histogram should resemble a hill, with the bottom slopes of the hill ending neatly in the left and right corners of the histogram. Evaluate the image itself and study the data presented in the histogram, then make exposure adjustments until both the image and histogram indicate a proper exposure.

As the process flow chart indicates, once the proper exposure is achieved, you can take as many images as you like without further adjustment or delay. Of course, if you substantially move your position, or the position of the person being photographed, you will need to return to step 1.

But, what if you have achieved what is otherwise a perfect exposure, but the person just doesn't look idealized? In this case, you should alter the position of the light sources. Depending on where you are photographing, this could be a softbox (key light in the studio), an on-board flashgun (fill light outdoors), or a reflector. This is where the artistic side of the equation starts to take shape—one's ability to examine the qualitative aspects of the photograph. At this point, return to step 5 and make adjustments to the way in which light is illuminating the person being photographed with either light sources or revised camera controls.

Here is an example of a simple pose combined with strong bokeh.

This is an example of a good pose and good exposure—but the background is questionable. The highlights in the background detract from the subject.

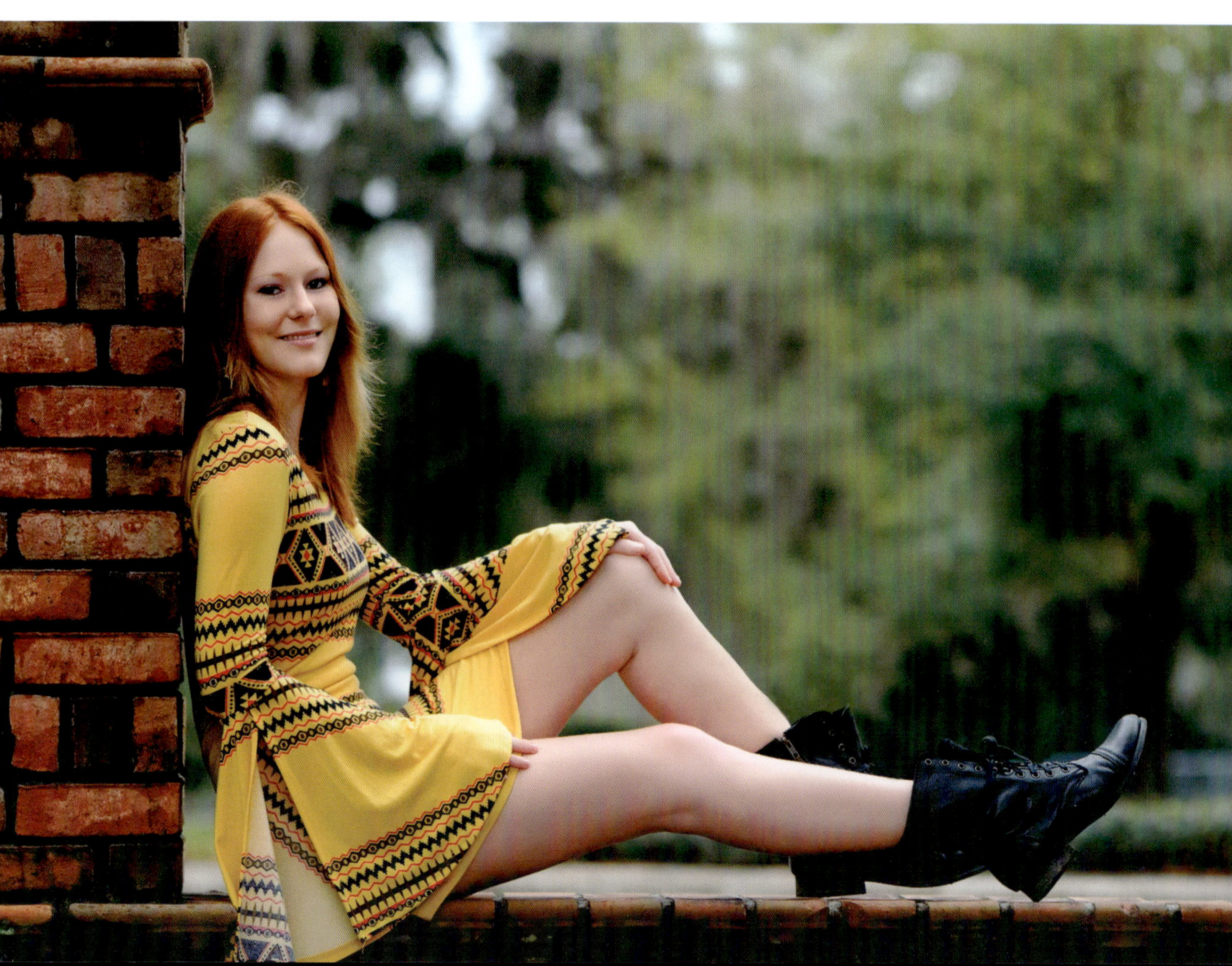

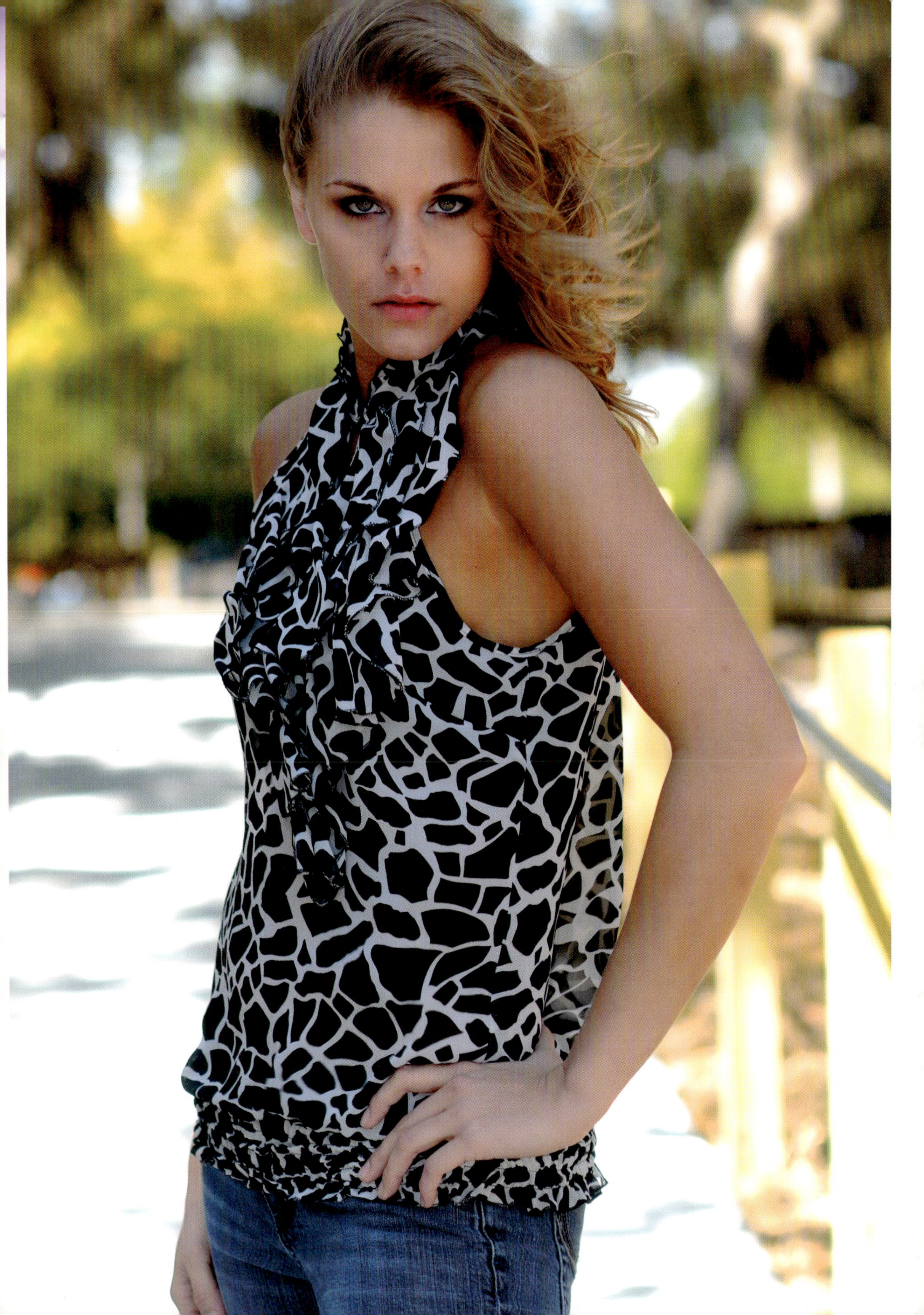

4. Outdoor Portraits

As much as I like the controlled environment of a studio, I never get tired of photographing people in the great outdoors. It could be that I see a river, a city street, or majestic landscape—whatever catches my eye more often becomes the backdrop for portraiture. Themes and moods that could originate only from the outdoor environment add such incredible beauty and drama to the overall image. As well, taking photographs outdoors ensures that every project is different—even if the same location is used in a redundant manner. The seasonal changes in the environment, weather, and sunlight offer unlimited possibilities.

▼ With an overcast sky, the light was near perfect for outdoor bridal portraiture. All that was necessary to obtain an excellent result was to add appropriate fill light. An on-camera flashgun was used to add a minimal amount of light.

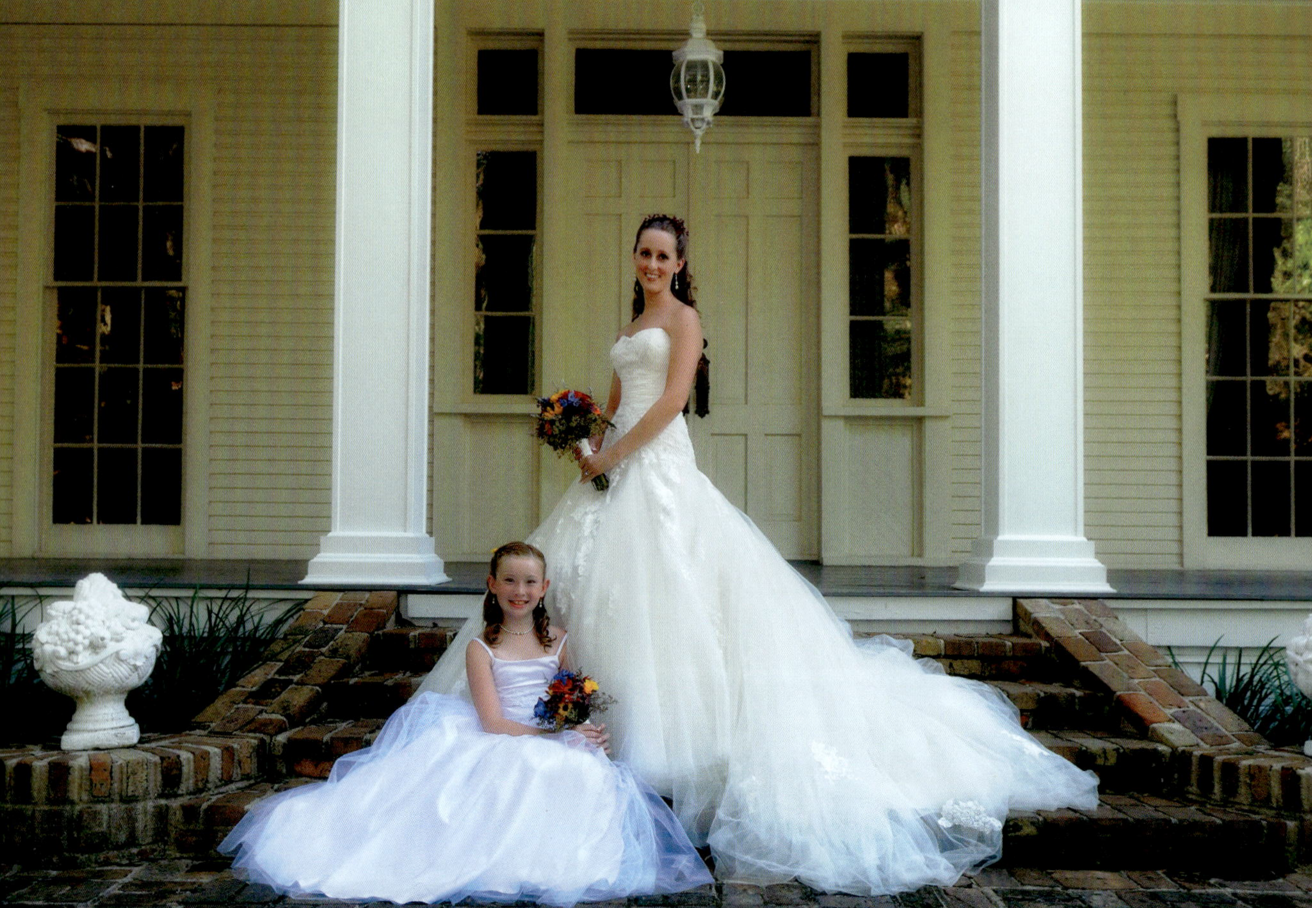

As we discuss outdoor portraiture, we'll consider the composition, pose, and lighting, but without the four walls and roof of a studio environment. Hence, you will once again be using the process to move from beginning to the end of a successful session. Prior to outlining the process for outdoor portraiture, let's talk about the major strategies used when working outdoors.

The Person Is the Central Object of Your Photograph

Since we are talking about portrait photography, we must ensure that the final image is about the person or people in the photograph and not the scene (because then we would be discussing landscape, architectural, or geographic photography). You may be thinking, "What is Bill talking about? If there is a person in the image, then the image is a portrait, and it is about the person." Not true. We can and often do get caught up in an internal conflict in our creative minds over the person versus the scene. The reason is simple: unlike the studio, the outdoor scene is usually unbound and *big*. We want so dearly to capture that scene with our person in it that the final image can be more about the scene than the person. I'm not going to declare some magical number or ratio of how much space the person should occupy within the frame. It's a judgment call; you know it's right when you see it. We are in the artistic realm of photography here. Ask yourself, "Is this about the person or persons? Yes or no?"

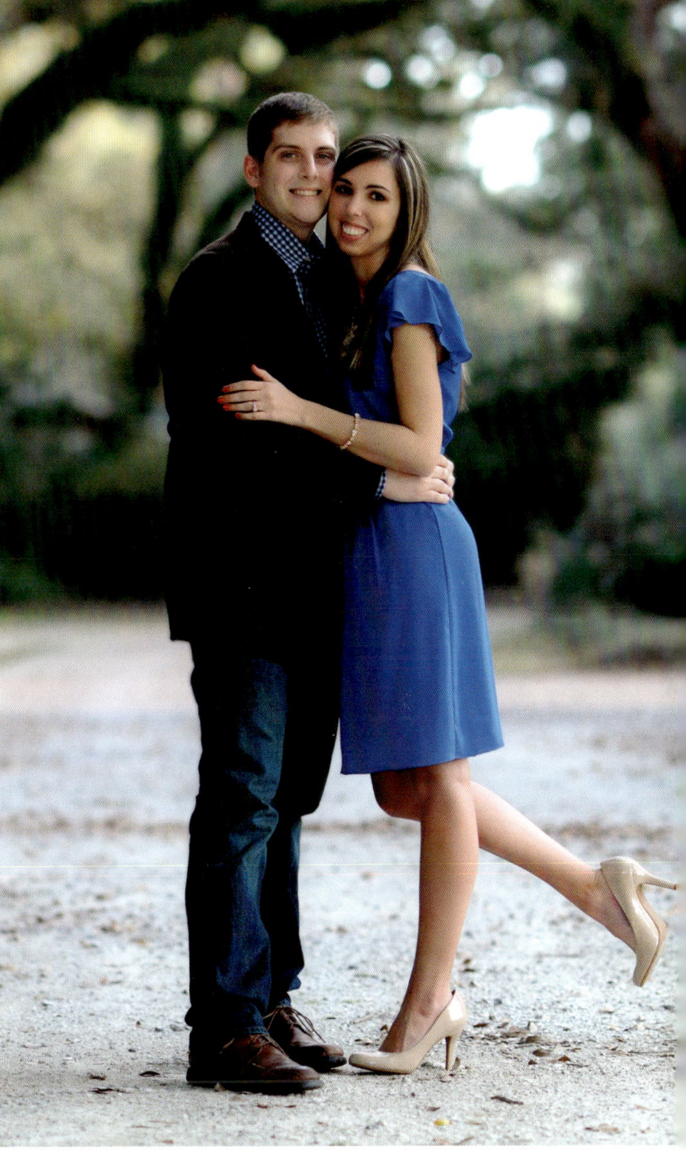

▲ This engagement photo involves a simple embrace, smiles, and terrific bokeh, resulting in a highly flattering portrayal.

The Background

When choosing the background, I decide up front on one of three types of backgrounds: close (within 1 to 10 feet), distant (separated by tens or hundreds of feet), or panoramic. This involves the careful composition of the image, and in turn lens selection and creative use of depth of field (DOF).

 # Lens, Aperture, and Depth of Field

Depth of field (DOF) describes both the closest and farthest distances from the lens that remain in focus. Within the DOF, there exists a precise point of focus. Strictly speaking, distances immediately forward and rearward of the point of focus begin to blur. However, for practical purposes and certainly for photography, objects that appear within the DOF are in acceptable focus.

DOF is inversely proportional to the diameter of the aperture. The larger the diameter of the aperture, the smaller the DOF; the smaller the diameter of the aperture, the greater the DOF. For example: f/2.8 has a shallow depth of field, whereas f/16 has a large DOF.

For portrait photographers, DOF is a creative tool that can greatly enhance interest by separating the subject from the background. Using this technique, a three-dimensional effect is produced with the subject as the center of interest and visually "popping" off of the page.

In conjunction with the aperture, the focal length of the lens contributes to the DOF. Given an arbitrary aperture setting, the shorter the focal length of the lens, the greater the DOF and conversely, the greater the focal length of the lens, the smaller the DOF. The property of a lens to produce shallow DOF and therefore a background which is out of focus is called bokeh (blur). Thus, bokeh can be achieved more easily with a focal length of 200mm versus 35mm. The 70–200mm f/2.8 zoom lens is very popular with portrait photographers, partially because of the flexibility of the zoom and the shallow DOF and bokeh that is achieved.

The relative distances between the camera, person being photographed, and the background have an effect on the outcome of the image. Achieving a blurred background is difficult when the distance between the subject and the background is small. Unless the DOF is very shallow, it is likely that the subject and background will both fall within the DOF and be acceptably sharp. A DOF table for a given lens helps you to understand the relationship between focal distance and DOF. Armed with this information, you will more readily and easily be able to position your subject at appropriate distances to a given background and achieve the desired level of bokeh.

When bokeh is not desired and the goal is to have the subject and background completely in focus, the hyperfocal distance comes into play. For a given aperture setting, the hyperfocal distance is the closest point of focus to infinity where all objects are in focus. It is recommended that you obtain DOF tables for the lenses in your kit and learn how to adjust the lens to the hyperfocal setting. You will then be prepared for both styles of portraiture and easily achieve the desired result.

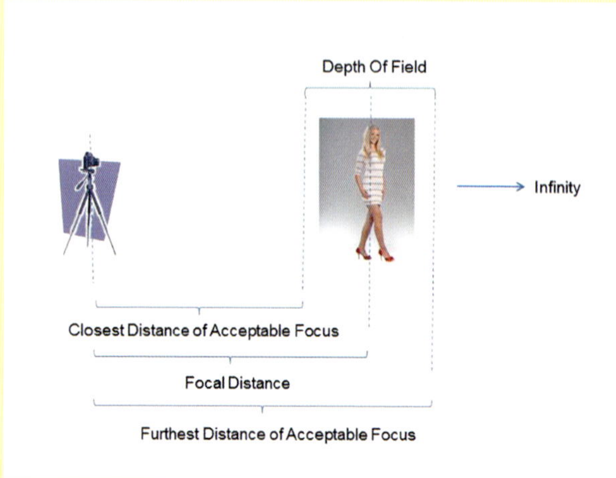

▲ This diagram depicts the fundamentals of depth of field (DOF).

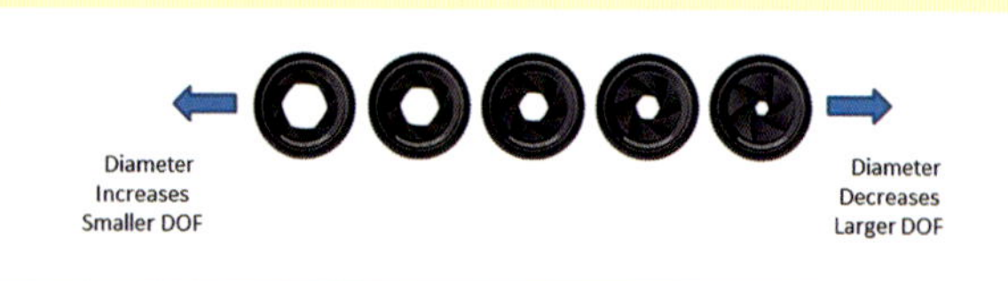

▲ This diagram illustrates the inverse relationship between f-stop and depth of field.

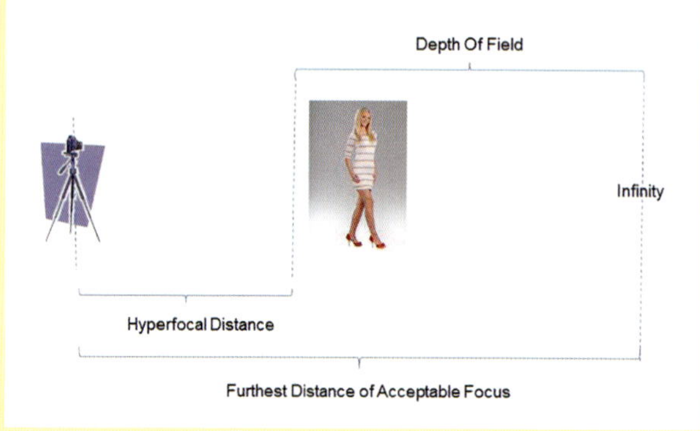

▲ This diagram depicts the relationship between the hyperfocal distance and DOF.

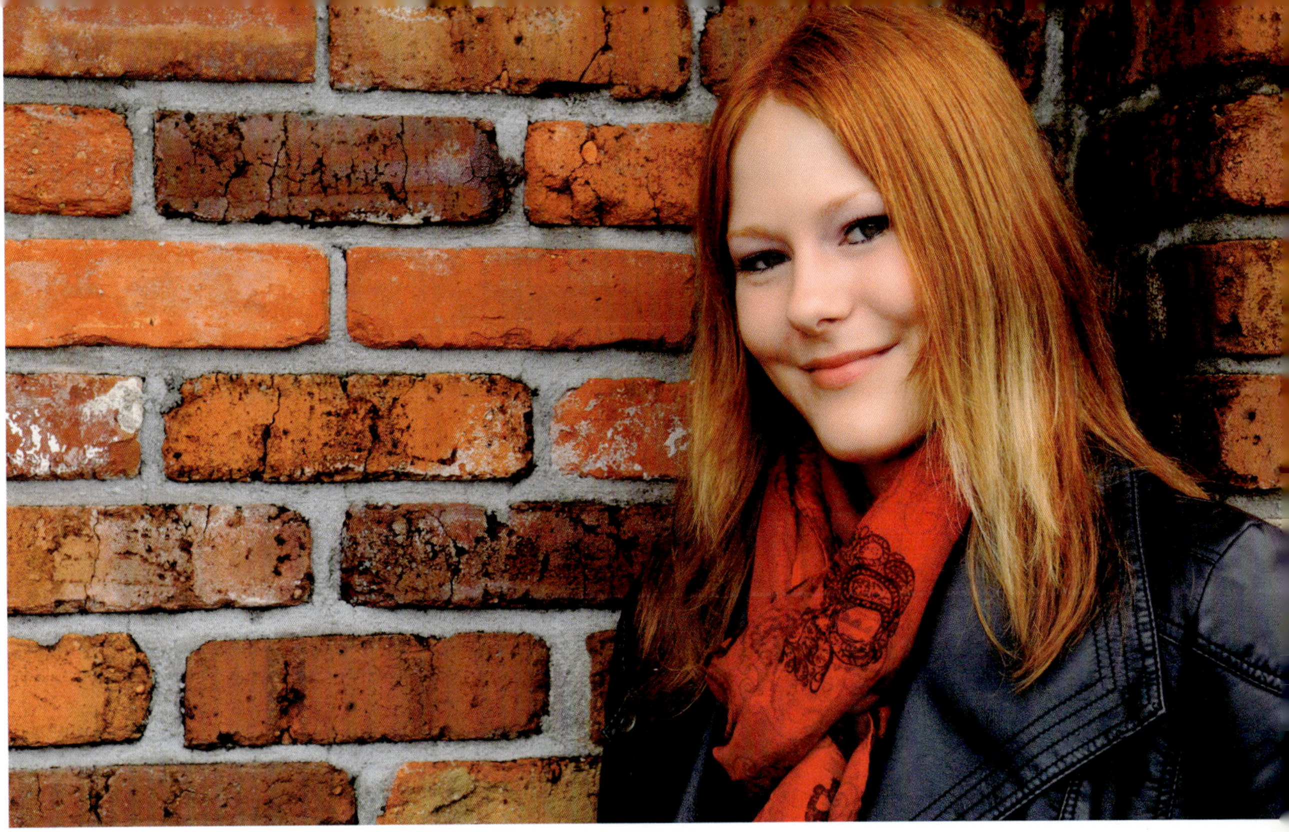

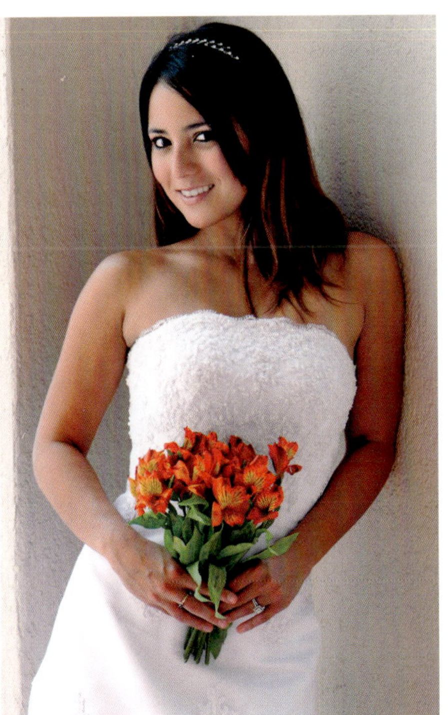

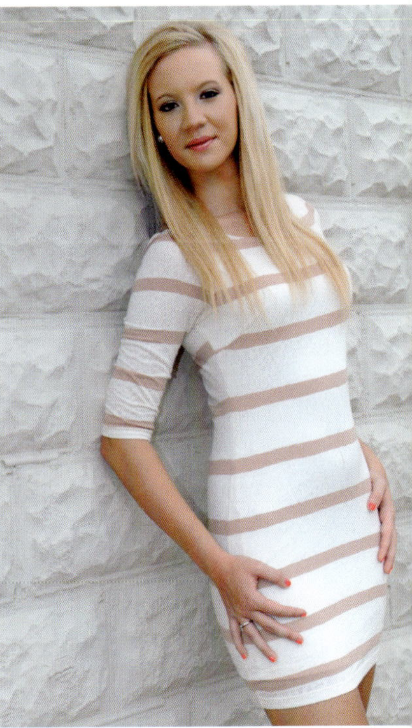

Close Background. With a close background, the person is almost leaning against or touching the background surface. The background surface texture and color is in and of itself interesting to the photograph. For a close background, I generally use a 35–50mm focal length lens at upwards of f/5.6. Whether the orientation is portrait or landscape, I am not expecting to blur the background—the texture and detail of the background is important to the photograph. Backgrounds that work well in this setup include a barn door, the front porch of a house, or the wall of an urban building.

All three of these images depict a close background. Note the effect on the subject and the overall image.

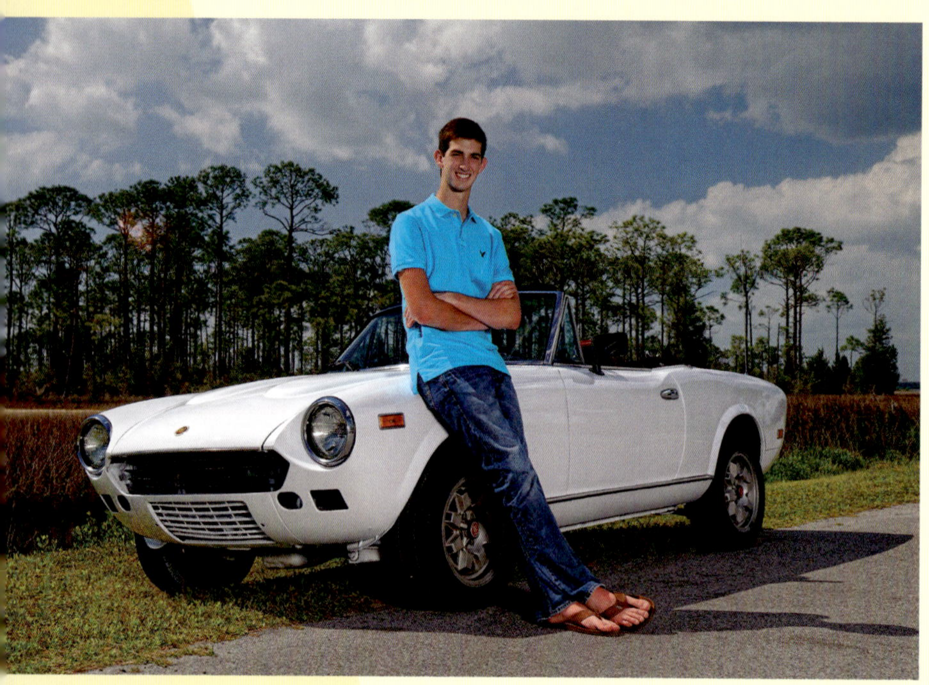
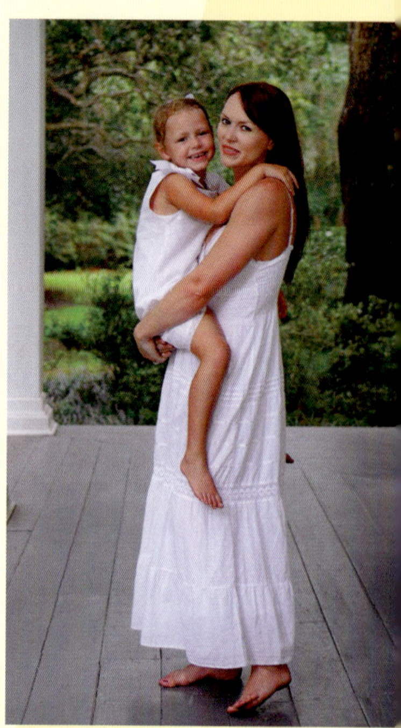

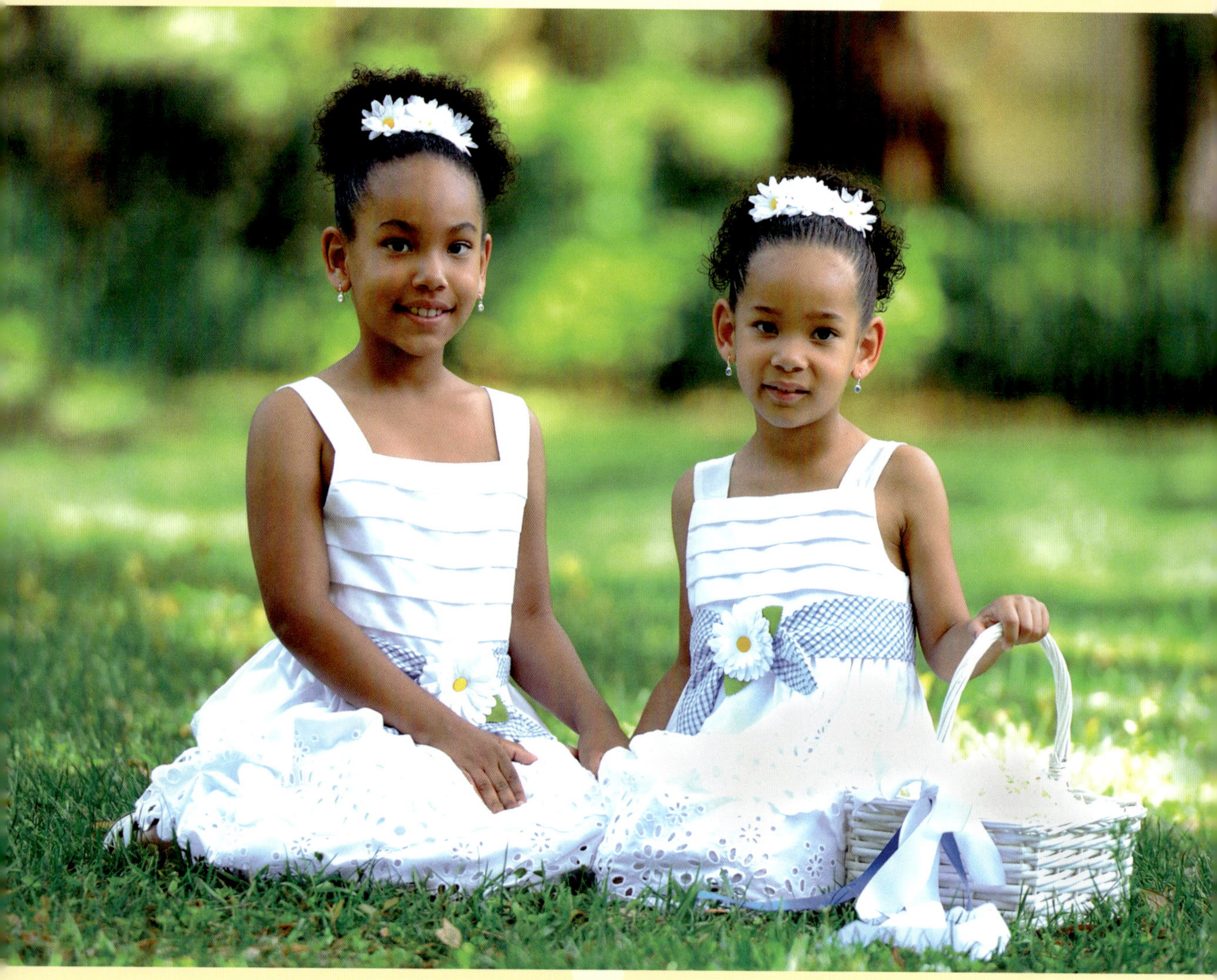

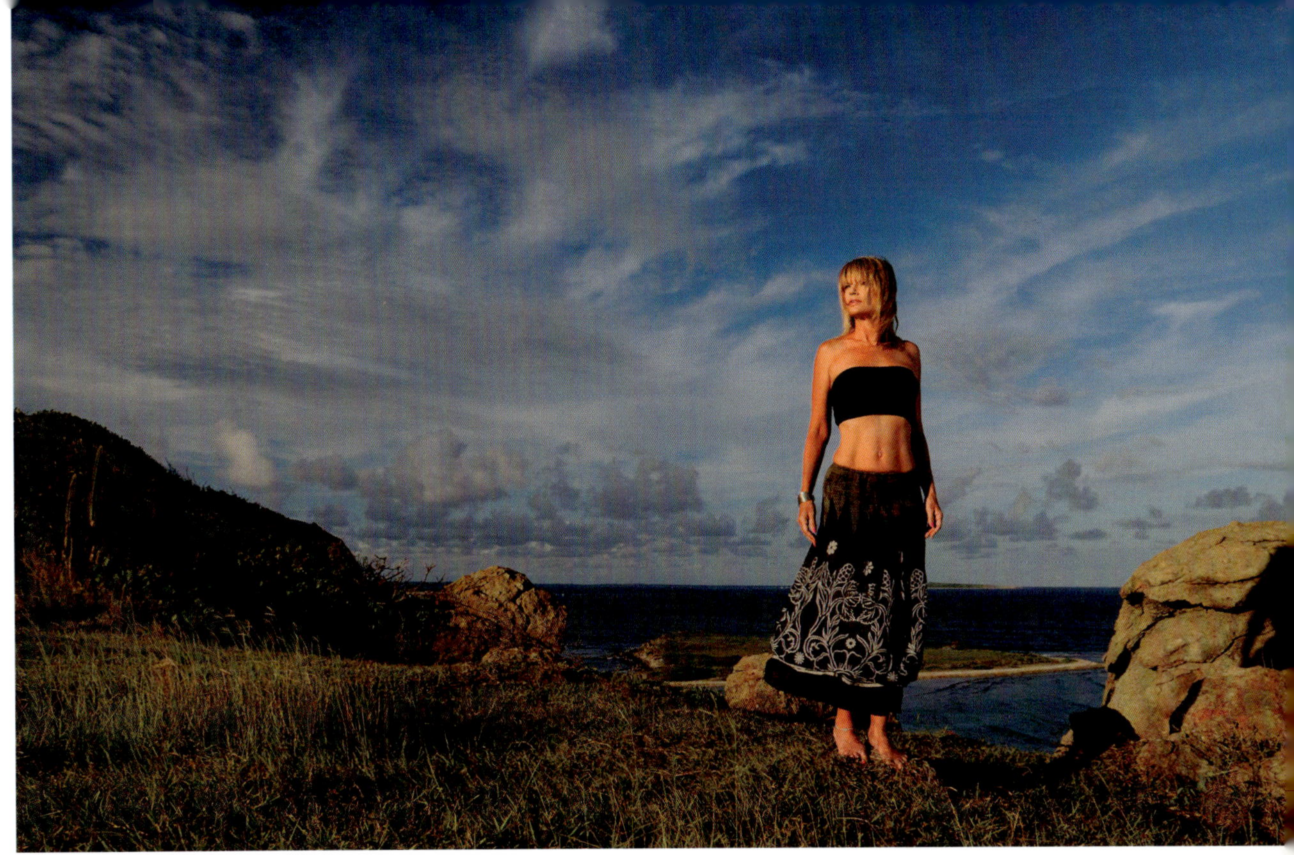

◄ All three of these images were shot with a distant background. The bokeh varies appropriately as a function of the intended image.

▲ Although the scene is panoramic, the image remains about the subject and can be considered a portrait.

Distant Background. The person is tens of feet or more away from the background surface or surfaces. The background and color are interesting but are intentionally blurred—or can be in focus; it's your choice. In the final image, there will be very little detail in the background. For a distant background, I generally use a telephoto lens with a focal length greater than 135mm at f/2.8 to f/4. Whether the orientation is portrait or landscape, I am intentionally blurring the background. Examples of a distant background are a forest, waterfall, and an urban setting involving a large building.

Panoramic Background. With a panoramic background, the background itself is sufficiently far from the person that you effectively have an infinite depth of field from the subject to the horizon. In this type of background, the scene itself is important and adds great context about where the person is and how they are interacting with the environment. For this type of photograph, I generally shoot with a wide-angle lens in landscape orientation with a focal length of 24mm. Examples of panoramic backgrounds include the horizon of the ocean, rolling landscapes such as the prairies of the midwest United States, or the fjords of Scandinavia.

Diminishing Line and the Horizon. When choosing a distant or panoramic background, try to identify artifacts that provide a diminishing line from the person being photographed to a vanishing point. This can be a trail, fence, telephone poles, etc. The result of incorporating a diminishing line is increased three-dimensionality, interest, and greater overall image impact.

Use the horizon sparingly in your portraits, as it normally creates a horizontal line that runs through everything in your photograph. You might opt to blur the horizon if the photo has a distant background. If the image has a panoramic background and the horizon is in focus, ensure that the person or persons being photo-graphed fall below the line that is formed by the horizon.

Sunlight

In order to create beautiful and interesting portraits in the great outdoors, you must adapt your equipment to different types of sunlight. I used to believe that it was only during the late afternoon that good light (and therefore good portraiture) could be had. Not true. The type and quality of sunlight varies, but in most cases all sunlight throughout the day can be used with great success. I'm going to define three categories of sunlight: (1) bright and sunny, (2) shade from bright sun, and (3) overcast or cloudy skies. We'll discuss each of these three categories and how to calibrate both the camera and auxiliary light sources in each situation to produce a professional result. If you haven't already, read over the section on light.

Regardless of the category, remember that sunlight must evenly cover the person or persons being photographed. I cannot emphasize this point enough; if the sunlight is not

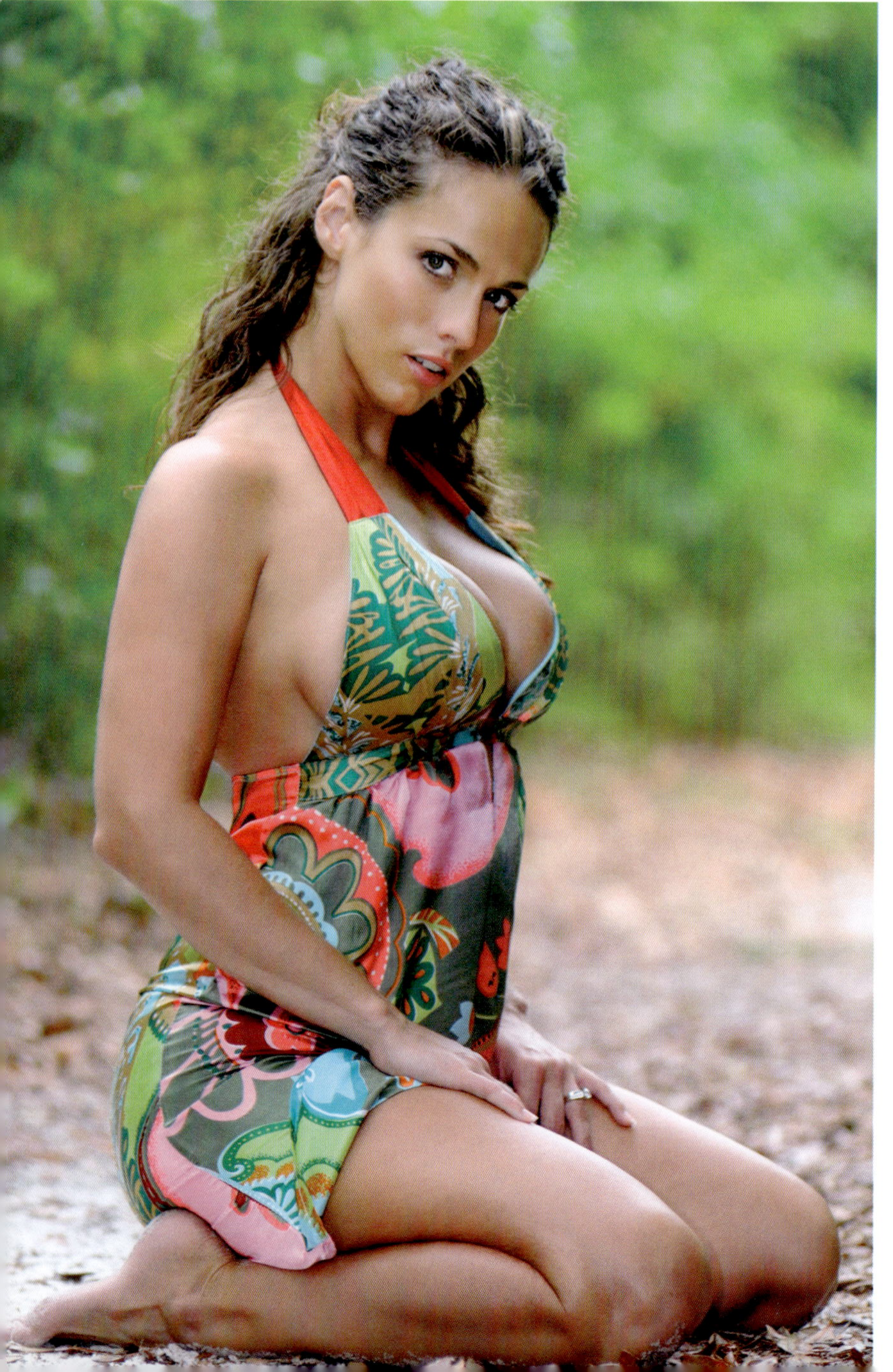

➤ This image shows a great example of a diminishing line. The road goes off into the distance to a vanishing point. Along with terrific bokeh, the young lady practically pops off the page.

◄ In this image, the sunlight was diffused by heavy cloud cover. This made for extremely soft and even illumination. With a minor amount of fill light via an on-camera flashgun, a great glamour image was produced.

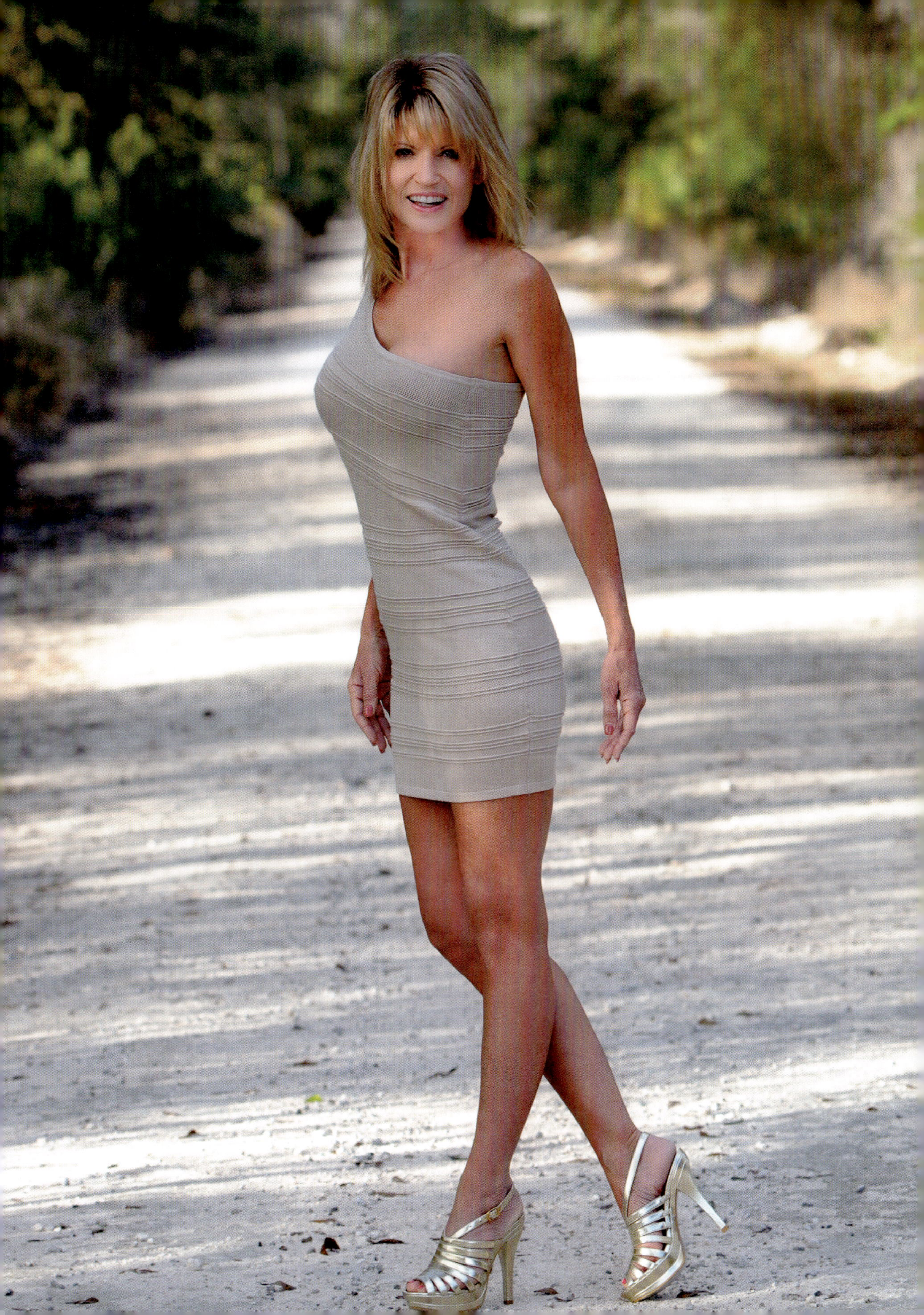

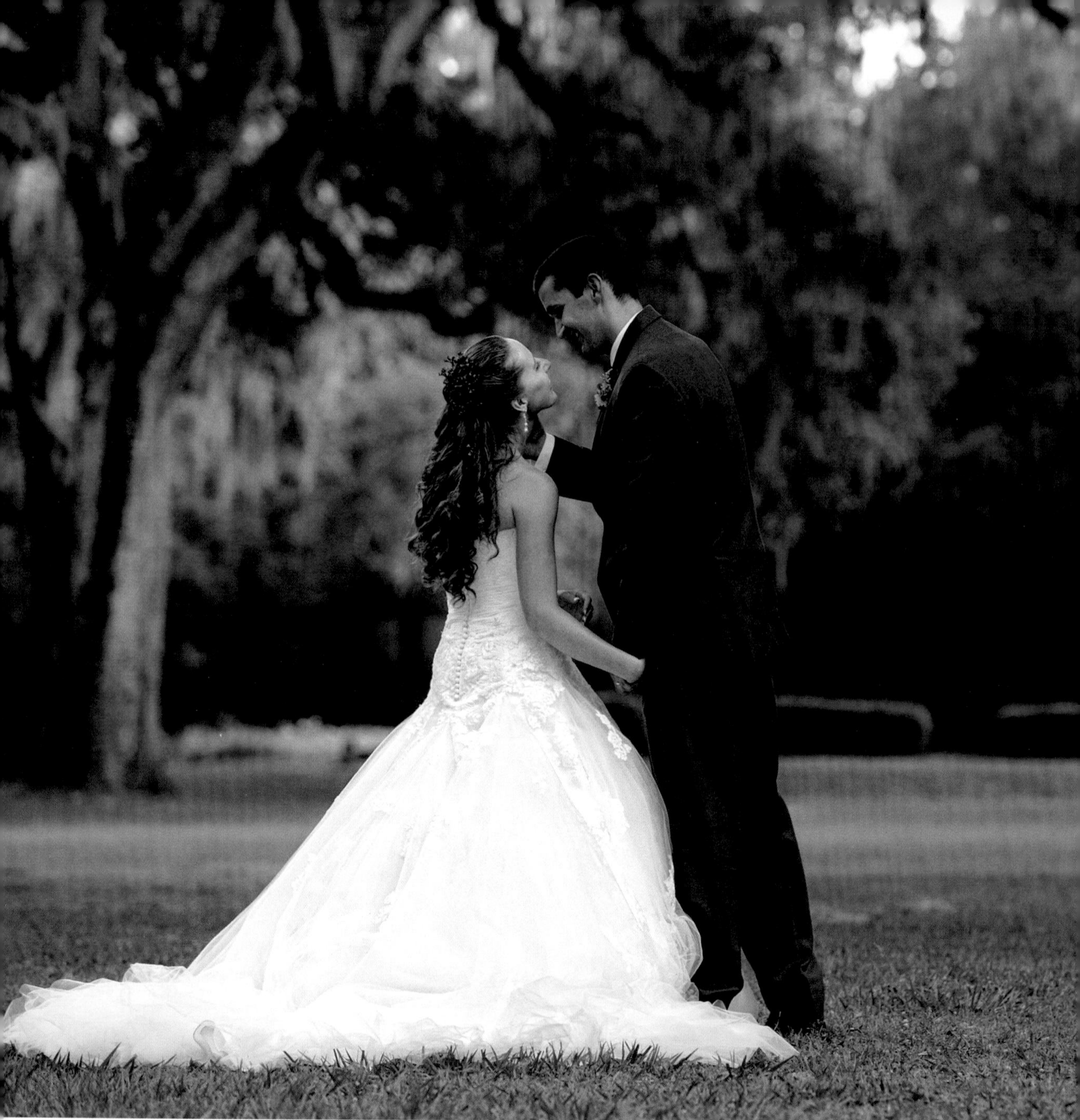

With the wedding ceremony over, it was getting late in the day and subsequently dark. My camera settings were ISO 800, f/3.5, and $^1/_{250}$ second in order to achieve a good exposure. Why did I shoot at $^1/_{250}$ second if it was getting dark? I had to choose a relatively fast shutter speed so that my tired, shaking arms would not blur the shot.

even, the potential beauty of the photograph is greatly hindered, resulting in blotchy, high-contrast photographs that do not please the eye.

Bright and Sunny Sky Techniques. For high-impact, "wow" portraits, the middle of a summer day provides all of the sunlight your

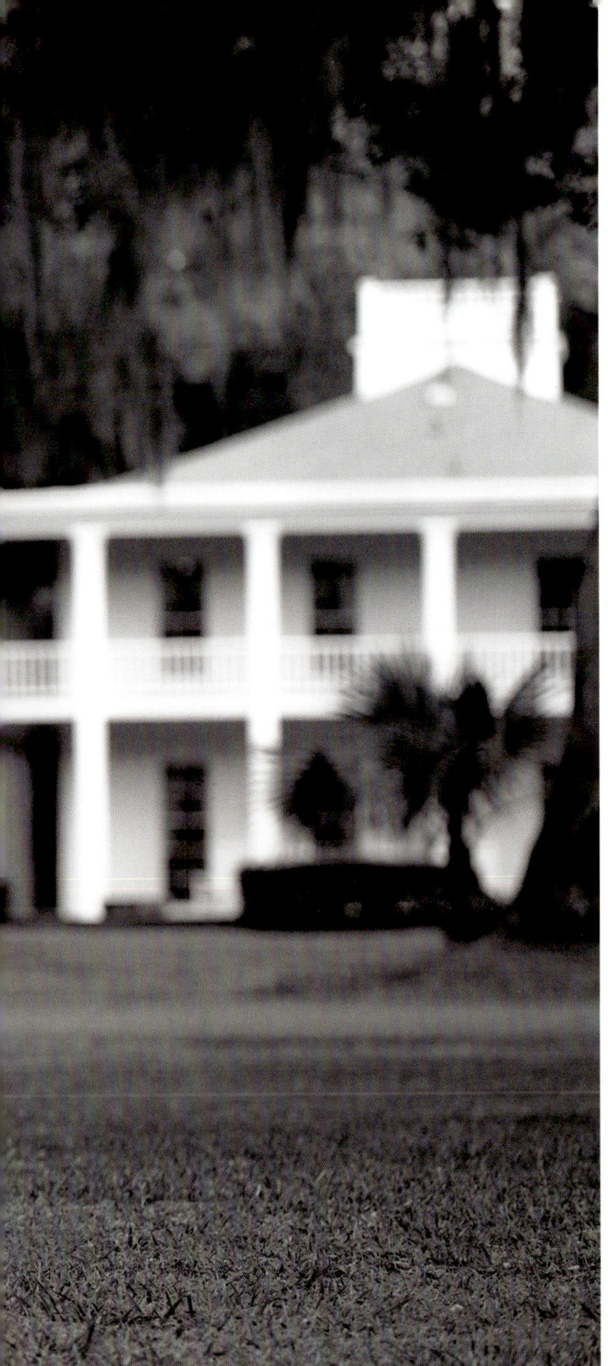

DSLR can handle; we are talking about the summer hours of 11:00AM to 2:00PM. The sun is your key light, while the fill will be in the form of either an on-board flashgun or remotely controlled strobes. I simply do not use reflectors, as the chance of reflecting the sunlight into the subject's eyes is not worth the

risk. You will have your camera set to ISO 100 for this situation. I typically have the subject positioned so that the sun is striking them from an angle somewhere from 15 to 30 degrees to camera left or right. Without any obstruction, the person should be covered in high contrast, specular, bright sunlight—and that is the goal. However, at midday, the sun is high in the sky, which is the cause for shadows under the nose, eyes, and chin. By introducing fill light, we prevent shadows from being formed under the eyes, nose, and chin as well as the shadow side of the body. You can use your on-camera flashgun or off-camera strobe.

Fill light was added with an on-camera flashgun.

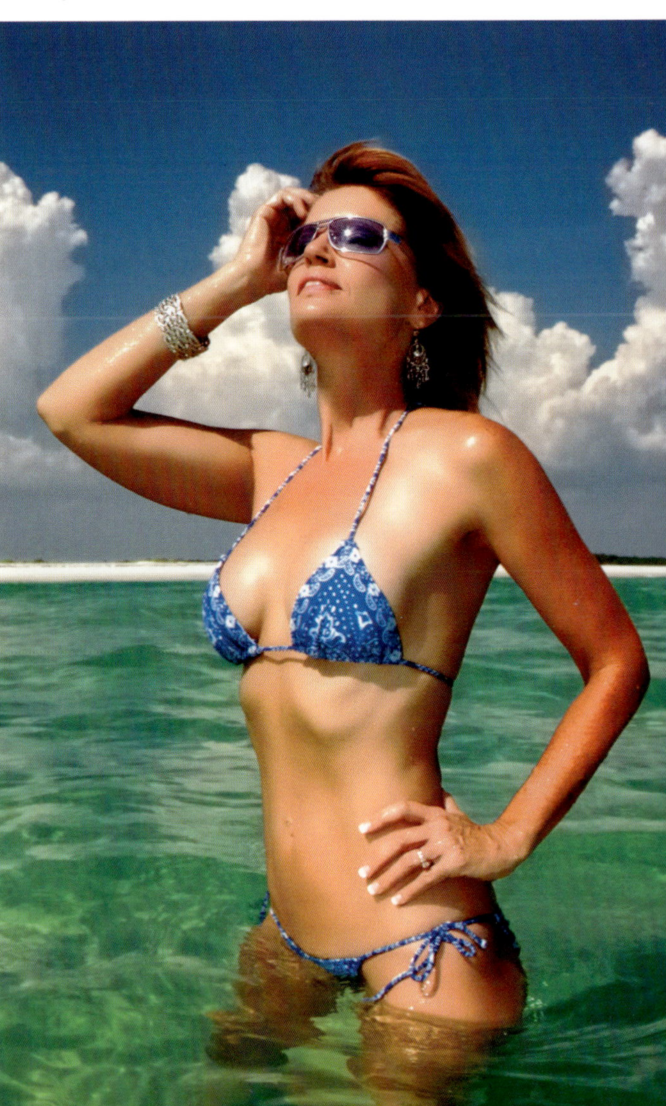

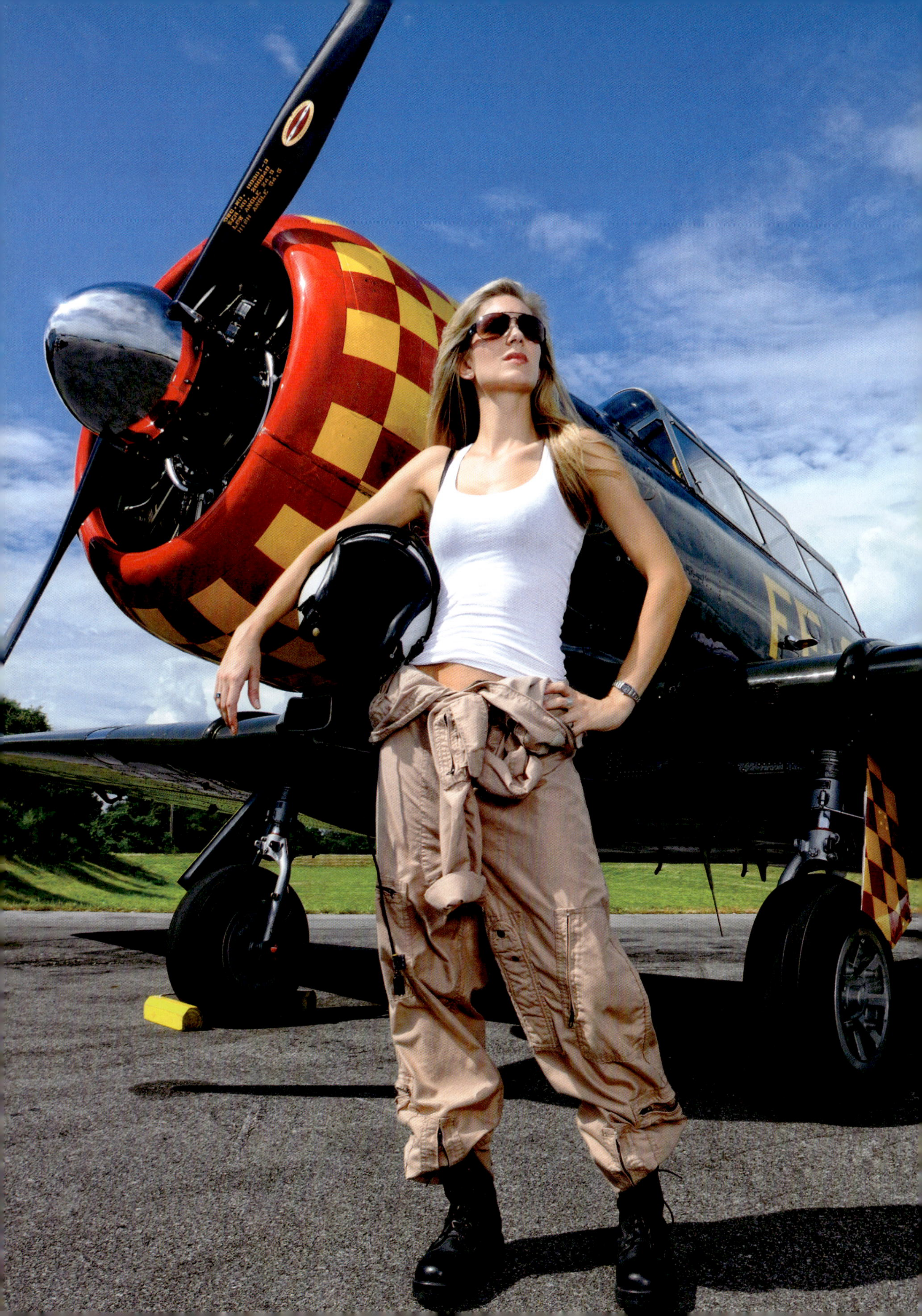

Using On-Camera Flashgun. The beach photo on page 81 was taken with an on-camera flashgun. The ambient light was metered at ISO 100, with a shutter speed of $^1/_{250}$ second, and an aperture of f/8. Neither a UV filter nor a polarizer was used. The flashgun was set to maximum power and a FOV of 24mm (wide) was chosen to match the sun's illumination on the model's face and body. By performing steps 5 and 6 two or three times, the correct exposure was achieved by simply moving closer and closer to the subject. Since we were alone in 3 feet of water 100 yards off of a Florida beach, the flashgun was the only option for a fill light.

Using Off-Camera Flash (Mobile Strobes). In the next example (facing page), an off-camera strobe was used. Step 4 was undertaken in the following manner: since it was a bright, sunny day, we started with ISO 100 but chose ISO 200 so that the strobe had a better chance of illuminating the shadow side of the model and the aircraft. The ambient light was measured at a selected shutter speed of $^1/_{250}$ second, and aperture set to f/13. The camera

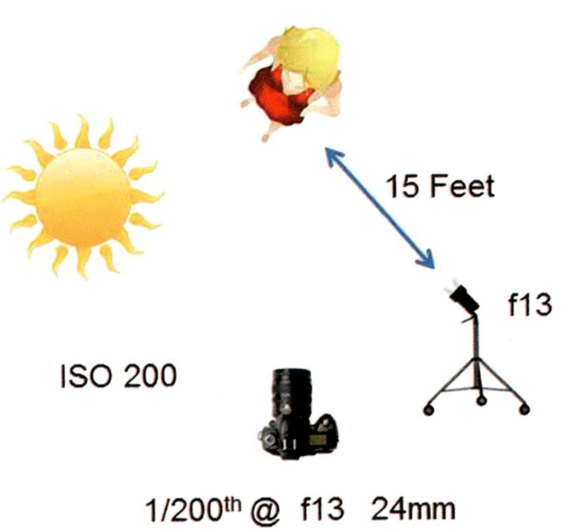

◄ ⌃ Fill light was added with a portable off-camera strobe. The setup is shown above

> ## [It] begins with a good educated guess at what you believe the shutter speed and aperture should be at a given ISO.

was set to these three parameters. Steps 5 and 6 involved switching the light meter to incident metering, and placing it under the model's chin, aimed at the strobe to camera right. The power of the strobe was increased until the light meter read f/13 (equal to the intensity of the sun). The goal was to set the power of the strobe such that it would illuminate the shadow side of the model. The result was an award-winning photograph.

Step 4 (setting the ISO, shutter speed, and aperture) could have been performed by trial and error to arrive at the same settings and result. Trial and error begins with a good educated guess at what you believe the shutter speed and aperture should be at a given ISO. Since we want the background to be exposed properly (that beautiful blue sky) we choose the highest shutter speed that we can sync our remote strobe to—$^1/_{250}$ second. By repeatedly taking exposures and examining the histogram, the aperture was narrowed to a final setting of f/13.

In the next example, the sun is both the key and rim light. Some may protest or argue about how the sun can be the key and rim simultaneously. My response to this is in the form of a question: If no fill is used, then what is the key? The sun, of course! As the key, the sun provides the *ambient* light; by positioning the subject at an extreme angle to the sun so that the sun illuminates the edge of their body, rim lighting is produced. The image of the female was taken with an 85mm prime lens with an on-camera flashgun providing fill. Step 4 involved the trial-and-error method of establishing an educated guess, then steps 5 and 6 were used to set the flashgun to the proper power. The image of the woman in the sunglasses (below) was made with a telephoto lens set to a 135mm focal length. The ISO was 100. The ambient light was measured for a shutter speed of $^1/_{200}$ at f/10. I used an off-camera flashgun for fill. This image proves how well the fill light can perform on a

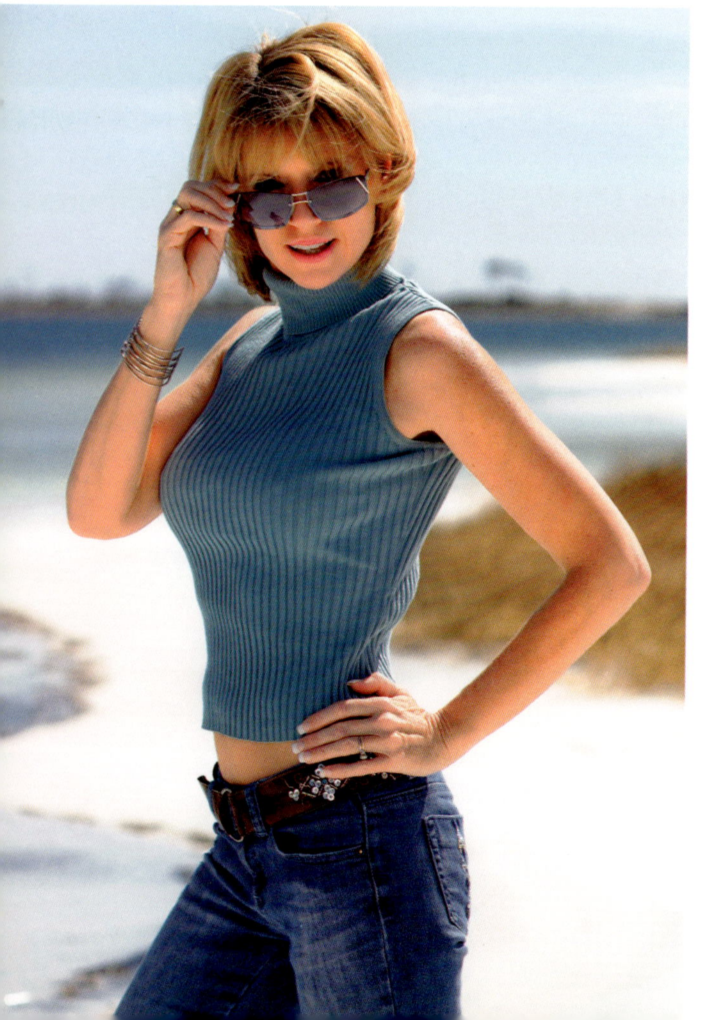

An on-camera flashgun added fill light.

bright, sunny day to illuminate the shadow side. With the flashgun just 12 feet away from the subject, it was discharging at close to maximum power—to compete with the sun!

Shady Areas Under Bright Sun. On a bright, sunny day, good light can be found in the shade. Specifically, I look for overhanging roofs, breezeways, or deeply inset doors. In settings like these, you will find light that beautifully illuminates your subject. Typically, the sun is on the opposite side of the building so that the rays of light are indirect. The diagram on the facing page illustrates what I am talking about. The sunlight is diffused by virtue of the fact that is not directly illuminating your subject. You will notice that as the person being photographed moves closer to the edge of the shadow line, the light starts to change and become harder; moving closer to the depth of the shadow, the light changes to softer. Where you place the individual is up to you and involves the time of day and the reflectivity of the light on that location. This technique and use of the sun as your key light renders photographically dense, colorful, and interesting portraits.

When creating this type of image, once again the sun is your key light. Normally, there will be plenty of soft, even light available to illuminate and flatter your subject. Unless the subject is young and has a perfect complexion, adding fill light is necessary. Again, the fill decreases lines, shadows, and any dark areas under the eyes. Since the sunlight is indirect, a gold reflector *carefully* positioned will also provide just enough fill light to render a beautiful result.

Since we are on the shadow side of a building or architectural overhang, the use of a reflector is okay. If you elect to use a mobile strobe as your fill, you will employ either a softbox or

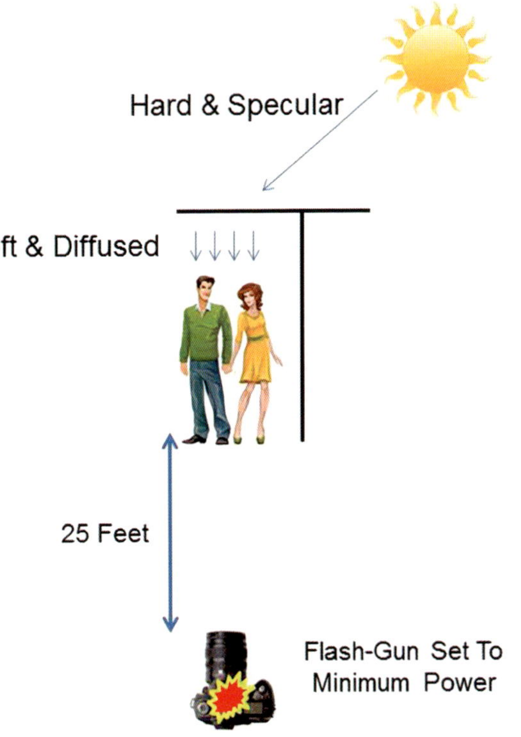

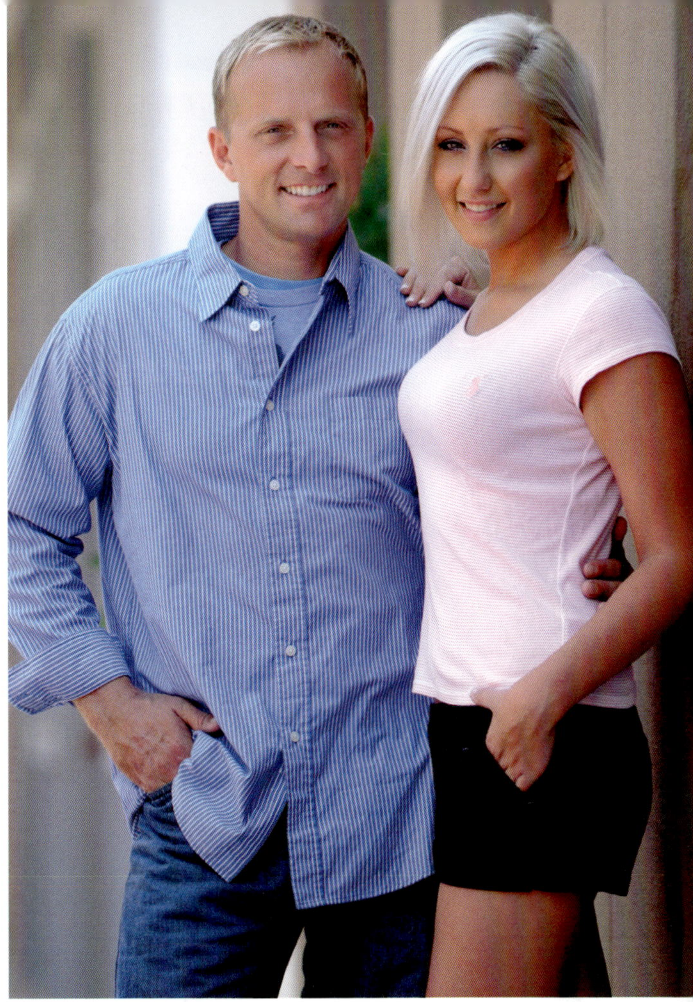

Sunlight was diffused under an overhanging architectural element.

This image is a great example of soft daylight found on the shaded side of a building.

beauty dish (both equipped with a front diffusion panel), as a minimum of power is necessary in this type of lighting situation. If the fill is an on-board flashgun, it will likewise be set to the lower end of its power range. If the fill is too strong, the face will range from being slightly glittery, with kind of a specular metallic quality, to blown out. For the face to look natural, you must pay close attention when performing step 6 and examining the image on the LCD.

When creating an image with this technique, I prefer to use an on-board flashgun. This equipment configuration provides a lightweight and flexible solution to adding fill. I can rapidly accommodate the given light conditions presented by the sun (and therefore the shade I am working under) by adjusting both the power and zoom setting of the flashgun. The image of the young couple (above) was taken at around 11:30AM on a sunny day. They were positioned on the shady side of a large building on a downtown street. A 70–200mm zoom lens was used at approximately 170mm focal length with a crop factor of 255mm (APS-C sensor). The ISO was set to 100, and I chose a shutter speed of $^1/_{200}$ second. Using my light meter, I measured the ambient light where the couple was standing; the meter computed an aperture of f/3.5, and I set my camera accordingly. Next, using steps 5 and 6, I determined the power setting of the on-camera flash. The camera and flashgun were on a tripod roughly twenty-five feet from the couple; the flashgun was set to just above its minimum power. The result is a remarkably soft, flattering image of the two. In the absence of the fill, the eyes are not as bright, lines can be seen on the facial skin, and dark areas appear under the eyes.

Overcast and Cloudy Sky Techniques. When you see that the sky above is overcast or cloudy, you should grab your gear and take advantage of this natural, soft, and beautiful light. Although not all cloudy days are equal in the type and quality of light that is produced, this type of light is the most desirable for outdoor work, as it is a low-contrast and soft light that will flatter most if not all of your clients.

Once again, the sun is your key light, except that now you are working with the largest softbox on the planet—the overcast or cloudy sky.

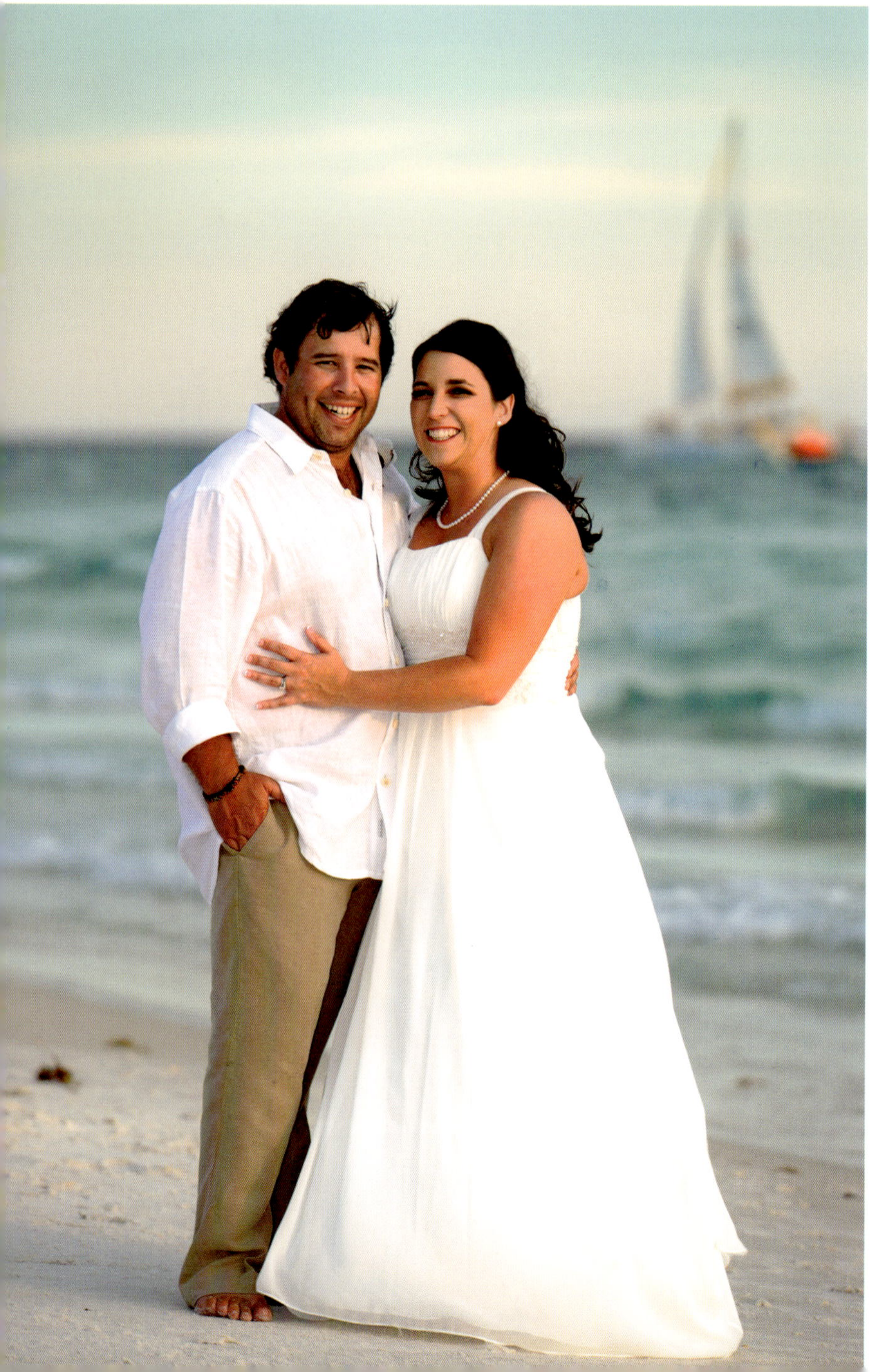

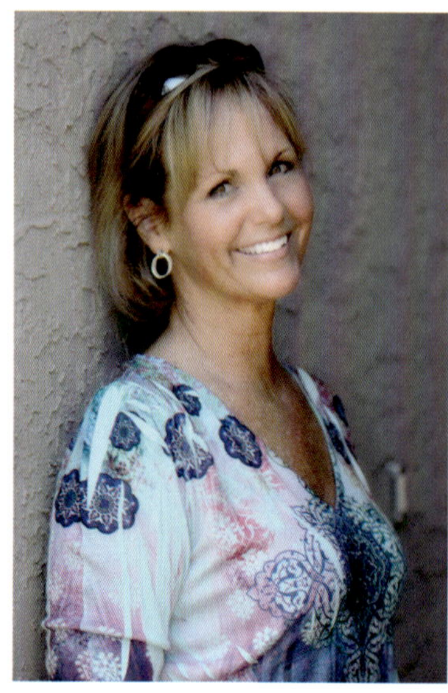

▲ This image is a great example of the use of soft light found underneath an architectural overhang.

◄ In this situation, the fill was used sparingly. It does not take a lot of energy to provide the necessary fill light.

 # RAW versus JPEG

Right up front, I'm going to emphatically recommend that you set your camera to RAW (right now), and leave it there. When you set your camera to RAW, you are maximally capturing all that the camera is capable of sensing (data), registering camera settings (metadata), and storing all of the information with your image file. Conversely, if you set your camera to JPEG (even Fine mode), then you are both throwing away important data and giving up control over the look of the final image. Purchasing an expensive DSLR, a great lens, and then setting the camera to JPEG would be like purchasing a Ferrari, and then letting half the air out of all four tires, pulling a couple of spark plugs out of the engine, and setting the emergency brake on while wanting to go fast and experience the thrill of Italian automotive engineering. That wouldn't make sense, would it? Neither does setting a DSLR to JPEG.

RAW files vary by manufacturer. If you shoot with Sony, the internal structure of the RAW file will be different than the RAW file that comes from a Canon body. Despite the fact that there is not an industry standard for RAW, you should start every shoot in RAW and develop a process to properly convert your RAW files to final images. In order to perform the conversion, you will require a software application called a RAW converter. A RAW converter can either be a plug-in to a bit-map image editor such as Adobe Photoshop, or a complete stand-alone application such as Nik NX2, which is used specifically for Nikon RAW files.

If you do set the camera to JPEG, then when you take an exposure, software that is internal to your camera will produce a JPEG file. JPEG is one popular image file standard because it was originally designed to save space by compressing the overall size of the file. The problem is that the compression is "lossy," so some data is lost during compression. It is the "some data" that you are losing that you don't want to lose! Furthermore, based on camera settings (which you can change) criteria such as saturation, brightness, and contrast are incorporated when the JPEG is created. Thus, as a photographer, when using JPEG mode, you are giving up both important data that constitutes your image and artistic control. I have my DSLR bodies set to RAW with neutral settings. That way, I can make necessary changes in postproduction.

Although it's not exactly the same as a film negative, a RAW file is the original image which contains both data and metadata at the moment the image was captured. In this case, data represents the image, while metadata represents parametric information such as the ISO setting, shutter speed, aperture, etc. At the completion of a shoot, you should back up or store the RAW image files. Make a working copy of the original RAW file (leaving the original intact) to do such things as editing and printing. Doing so will ensure that you will maintain a master copy of the image for future use.

Depending on the brightness of the light filtered through the cloud layer, your camera will be set between ISO 200 and 400. The light of this category is best between late morning and late afternoon. If you shoot too early or too late in the day, the sun will be low in the sky and the resulting photos may lack tonal contrast and appear flat. Use your own judgment on this point, but I usually quit by late afternoon. I highly recommend that you join the camera to a tripod or strap the camera to your arm and enable vibration reduction if your lens is so equipped. The reason is that you will be setting your shutter speed anywhere from $^1/_{60}$ to $^1/_{200}$ second, and on

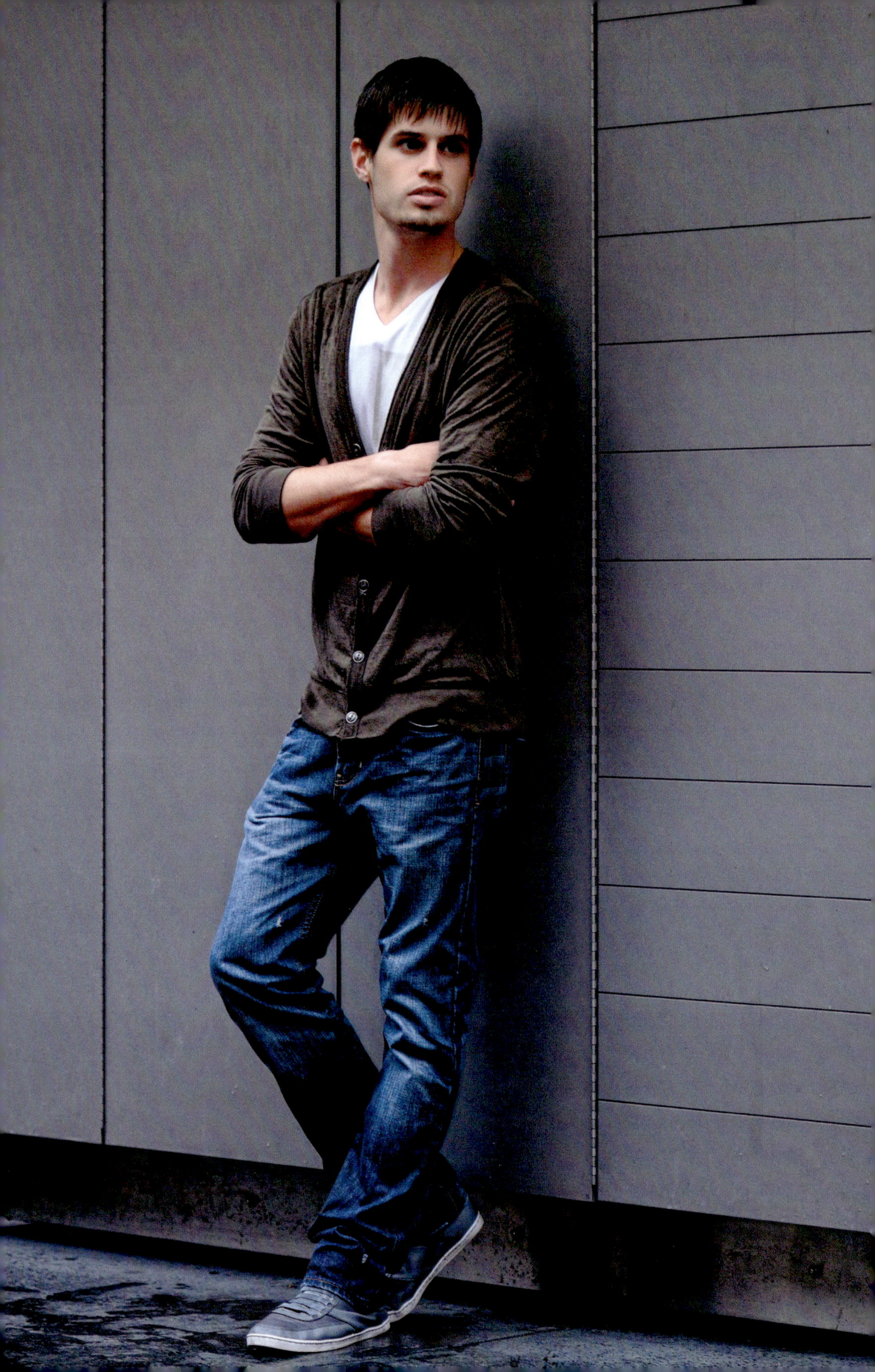

the lower end of the scale, isolating the camera from vibration will be absolutely necessary in order to avoid blur in the final image.

Beach Photography

What we have just gone over in terms of creating an outdoor portraiture holds true, but let's take a closer look at working at the beach. The beach offers a couple of unique challenges that I thought we should address. Normally when photographing people at a shoreline, we gravitate toward positioning people where the water meets the land. So, the first challenge comes with the horizon and realizing that a horizontal line will show up in the image. If it is a sunny day, then there will be an abundance of light

◄ This image was shot on a rainy day in downtown San Diego. The ambient light was soft. The shopping area had plenty of features, and it was decided that a gray steel wall would be used for the background. I asked the young man to pose in a natural position by leaning against the wall. ISO 400 was selected, and a shutter speed of $^1/_{100}$ second was chosen. An ambient light meter reading calculated an aperture of f/3.2. I set the camera accordingly. Using a 70–200mm zoom, and positioned 20 feet away, I got down low to his knee level. By repeating steps 5 and 6 twice, I narrowed the power of the on-camera flashgun to just slightly above minimum power and a zoom setting of 120mm. I took a series of ten exposures, the best of which you are reviewing. It took all of about three minutes to obtain this photograph. I believe the young man liked it too.

▼ Soft late-afternoon sunlight combined with a prop suitable for children, yielding this image.

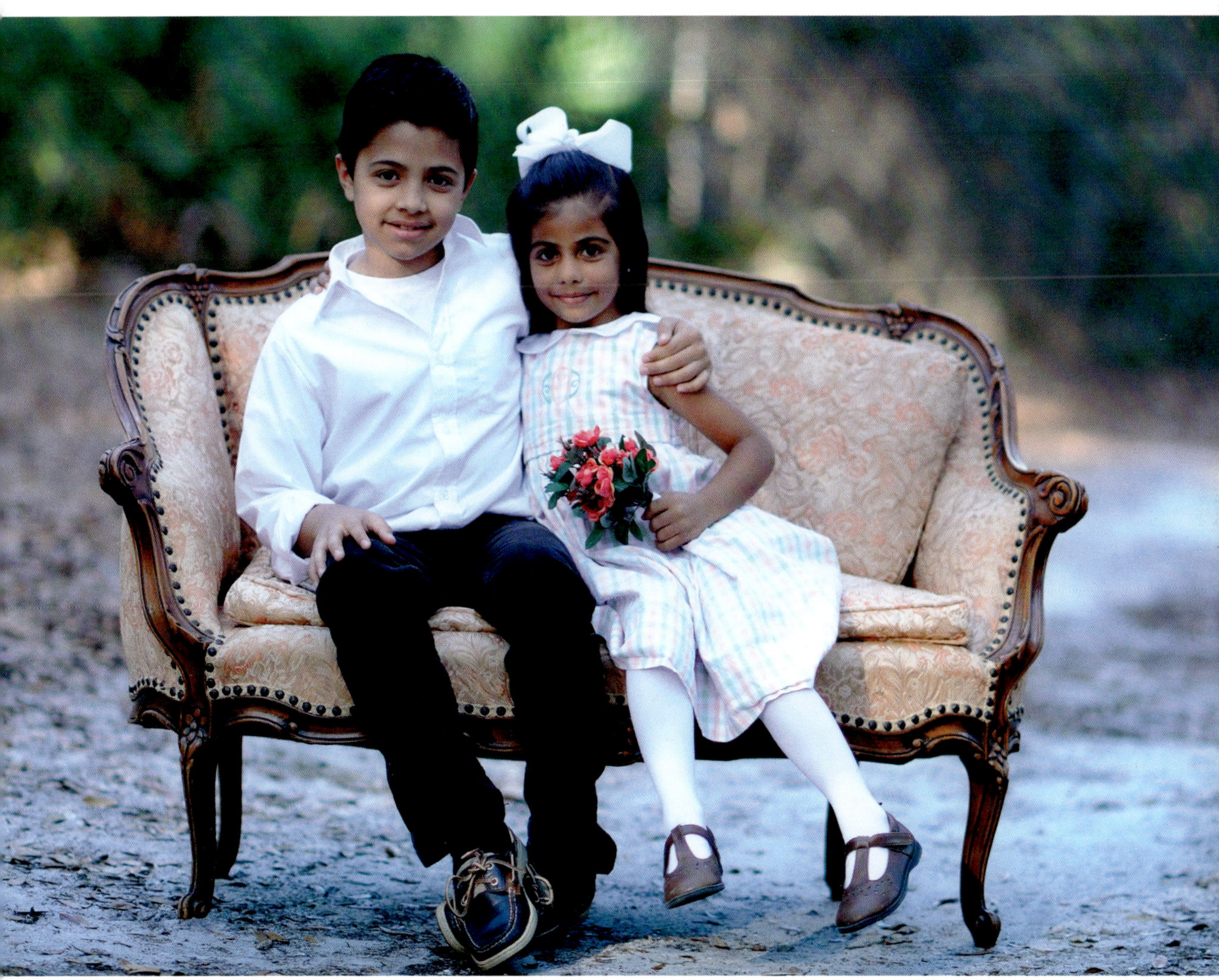

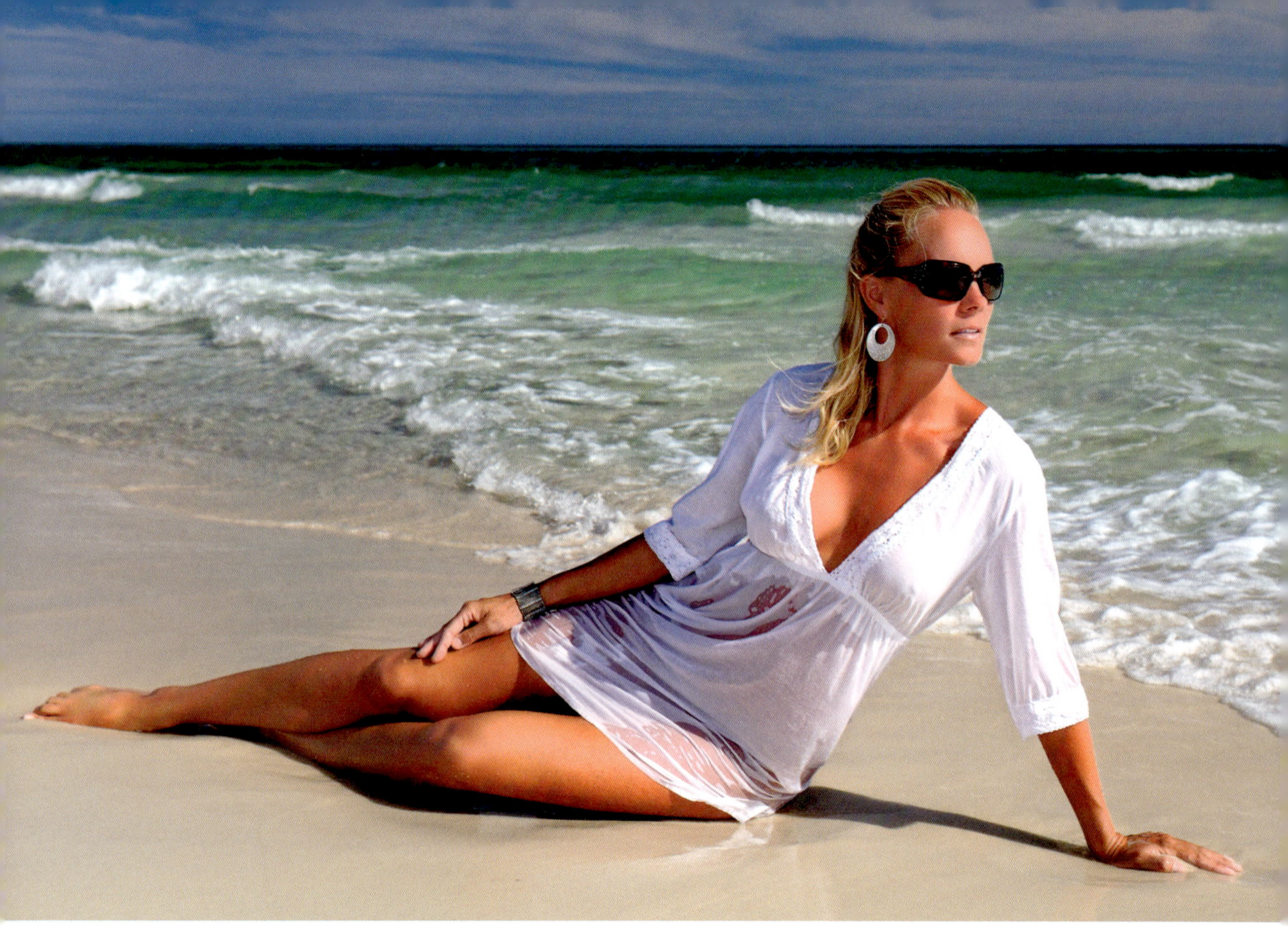

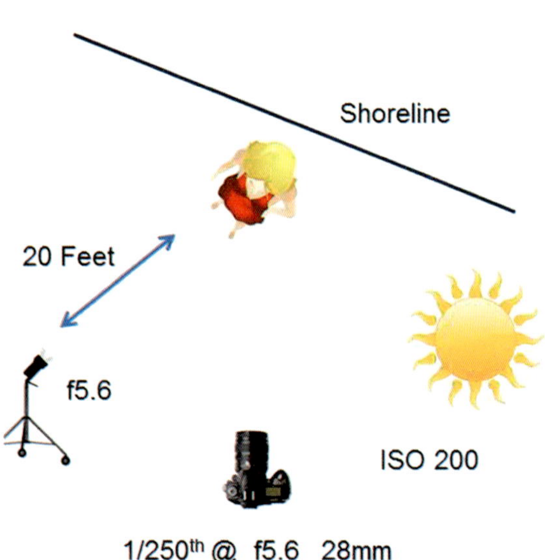

◄ This diagram depicts a typical shoreline beach portrait using portable off-camera strobe.

▲ Here is the final result, a fashion image. The subject was positioned below the line formed by the horizon, illuminated by the sun as the key light, with fill light illuminating the front and right side of the model.

reflecting off of the sand and water. If it is a cloudy day, then the sky and water may blend together, creating a featureless and potentially uninteresting background. And of course, there is often wind.

The image above adheres to two guiding principles. First, the subject was positioned below the horizon. Second, the placement adheres to the rule of thirds. Taken in the late afternoon, the sun was approximately 30 degrees azimuth. The sun was the key light (this can be determined by noting the shadows on the sand). To camera left, an off-camera strobe was used to fill the shadow side.

Careful use of a 28mm focal length developed an interesting perspective with the diminishing line of the beach and the horizon.

The next image, a dramatic black & white shot, was taken just moments later. The identical settings and position of the camera were used to yield an award-winning photo.

The photograph has a great deal of density. Sure, the horizon bisected the photo (that's a no-no), but the strength of the image's other aspects carry the shot. Note that the model was placed in the left third of the frame for maximum impact.

Just out of the frame, an assistant held a scrim over the subject's head to cut the intense

Placed just above the subject's head and out of the frame, a scrim was used to cut the midday sunlight . . .

midday sunlight for a softer, more flattering look. A flashgun set to minimum power was used on-camera to fill the shadows.

Note the diminishing line formed by the waterline.

Both the color and black & white image were shot at ISO 100, $^{1}/_{250}$ second, and f/8. For both portraits, I shot with a 70–200mm zoom lens set to a focal length of 135mm. Using a polarizing filter helped to cut the glare, render more dramatic color (facing page), and add drama (below).

Using the identical lighting setup yielded a very different result. She is looking away from the lens entirely, but this image works!

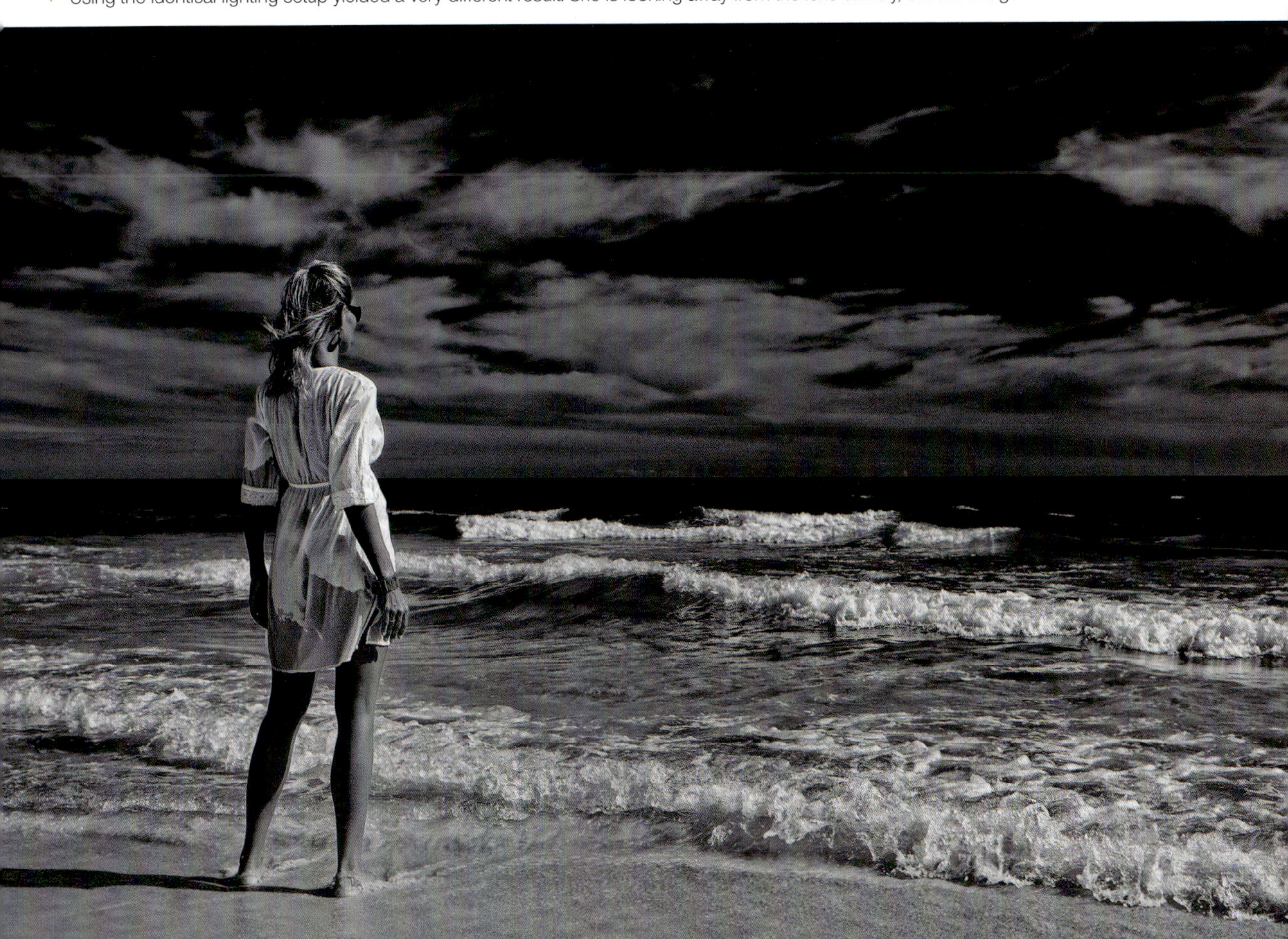

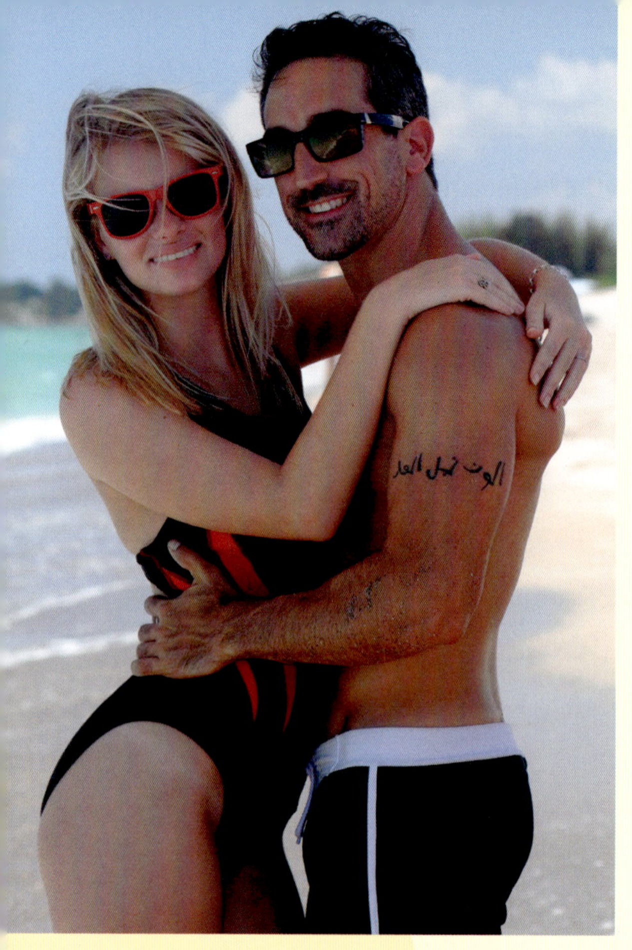

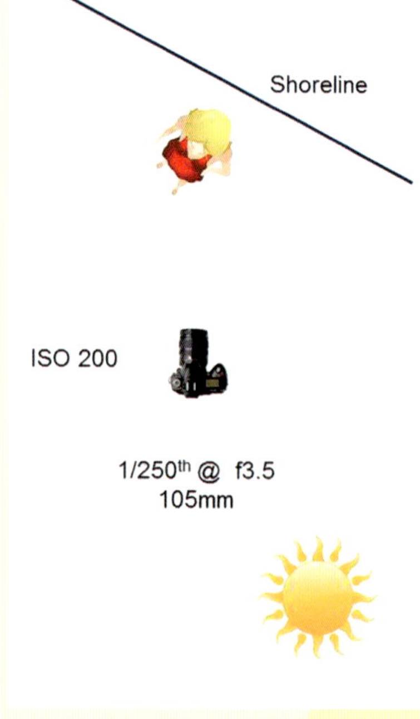

◄ ▼ These two beach images show the differences in how the sun is harnessed as the key light. The couple standing in the Gulf of Mexico was underneath a scrim, which greatly softened the sunlight. The young lady sitting on the beach in Destin, FL had the setting sun illuminate her, without a modifier. In both situations, an on-camera flashgun was used to ensure the shadows were removed. The diagram shows the setup used for the photo at the bootom of the page.

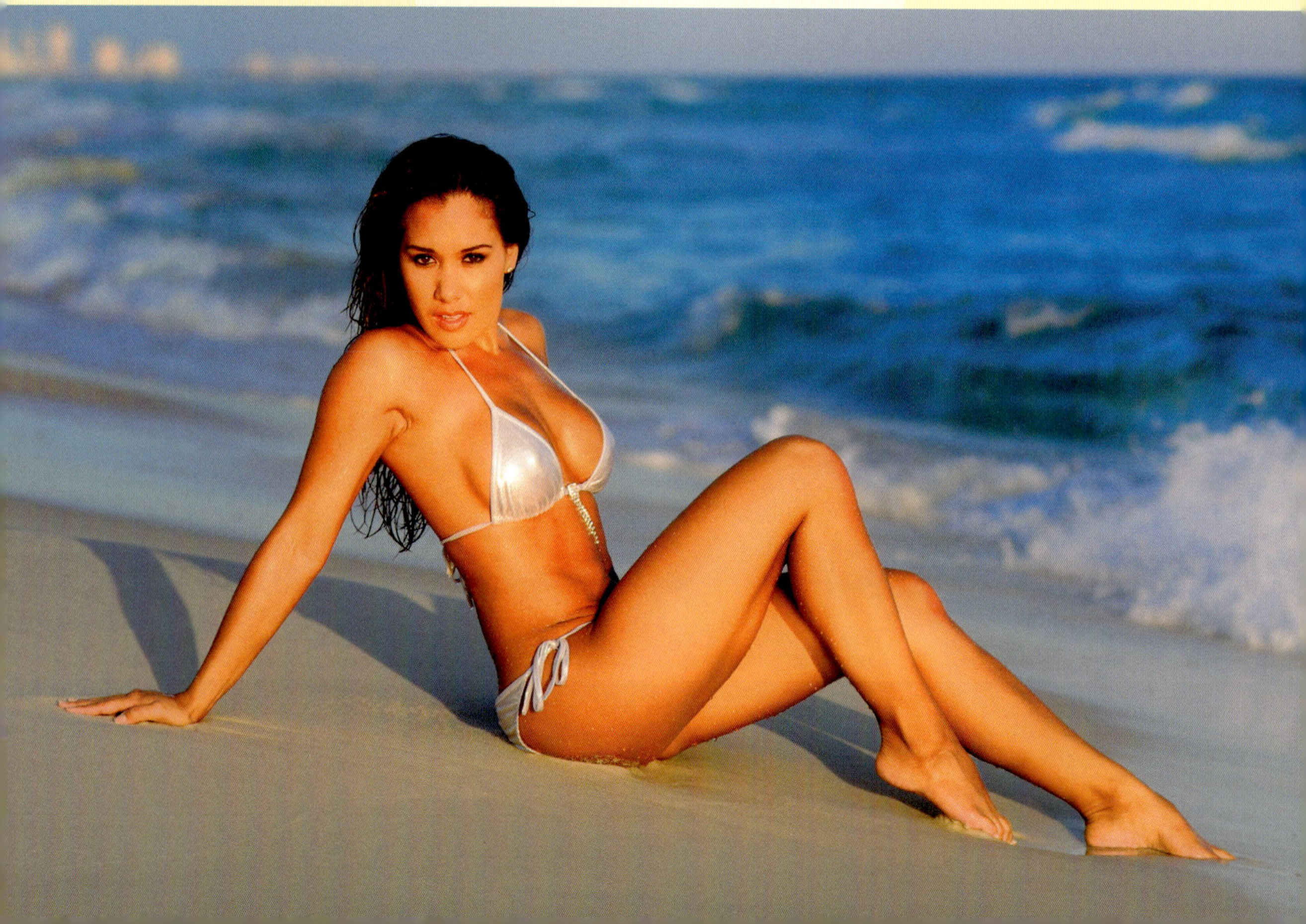

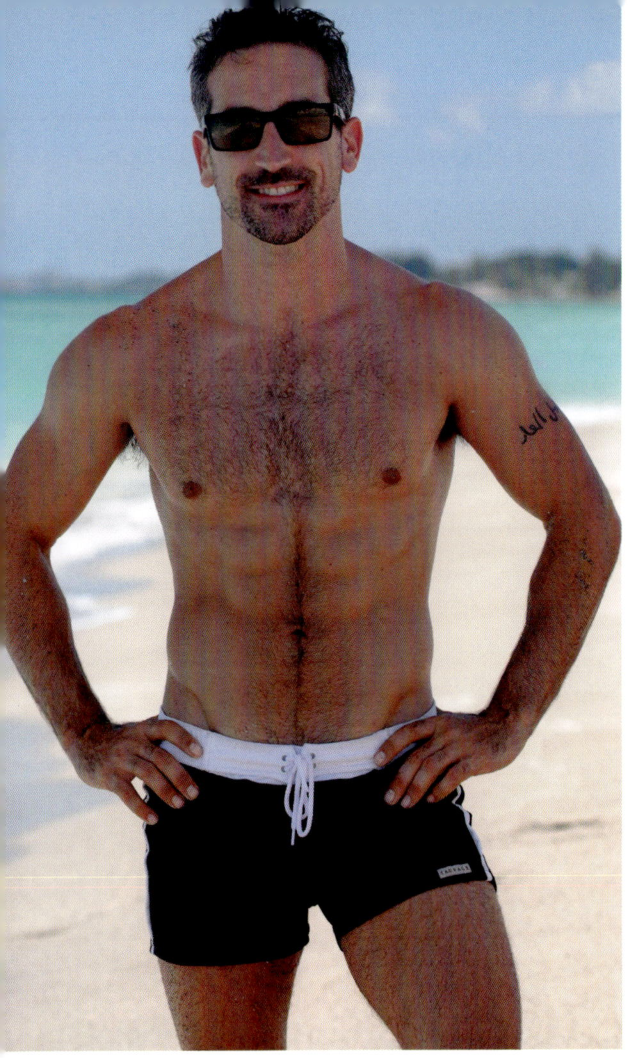

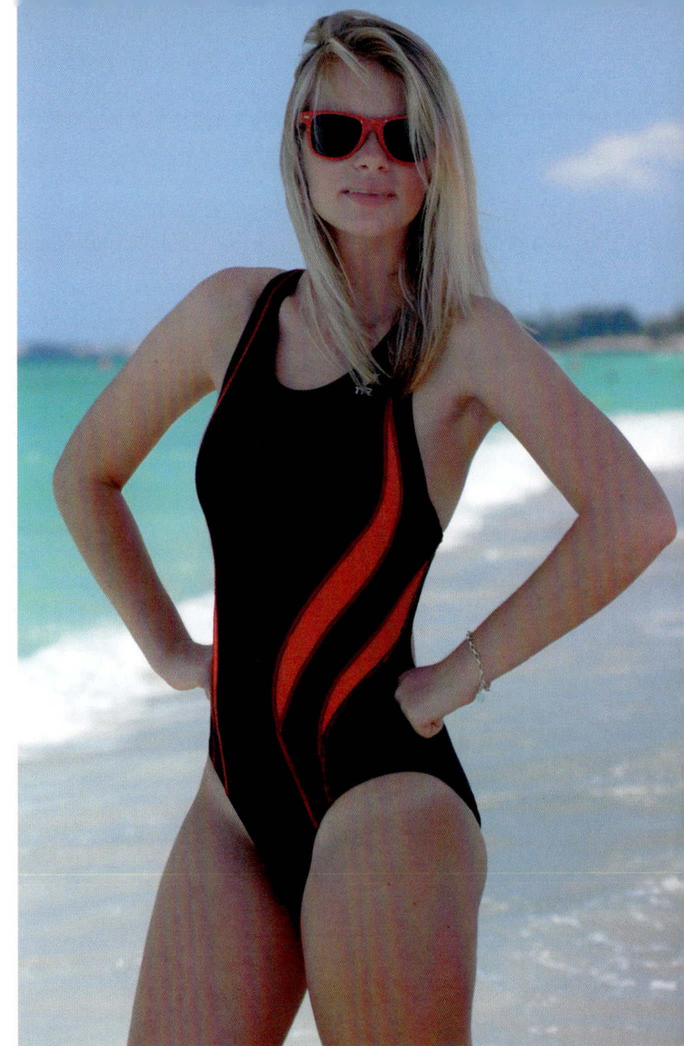

This is a typical yet effective setup used to diffuse sunlight at the beach. The glare of the sun was removed, leaving soft, even light.

(left and right) The result of using a scrim is a pleasing portrait.

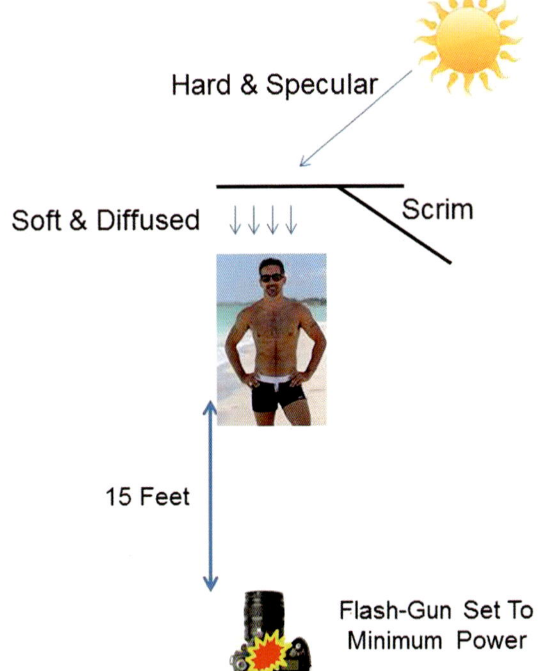

The next image (below), taken moments before the sun hit the horizon, is an example of the beautiful light that exists at sunset. With the sun as the key light, an on-camera flashgun was used for fill, which enhanced detail on the on the left side of the model. The result is a dynamic image of pose and context (taken on the North Shore of Oahu, HI).

To capture this photograph, I used a 17–35mm zoom at a 17mm focal length. The exposure was f/5.6 at $^1/_{250}$ and ISO 200. While I used a wide-angle zoom, I made sure that any bending or stretching of the model was kept to a minimum.

Whenever possible, avoid blowing out the sky. The sky should have some hue of blue and the detail of clouds if they are present. On a sunny day, set the ISO to 100 and choose a shutter speed of $^1/_{250}$ second; your aperture will be a function of exposing your subject correctly.

As we previously discussed, your fill provides the illumination to the shaded side. In the final image in this chapter, both the sky and the person being photographed are properly exposed.

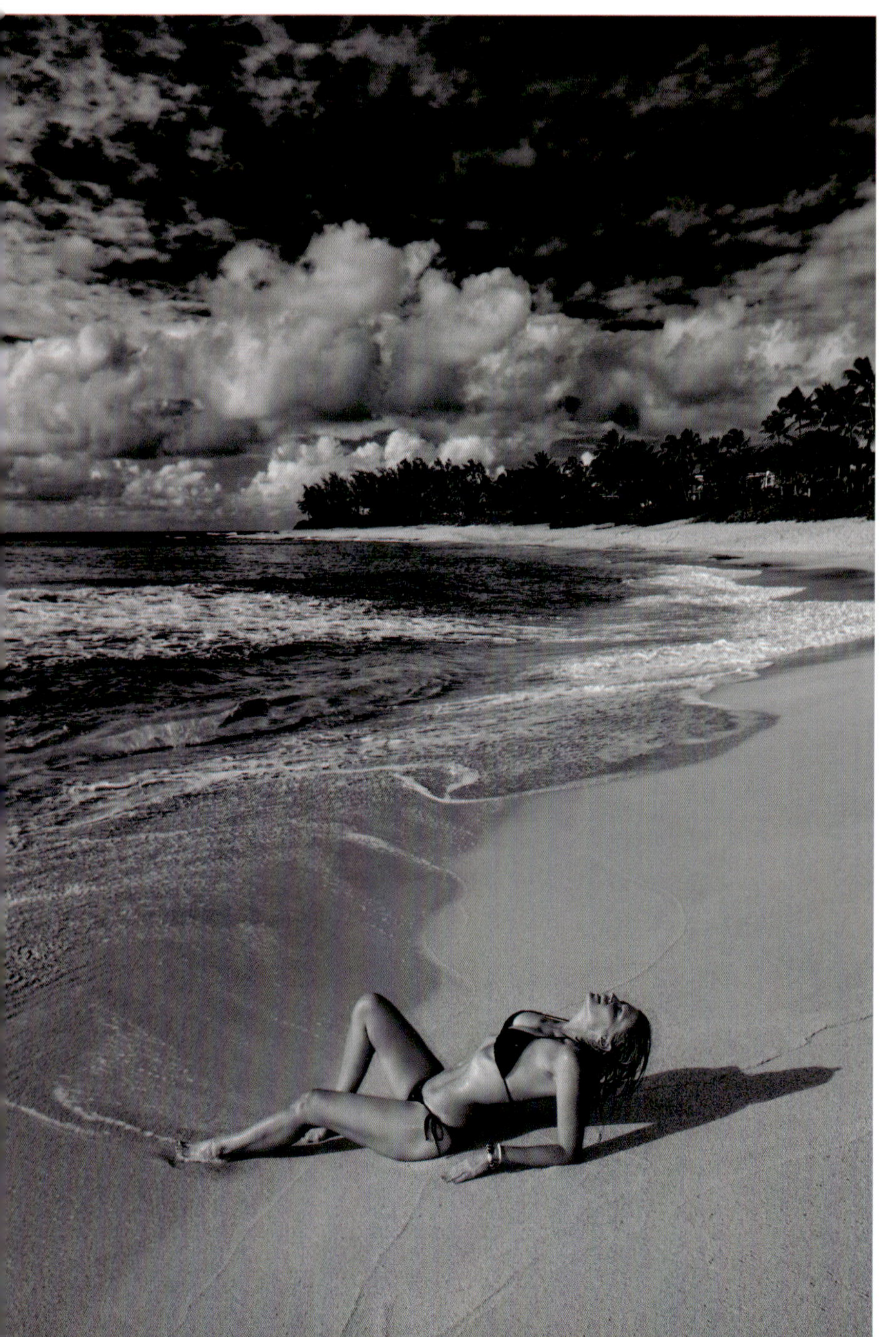

◄ Although this image was taken in the portrait format, I consider the photograph to be panoramic. Your eye is first drawn to the model resting in the sand, then upward to the surf, and then on to the beautiful sky. The image looks best rendered in black & white.

► Taken at high noon, and thirty minutes prior to sunset, the sky has color, texture, and adds greatly to the context of the images.

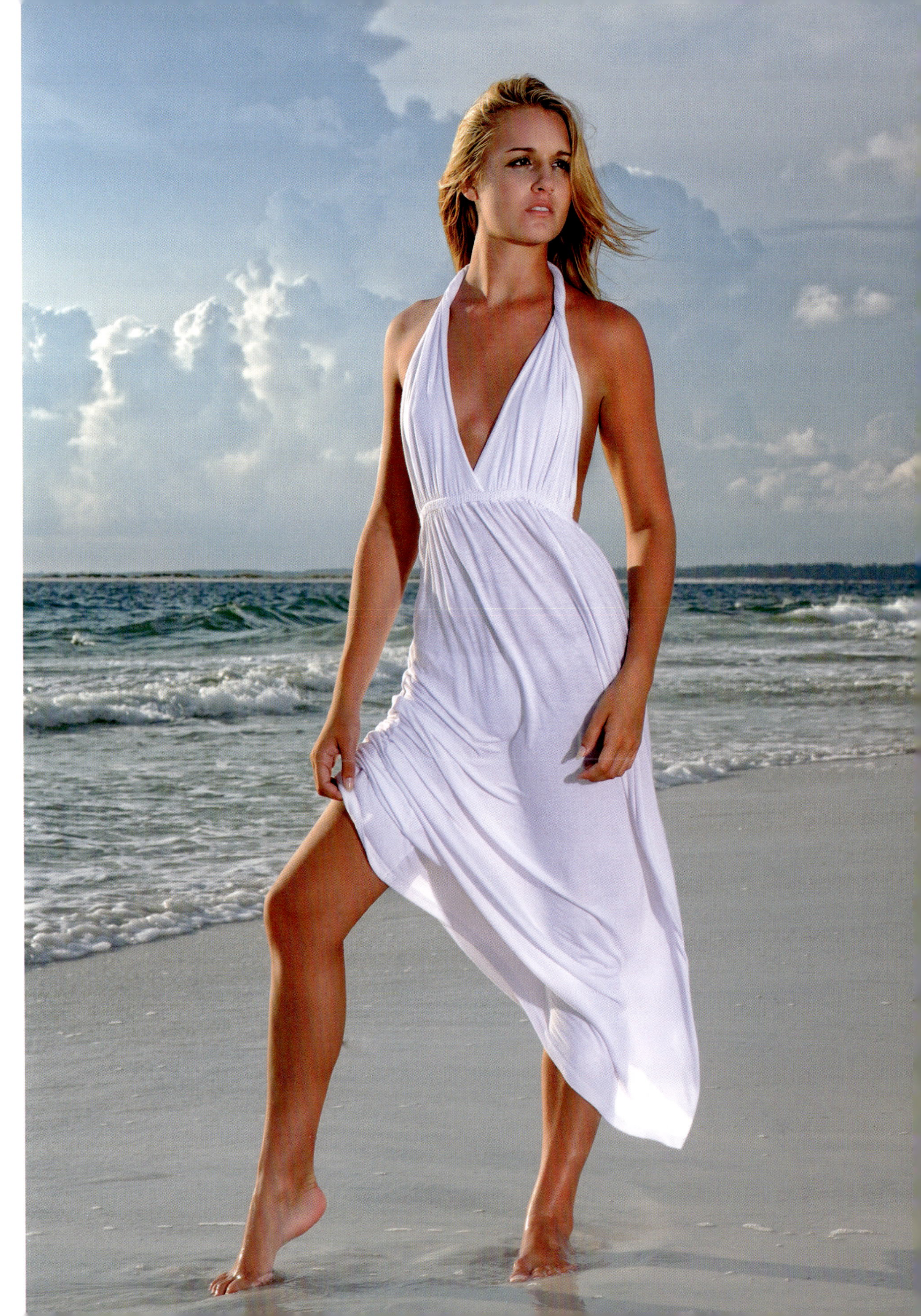

5. Studio Portraits

The Studio as a Workspace

Perhaps the most important aspect of a studio environment is control. Whether you are using a basic set of equipment or the most sophisticated lighting and camera controls, the studio is a terrific domain in which to express your creativity. With so many companies offering quality studio equipment, the choices are staggering. Products range from entry-level strobes and softboxes to computer-controlled lighting and sophisticated backdrop systems. I'm going to give most if not all of it a big thumbs up. But let's assume that you are just starting out, have a limited budget, and want to create great photos in your studio.

The studio that we are going to talk about does not have windows, nor skylights; we'll discuss those in chapter 6. The size of your studio is an important factor in what you will be able to achieve on portrait projects. The length of the room is the boundary condition for the lens focal lengths that can be properly used for headshots, three-quarter, and full-length images. The diagram on the facing page is representative of the point.

Incident Light Meters

The light meter is set to incident mode. An incident light meter is a very useful tool in the studio, on location, and outdoors, and it provides the ability to precisely measure the light that is illuminating your subject. I believe that it is important to know how to use a light meter, but it is not imperative to use one. For me, relying on a meter means that I can work more efficiently and eliminate guesswork or ensure that I have a light ratio set correctly. But, to be perfectly honest, after a while, you will get to know your lighting equipment and cameras, and using relative settings will become a natural habit. With the proper use (i.e., analysis) of the LCD and histogram, calibrating the camera and lighting equipment becomes straightforward—if not easy.

Lens Selection

Earlier, we discussed that in the studio, the choice of lens and focal length must take into account the distance between the person being photographed and the camera, whether it be a head shot, three-quarter portrait, or full-length image (which in turn is a function of the size of your studio). We should be thinking about this because in smaller studios, there is a tendency for photographers to choose a wider lens (17–30mm) to get that full-length image. In my opinion, this is not a good idea. Yes, there

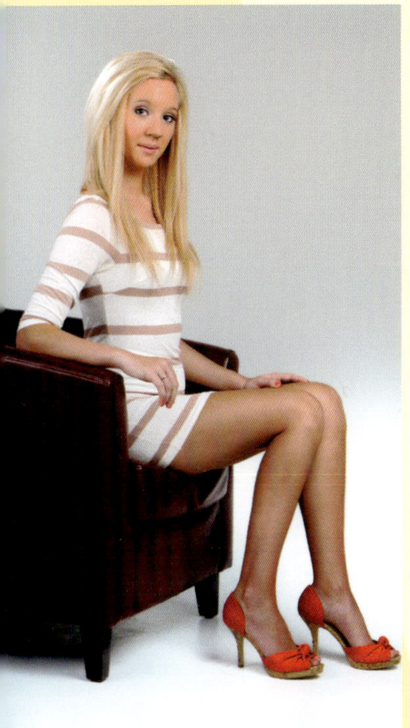

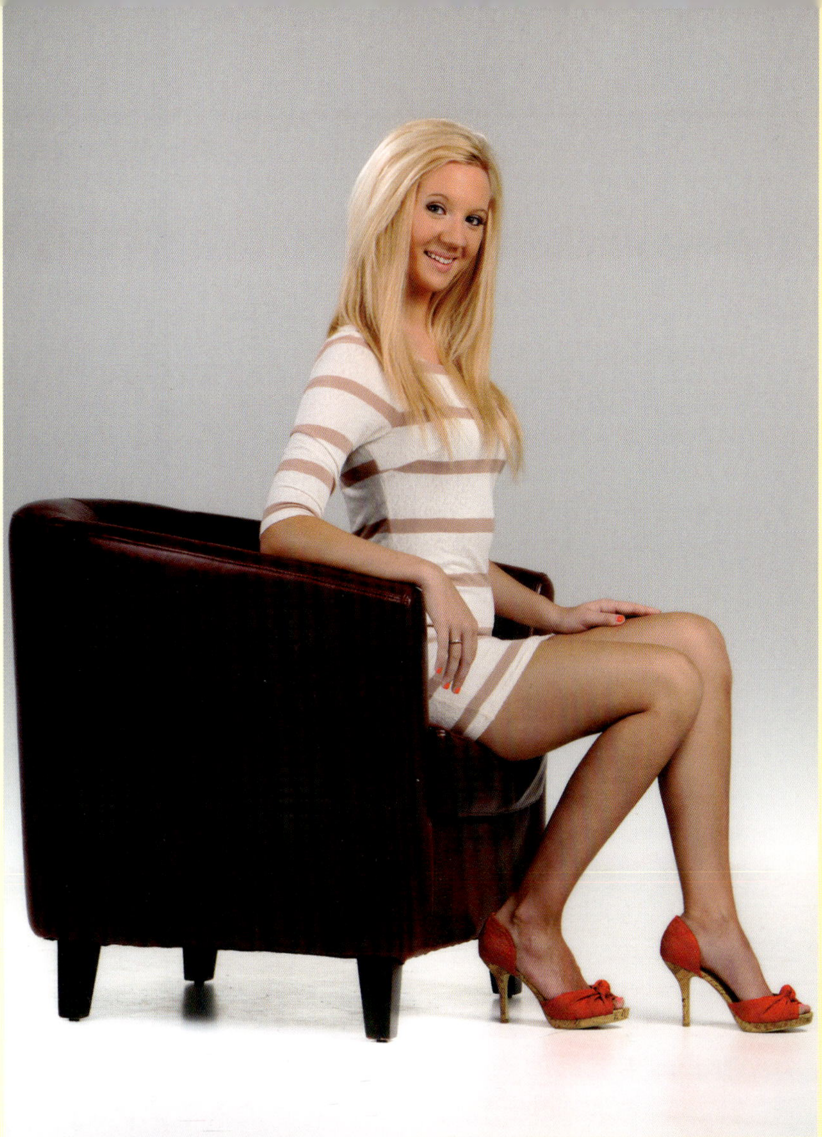

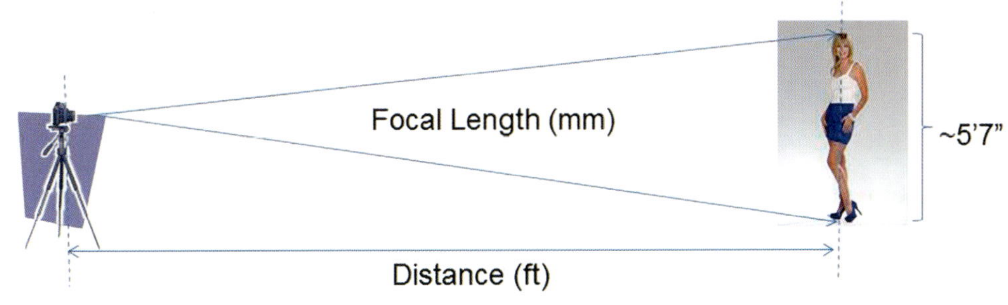

Focal Length (mm)	Distance (ft)
50	9.5
85	15
105	20
135	24
200	34

are creative modes, but we are discussing the fundamental aspects of portraiture. You might be thinking that using a wider lens will place you closer to the subject and thus translates to a smaller room or space. You could do this, but then you run the risk of anamorphic error of the person being photographed, resulting in bending and twisting their form.

Focal lengths ranging from 50mm to 200mm work very well. Careful use of focal lengths of 50mm, 85mm, and 135mm produce pleasing results with little to no perceptible distortion to the person being photographed. The diagram on the previous page illustrates the relationship between focal length and the relative distance from lens to subject—given a nominal height of the person being photographed.

Strobes

A strobe is a flash tube that provides an on-demand intermittent source of light. Strobes are efficient at taking stored energy and releasing it in the form of a brief burst of light (e.g., $^1/_{1500}$ second). Strobes typically range in power from 300 to 1200 watt/seconds and can be used in any combination that you may require. A watt/second is a rating of the amount of energy released by the strobe. I wouldn't get hung up on this. I use 600 watt/second strobes, and they provide *more* than enough light. May I suggest that if you endeavor to photograph large scenes with many actors, then 1200 watt/second strobes may be required.

An 85mm prime lens was used for this beautiful image.

Strobes can be used with or without light modifiers. Recall that our goal as portrait photographers is to idealize the appearance of the person being photographed. Unmodified

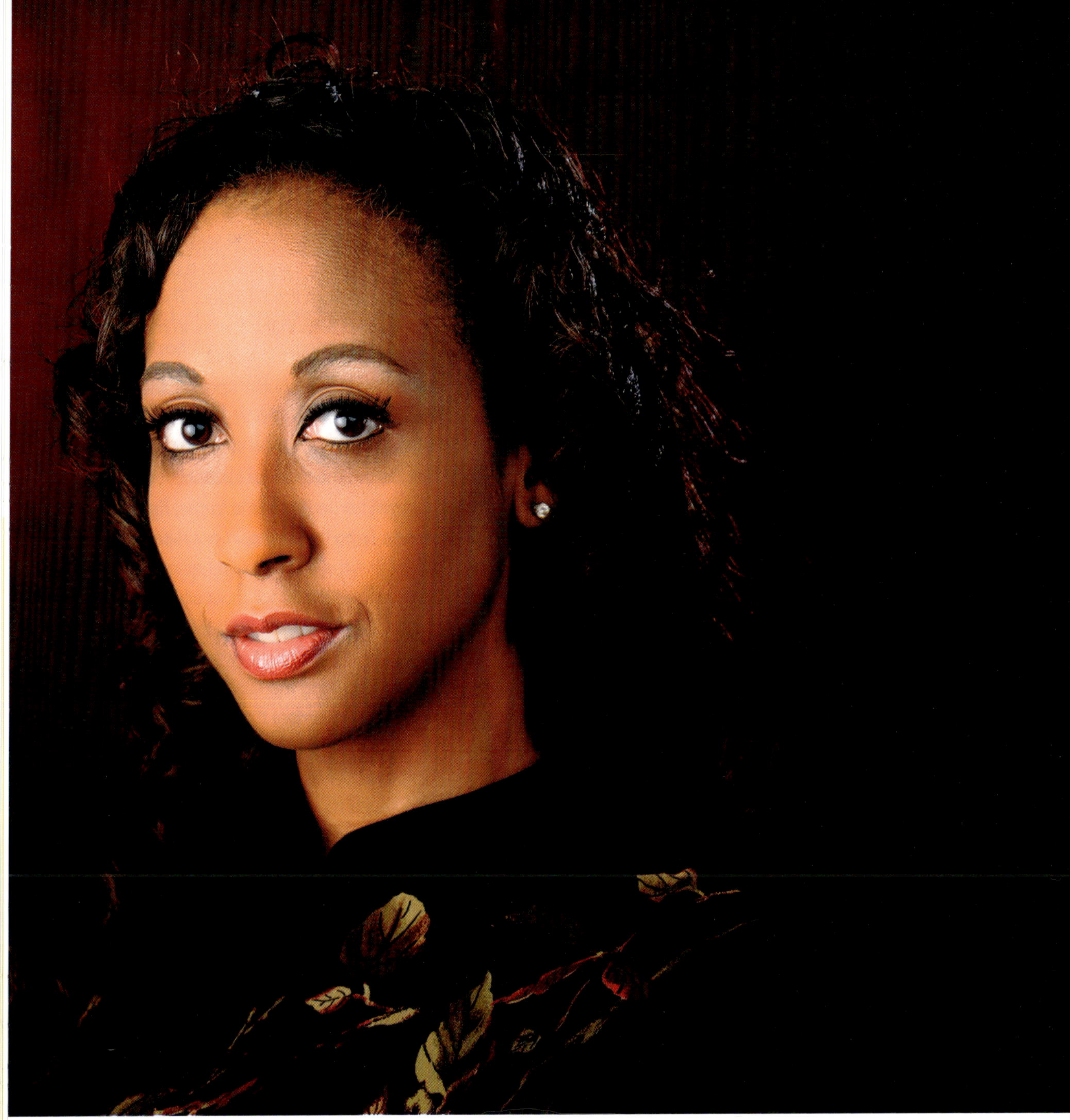

strobes produce harsh light. We must modify (soften) that light in order to make it usable. To do so, we use a softbox or an umbrella placed in front of and attached to the light source. The softbox and umbrella both have material which is slightly opaque (typically made of plastic or rip-stop nylon). This combination of opaqueness and surface area results in diffusing the light passing through; the greater the surface area, the softer the light. Strobes are activated by a wired or radio frequency (RF) trigger or electric cable from the camera, or from the light

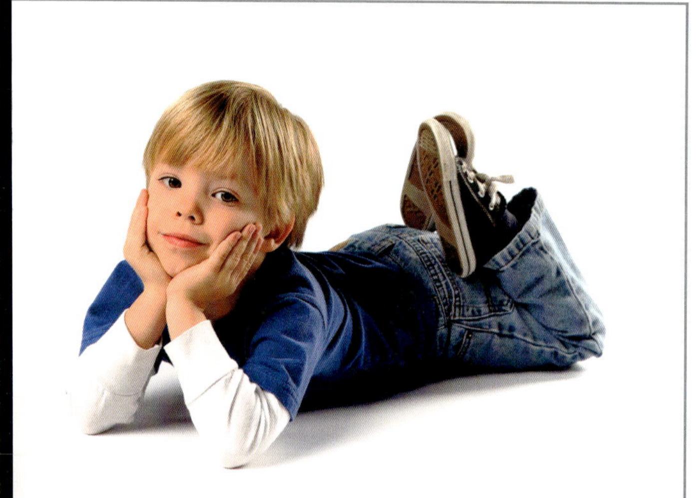

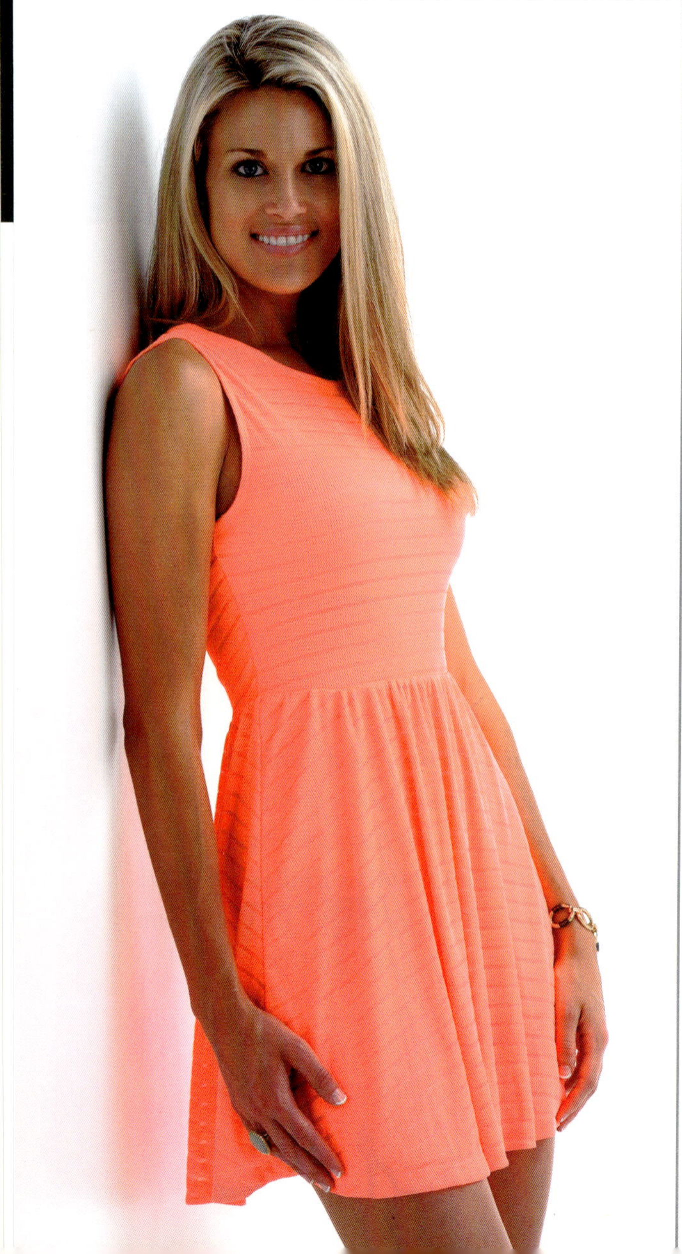

key portraiture works very well with children and families. The results are dynamic, specular, detailed images. Without a doubt, high-key is my favorite approach; I find that the expressive qualities of the person being photographed can easily be captured and even exaggerated.

I typically use a 5-foot octabox connected to strobes that are rated at 600 watt/seconds. Fill light is driven by the same strobe with a 24x36-inch softbox. Although not absolutely necessary, a 6-foot octabox is employed as an additional

◄ (top) This tyke posed in front of a 10-foot roll of white paper.
◄ ► The young lady and gent were asked to stand/lean against a wall in the studio. I used the key and fill lighting described above.
▼ A typical high-key lighting setup. This setup produces images with a dynamic, energetic feel.

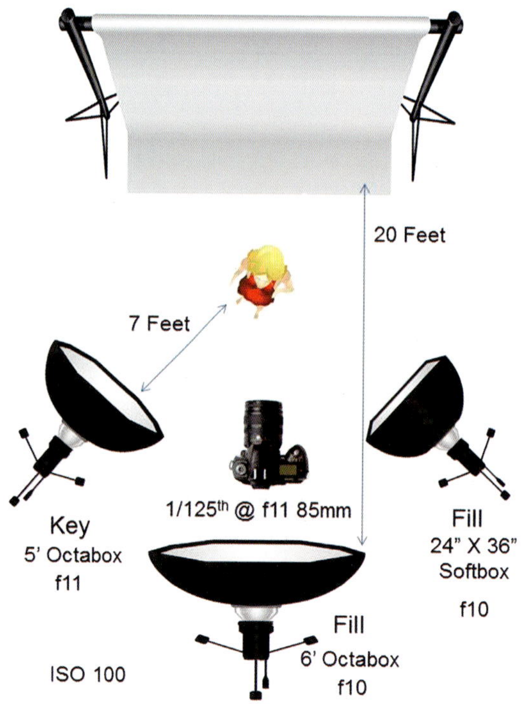

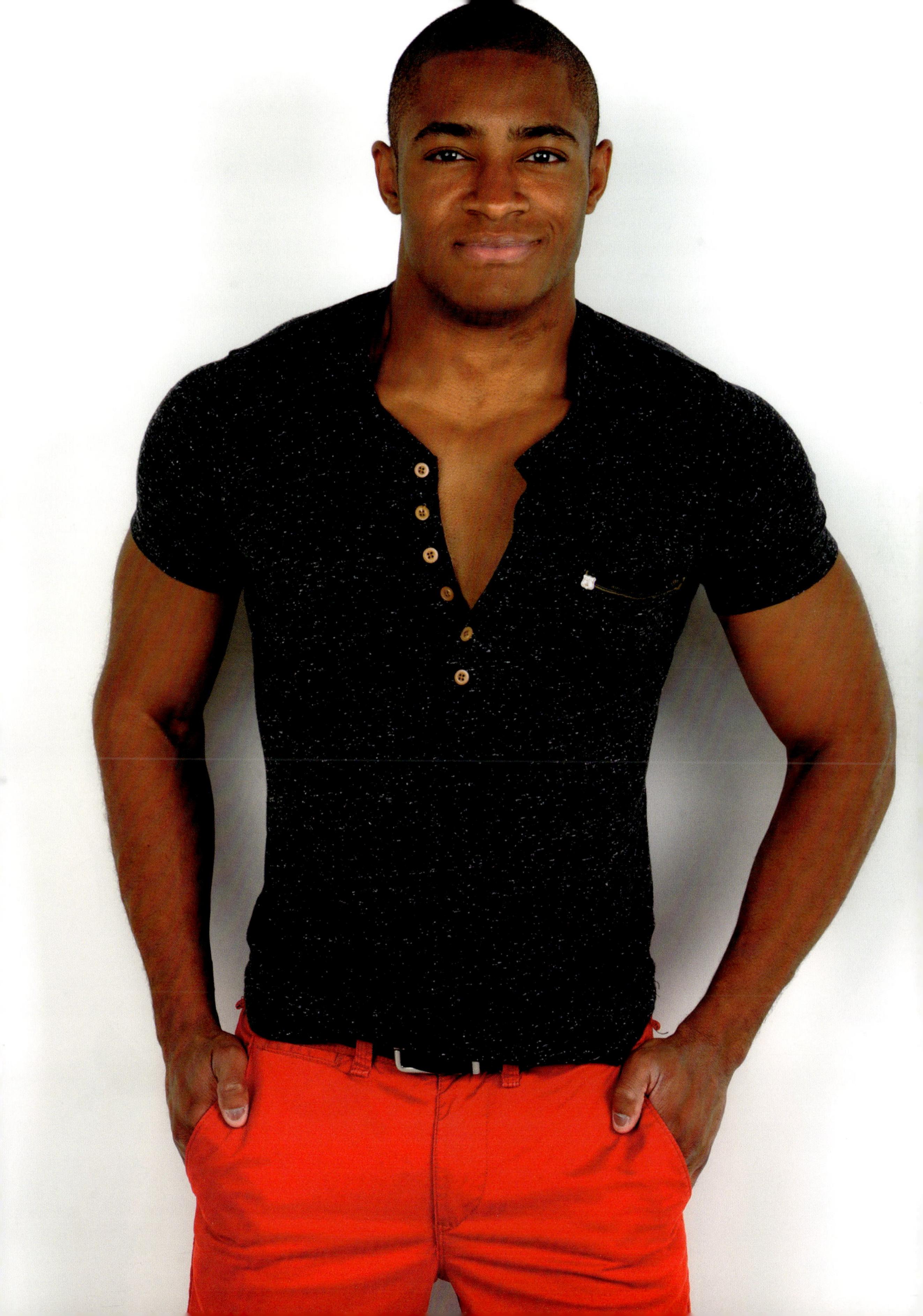

fill light and set 20 feet from the backdrop and behind the camera. I generally do not use a rim light for this type of project because there is already sufficient light, but a rim light could be added. To keep the light falling off the subject to a minimum, the subject is placed close to the backdrop and in some cases is asked to lean against a wall in the studio.

Steps 1 through 3 have been performed. The selection of backdrop (normally white), props, position, and pose are complete. Step 4 involves the selection of ISO 100 with a shutter speed of $^1/_{125}$ second at f/11, and the camera is set accordingly. The light meter is set to incident mode, placed under the chin of the subject, and aimed at the key light, which is metered to f/11 while both fill lights are measured and read $^1/_3$ stop below f/11, which is f/10. This is a very bright situation! If a rim light were to be used, it would be positioned to illuminate the edge of the subject and metered to a full stop above the key at f/13. I generally use 50mm, 85mm, and 105mm prime lenses, as well as a 70–200mm zoom for this type of work.

Mid Key. Mid key portraiture typically involves a moderate level of contrast and accentuates the shadow side of the face and body of the person being photographed. Mid key is almost

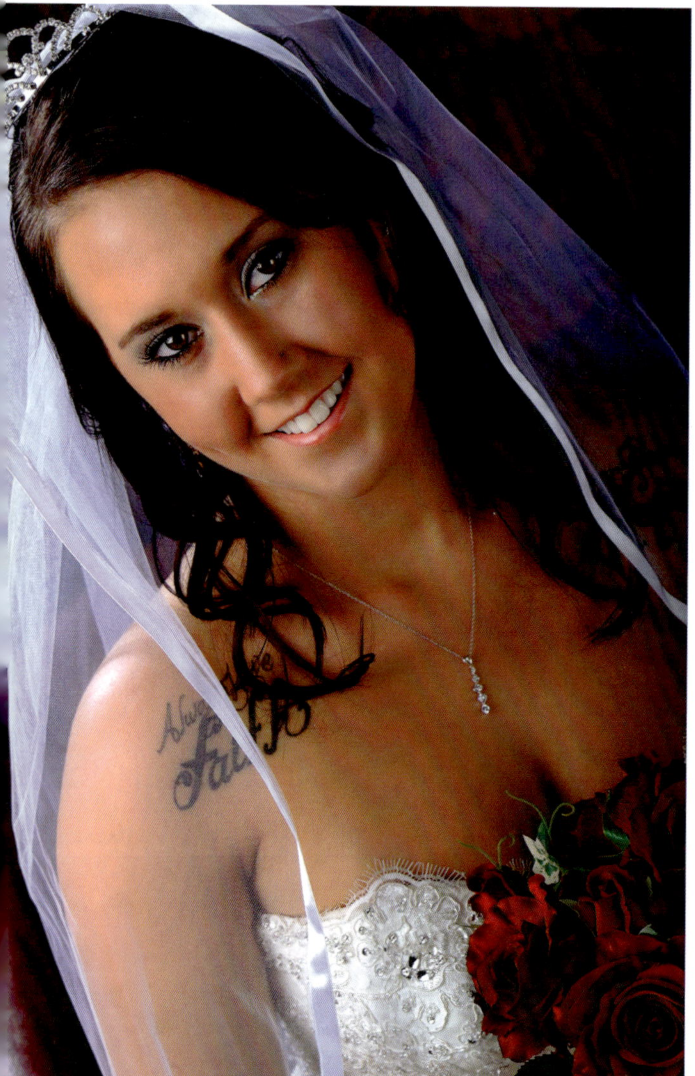

◄ Try filling the frame completely, as was done in this image. The result is a very personal essay of the subject.
▼ Typical middle-key lighting setup. This approach is excellent for general portraiture such as corporate headshots.

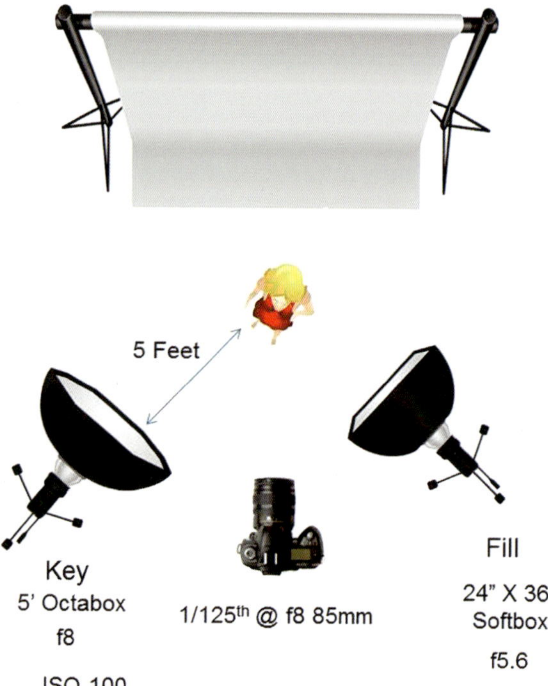

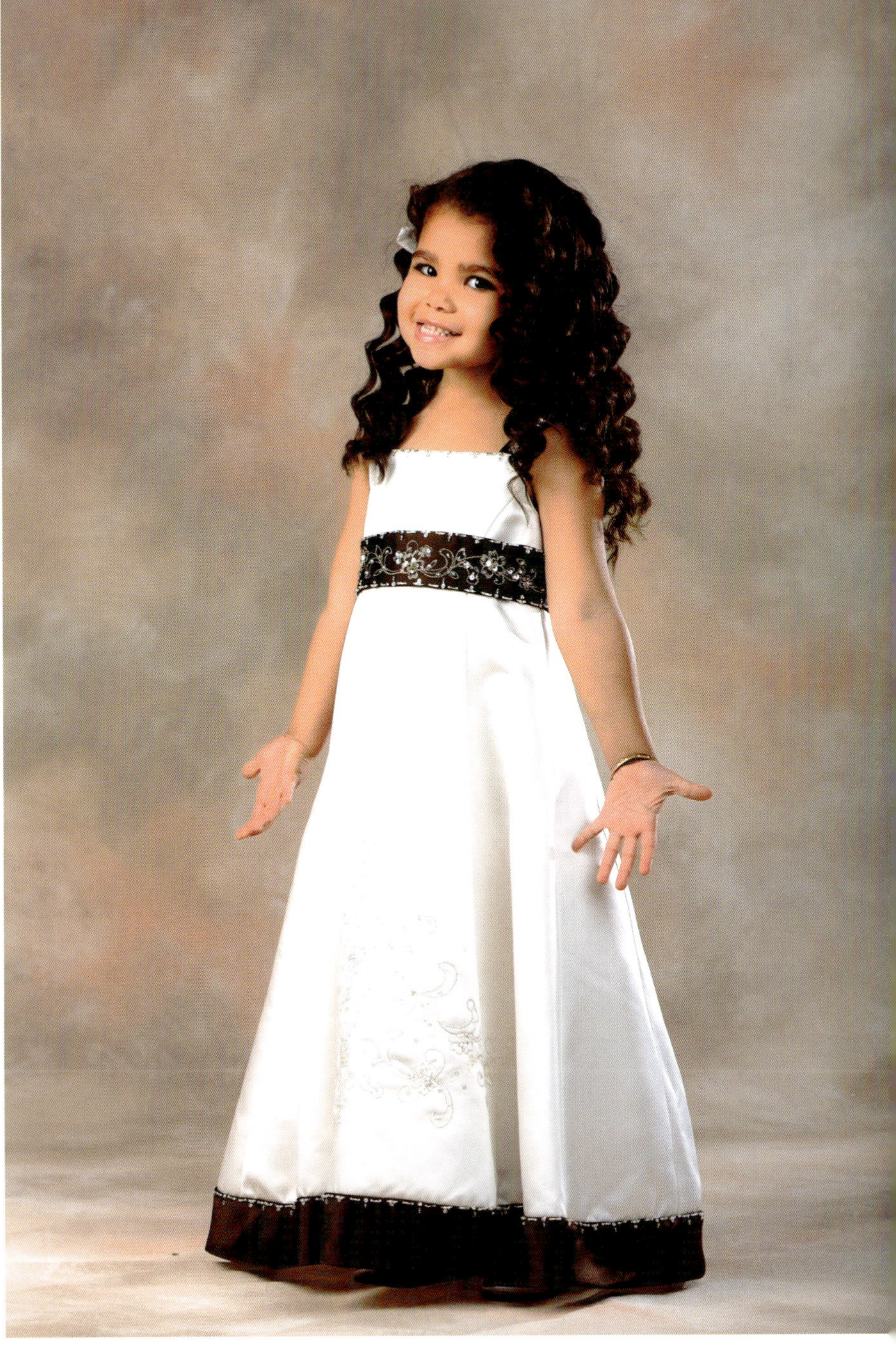

universal in its use. The result of a well-executed mid key image involves color density, beauty, and less specular highlights than that of a high-key equivalent.

For this type of image, I employ a 5-foot octabox as the key light and a 24x36-inch softbox as the fill light. Certainly, a rim light can be used. Recall that the shutter controls the brightness of the background. For mid and low key, pay attention to how you can darken and brighten the backdrop by increasing and decreasing the shutter speed of the camera. Furthermore, the position of the subject in relation to the backdrop for a given light source also has an effect on the brightness of the backdrop. This involves the inverse square law. (If you're interested in this technicality, review the Inverse Square Law Tech Tip.)

Steps 1 through 3 of the process have been performed. The selection of backdrop, props, position, and pose are complete. Step 4 involves selecting an ISO of 100 with an initial shutter speed of $^1/_{125}$ second at f/8. The light meter is set to incident mode, placed under the chin of the subject, and aimed at the key light, producing a reading of f/8. The fill is metered to be between one full stop below the key, at f/5.6. Steps 5 and 6 involve moving and feathering the key and fill lights, then analyzing the exposure to ensure that the desired contrast on the face is achieved. I generally use an 85mm prime lens for this type of work, as this lens offers excellent bokeh resulting in a beautiful blurring of the backdrop.

Low Key. Low-key portraiture involves high contrast that defines and exaggerates the shadow side of the face. Low-key portraiture works well with adults when the goal is to create a compelling or demure image. Low-key images are often interesting because they have a mysterious quality. Black & white nude images are a good example of the use of low-key lighting— although there are no examples of nudes in this book! Generally, I find low-key images to be beautiful and involving, with a timeless quality. There is an abundant creative space with low-key lighting. The images on pages 111 to 113 are examples of low key. A diagram of the setup is shown on the right.

Steps 1 through 3 have been performed. The selection of backdrop, props, position, and pose are complete. Step 4 involves the selection of ISO 100 with a shutter speed of $\frac{1}{200}$ second at f/8. The light meter was set to incident mode and was placed under the chin of the subject and aimed at the key light, yielding f/8. The

fill in this case was a silver reflector to camera right; set initially to f/11, the rim light, a strobe with a grid attached, added highlights to the hair. Blond hair and brunette hair (and

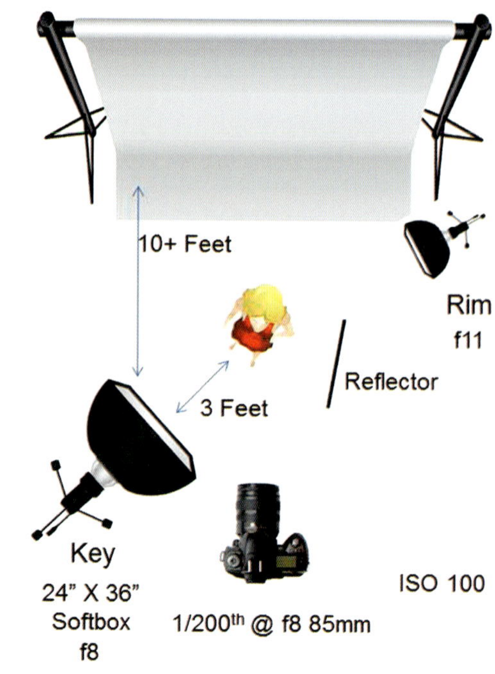

▲ Typical low-key lighting setup. Use this technique when your goal is to create drama, depth, gravity, or a moody feel or theme.

 # Inverse Square Law

Relative to photography, the Inverse Square Law means that as you double the distance between a light source and the person being photographed, the light intensity is reduced by one fourth. Another way of thinking about this relationship is that by doubling the distance, four times the light intensity will be required for an equivalent exposure. This is a good thing to know, especially in the studio. When doing studio work, the way that light "falls off" of a subject is an important artistic feature in the image. For example, a male being photographed 5 feet from the key light, while the backdrop is separated from the key by 10 feet, receives four times the light than that of the backdrop. Simply separating the subject from the backdrop can make a dramatic change in the look of the

image. The formula reads: the intensity of light is 1 divided by the distance squared. At 5 feet from the light source, the intensity of light is calculated to be $\frac{1}{25}$; the same light source at 10 feet has a calculated intensity of $\frac{1}{100}$, or four times less.

When photographing large groups where there may be two, three, or more rows of persons in the scene, employ the inverse square law. By setting the camera and light source at a greater distance, the relative difference in the intensity of light between the people in the first row, as opposed to the people in the last row, will be minimal and you will produce a better image of all those involved.

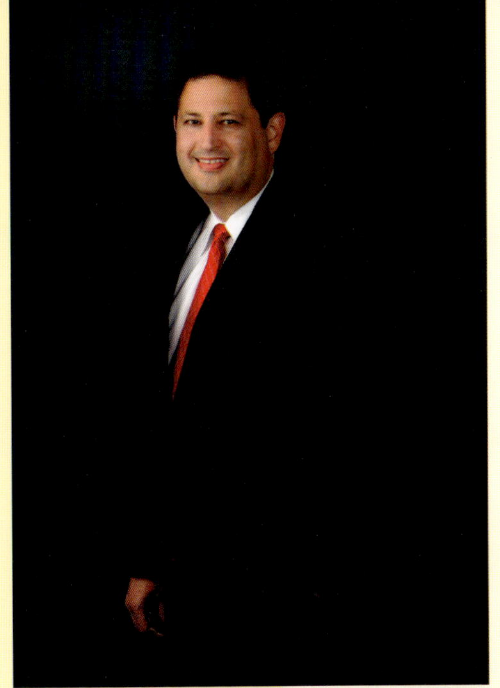

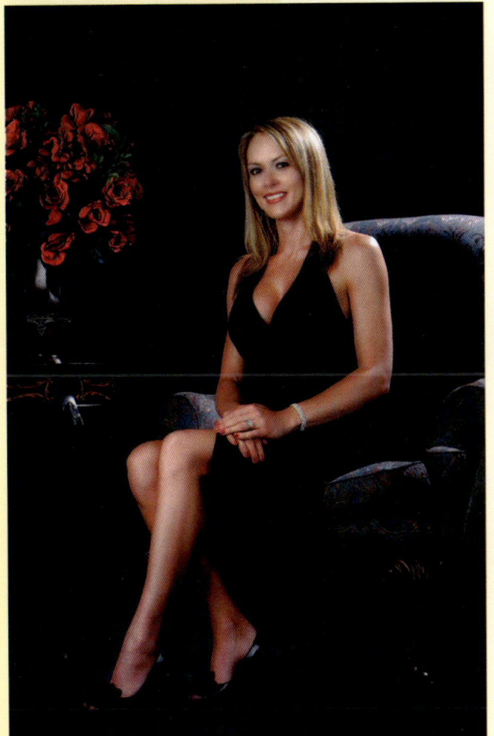

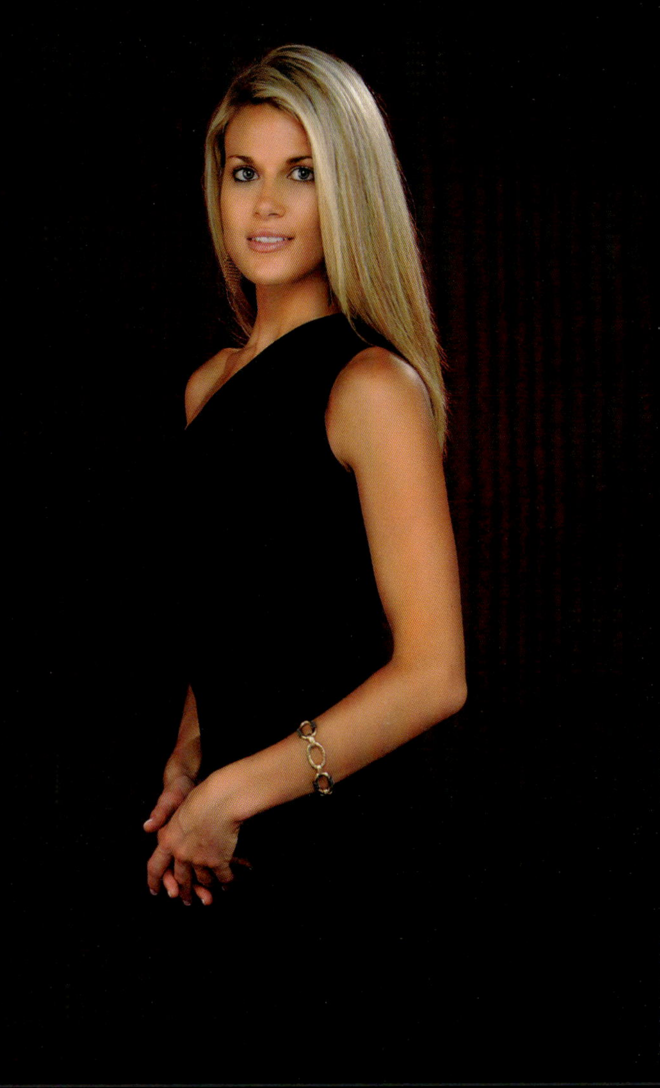

➤ This is a great example of a low-key, full-length portrait.

▲ Additional examples of low key portraiture.

If your analysis indicates proper exposure, then take all of the creative images necessary . . .

no hair) reflect light differently. Thus, there is no hard-and-fast rule for the power setting of a rim light. Set it to one stop higher than the key light, then during step 5, adjust the power according to how you want the hair to look. (Remember, step 5 involves both moving and feathering the key light and the reflector in order to achieve the desired contrast on the face.) Take an exposure (step 6) and analyze the histogram and image. If your analysis indicates proper exposure, then take all of the creative images necessary; otherwise, return to step 5.

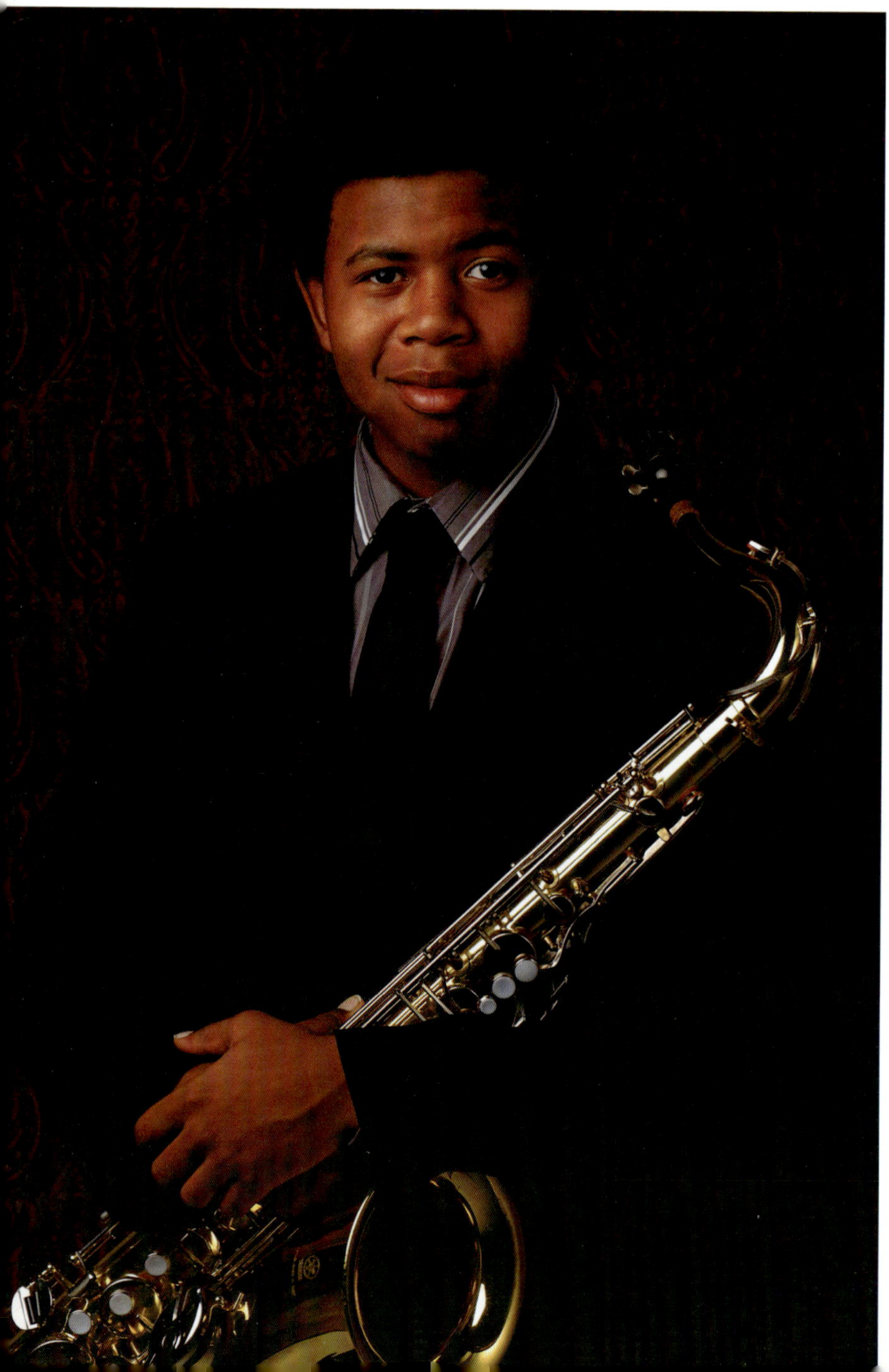

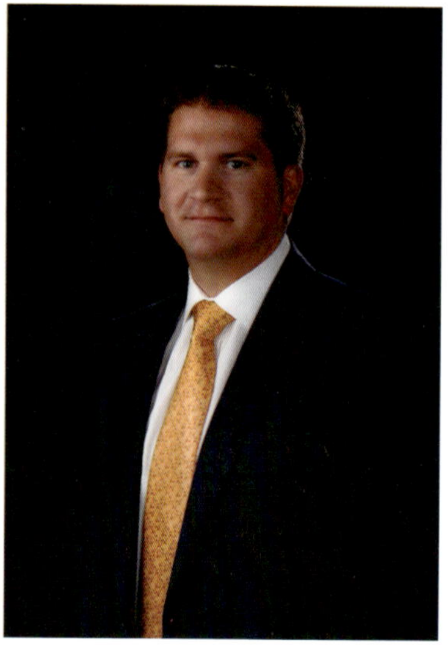

▲ A typical low-key headshot.

◄ This high-school senior brought his saxaphone to the shoot. This added authenticity and interest in the image.

► By allowing your clients to express themselves, as this woman did, unique and interesting results will produce indelible images.

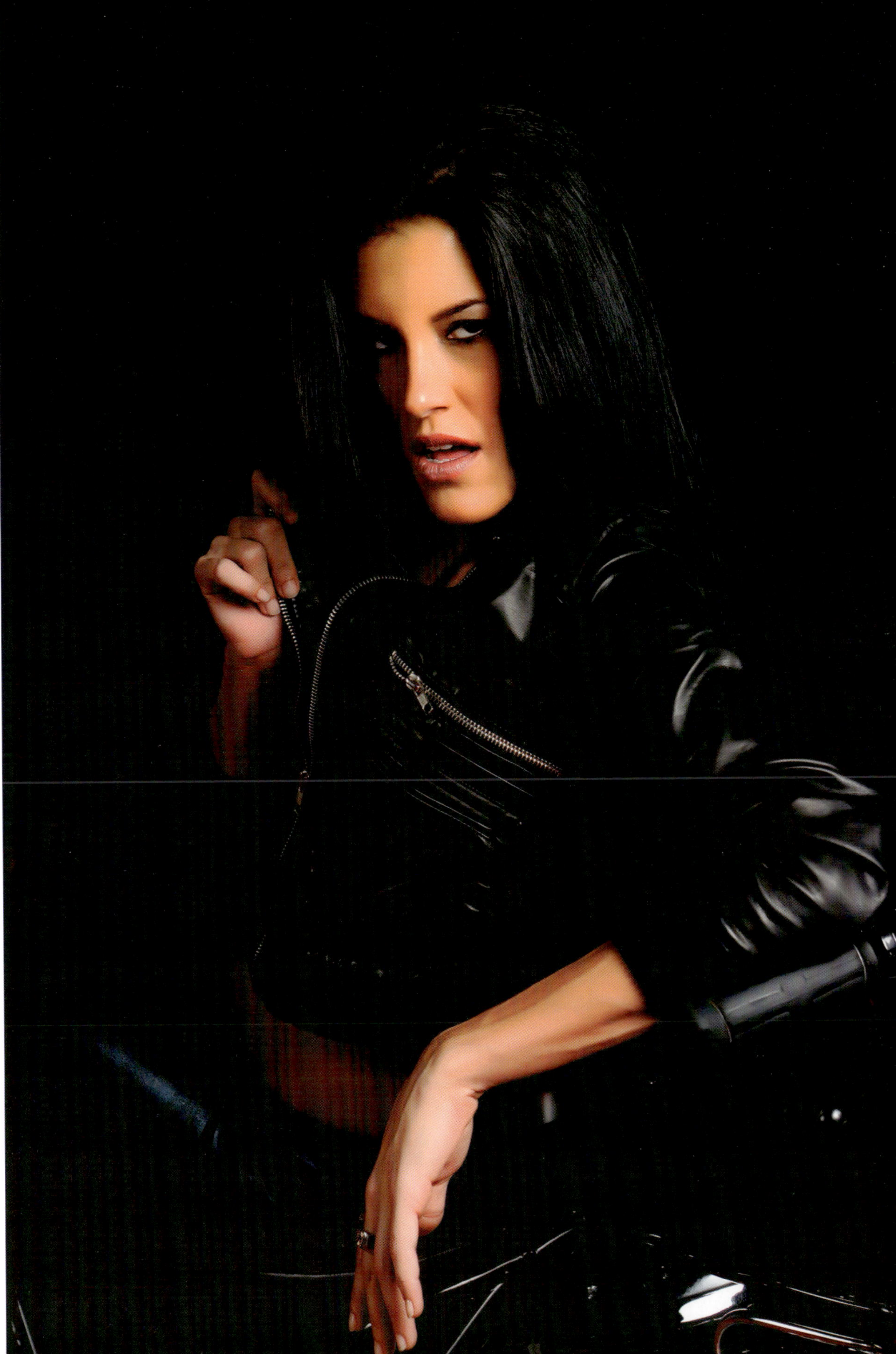

6. Indoor Portraits

From time to time, you may be required to produce portraits indoors, but without the controlled predetermined environment of the studio. Indoor locations include a client's home, a reception hall during a wedding, or perhaps the foyer entrance to a hotel. Producing professional images in this type of domain can be a challenge. The good news is that the fundamentals we have discussed do not change. A key light is required, with fill and rim lighting added if the space allows you to position the equipment properly. Since we have gone over fundamental studio portraiture, I'm not going to repeat the information in this chapter. Instead, I'm going to concentrate on two specific techniques that will increase the quality of your images. I use both of these techniques frequently. In both cases, all that I require is my camera and an on-camera flashgun; this is a lightweight, agile solution. I can move with relative ease, allowing myself more time to dedicate to steps 1, 2, and 3. With a little bit of imagination and practice, you will be able to assess an indoor environment and quickly adapt your equipment to produce beautiful portraits.

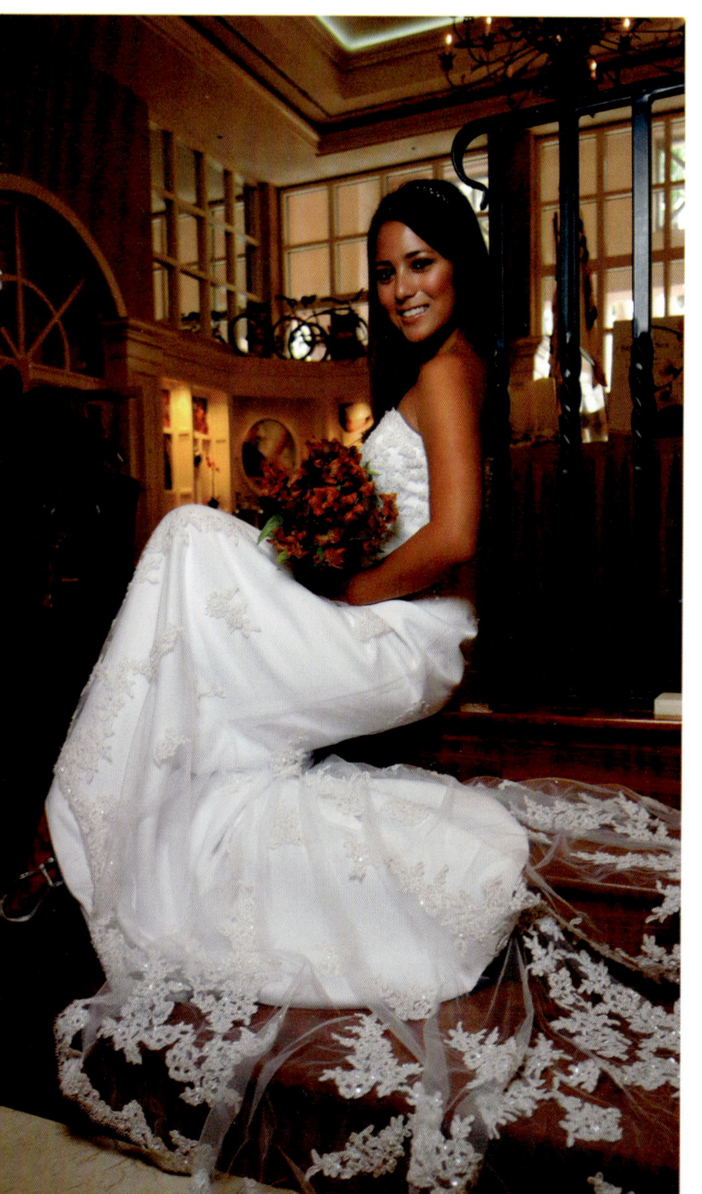

◄ To light this image, a portable strobe with a 5-foot octabox was placed just to camera left. Note the distortion in the vertical plane; she is slightly stretched. However, I had no choice in the matter, as my back was literally against a wall. I believe this to be a successful image.

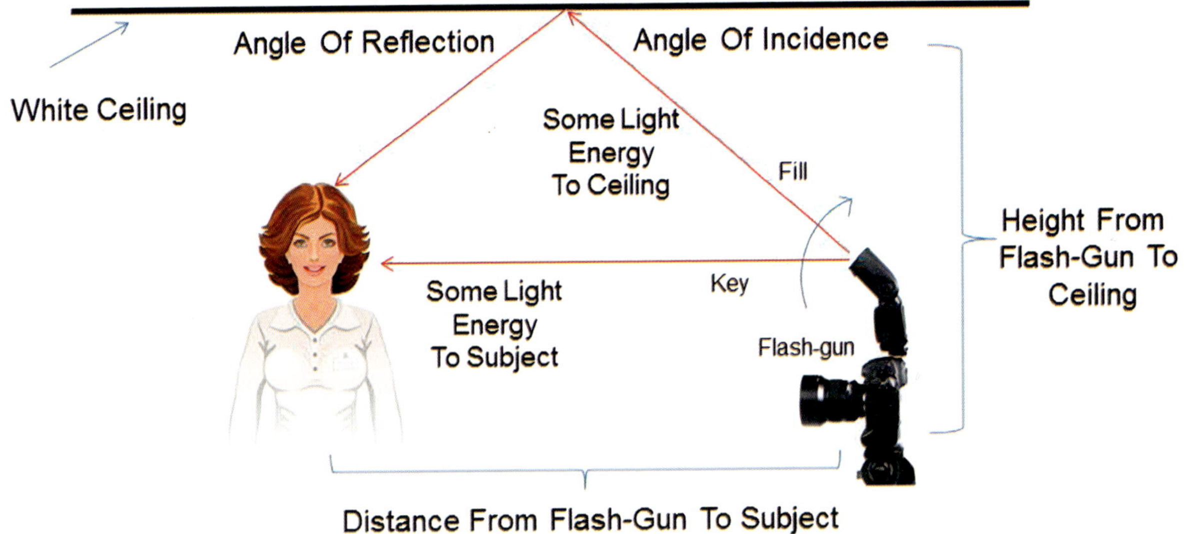

This diagram shows the relationship of the angle formed by the on-camera flashgun and the incident light, which forms the basis for key and fill lights.

Reflecting Light Off the Ceiling

Reflecting or "bouncing" light off of a surface such as a ceiling is an excellent means of illuminating the person being photographed. Provided the ceiling is white or at least very close to white, you effectively have a large softbox suspended over your subject. The reflected light takes on a soft, wraparound effect that is pleasing to the eye. I use an on-camera flashgun placed at an angle such that the light emitted is "split" between the ceiling and the person being photographed. The flashgun acts as a key and fill light simultaneously. The precise angle to which the flashgun is set is a function of the distance between the camera and the subject, and the height of the ceiling. The power setting of the flashgun is set by trial and error. I find that it normally takes two or three trial images to get the power and angle correct. The goal is to brighten the subject with the key, while providing soft light to remove shadows with the fill. It takes some practice. Remember that the incident angle is equal to the reflected angle. After performing this operation, you will get better and better at judging what angle and power setting are required given the distance from the subject and the height of the ceiling. Rest assured, it works!

This might sound radical—a key and a fill from one on-camera flashgun? Yes, it is both efficient and effective. The black & white image of the bride on the following page was made using this technique. The bride was standing in a hallway with a ceiling height of approximately eleven feet. The camera height was approximately three feet off of the floor. Using the process, step 4 involved choosing an ISO of 400, a shutter speed of $^1/_{125}$ second, and an aperture of f/4 using the trial-and-error method. Steps 5 and 6 involved adjusting the angle of the flashgun (similar to moving the position of light sources) until both the reflected light from the ceiling and direct light to the face were cor-rect. The portrait was taken during a wedding reception—there was neither sufficient time nor room to set up strobes and softboxes. With my camera and flashgun in hand, the image was taken quickly.

Using a Window as the Key Light

Quite often, sunlight that penetrates a window provides beautiful, soft light. In this situation, the window represents the key; the window pane itself is similar to a softbox. Either on-camera flashgun or off-camera strobes (with softboxes or umbrellas) are used as the fill source. For this image, step 4 involved using an 85mm prime lens. The trial-and-error method was used to arrive at ISO 800, a shutter speed of $^1/_{100}$ second, and aperture of f/2.0. The fill light, an on-camera flash-gun, was set to the absolute minimum power. Steps 5 and 6 involved angling the flash-gun away from the subject to provide just enough fill light to eliminate dark shadows on the face.

In the next photograph (facing page), the woman was posed in a theater lobby. Step 4 involved selecting an ISO of 400 and a shutter speed of 1/80 second at f/3.2. With a shutter speed of $^1/_{80}$, I decided

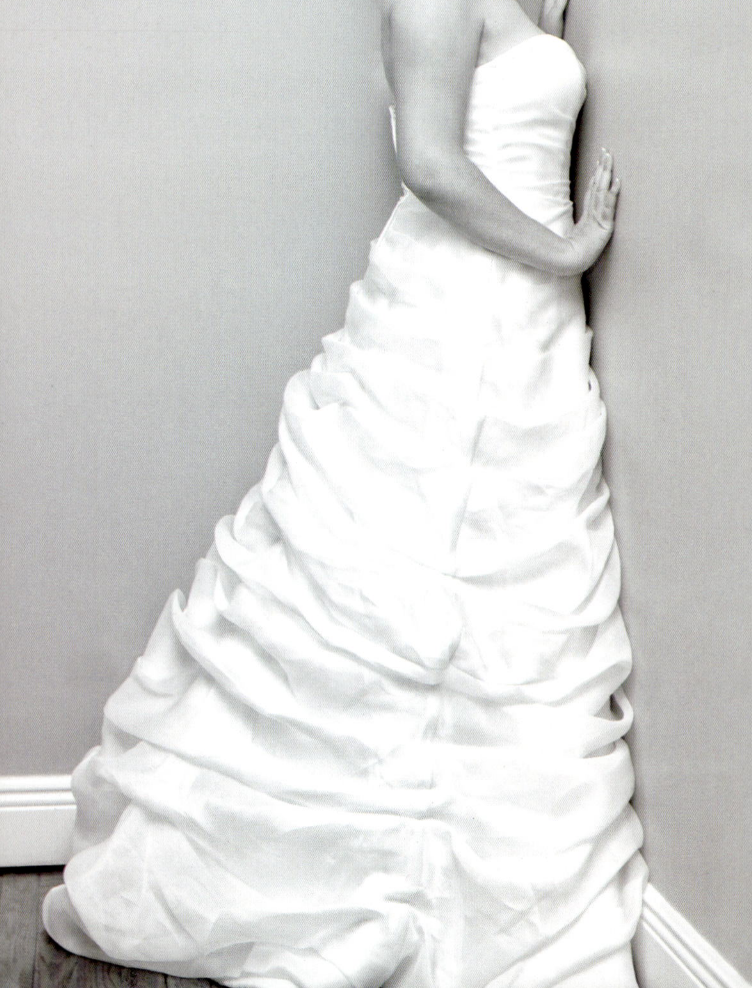

◄ By setting the angle of the on-camera flashgun to both bounce light off of the ceiling and directly illuminate the bride, a great bridal portrait was produced.

► Window light served as the key light in the image. The exposure was ISO 800 at $^1/_{100}$ second and f/2.0.

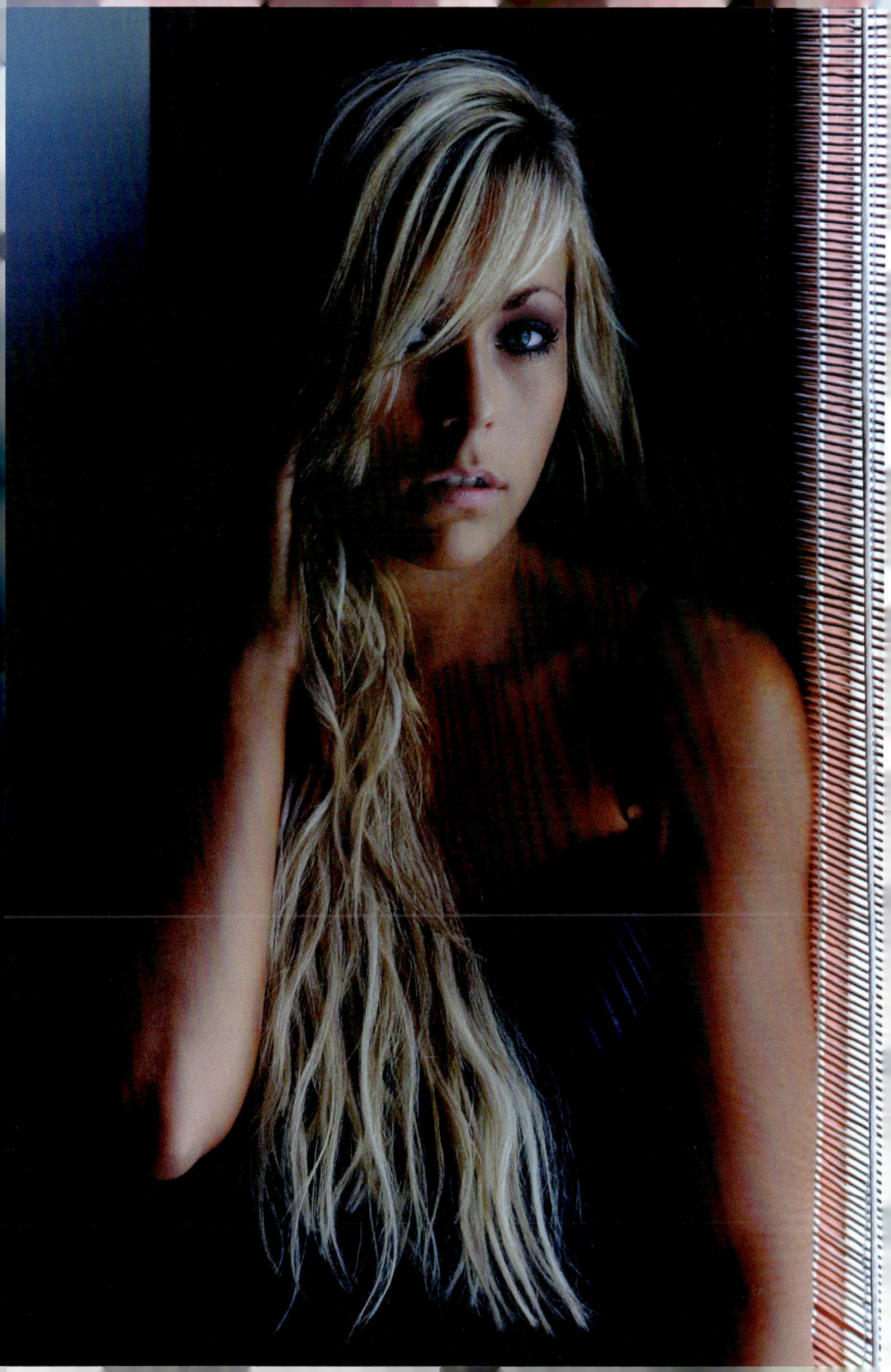

it was a good idea to mount the camera on a tripod. At a distance of 10 feet from the subject, a 35mm prime was used with on-camera flashgun for fill. Steps 5 and 6 involved arriving at a final power setting on the flashgun, which provided the precise amount of fill light (very little), thereby eliminating shadows under the eyes. Great care was taken to frame the individual in the center of the field of view of the 35mm lens to minimize any bending. I think I pulled it off—you be the judge.

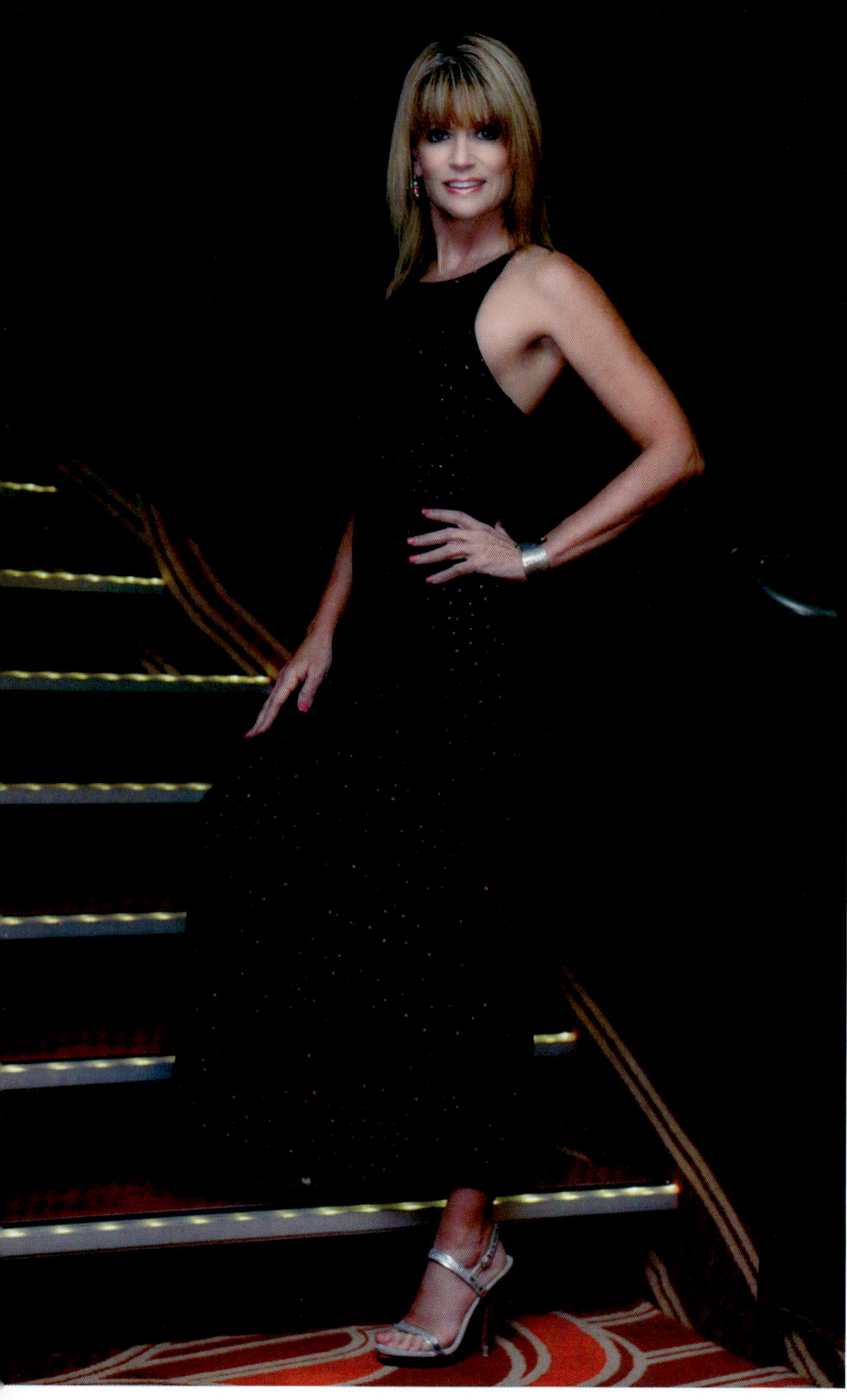

◄ By bouncing the light from my on-camera flashgun with just the right split in key and fill light, this terrific image was an impromptu capture, made in under two minutes.

➤ This mid-key portrait exudes beauty and emotion due to the soft light, pose, and personality of the bride.

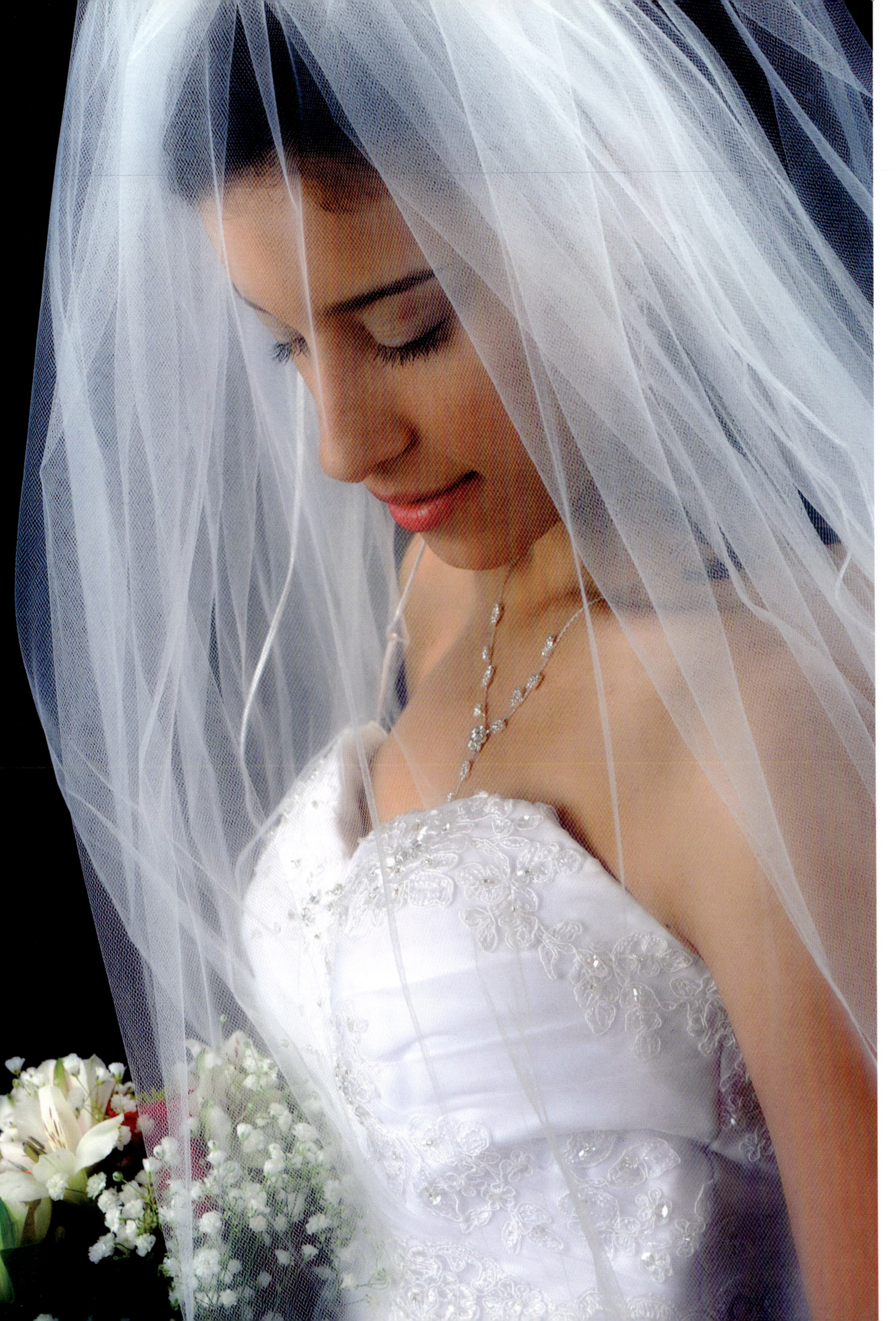

7. Practice, Practice, Practice

Now You Are Ready!

We have covered a wide range of topics concerning portrait photography. With the five pieces of equipment that comprise the basic portraiture photography kit, you are ready to go to work. We have covered the use of the DSLR, flashgun, and light meter sufficiently for you to produce professional indoor and outdoor results. With the addition of studio equipment, you have been introduced to equipment and techniques that will result in dynamic and exciting studio portraits. Is there more to learn? Absolutely! There is so much to photography that I believe it is a lifelong learning endeavor. In the digital age, computer equipment, sophisticated bit-map editing software, workflow, and web presence are just a few of the supportive elements to creating images.

Follow the Process

Use the six-step process introduced in chapter 3 whenever you are conducting a portrait session. The process represents a stable, repeatable approach to controlling the variables of composition and pose, camera exposure, and lighting. Take the time to evaluate sources of light; determine and use the best light possible—don't settle for average light. Ensure that you create a mental image of the photographic work. The mental image provides an objective that you work toward. This keeps the portrait shoot manageable and aligned—you are less likely to veer off course and lose your way.

To improve your ability and efficiency in positioning and posing your subjects, develop

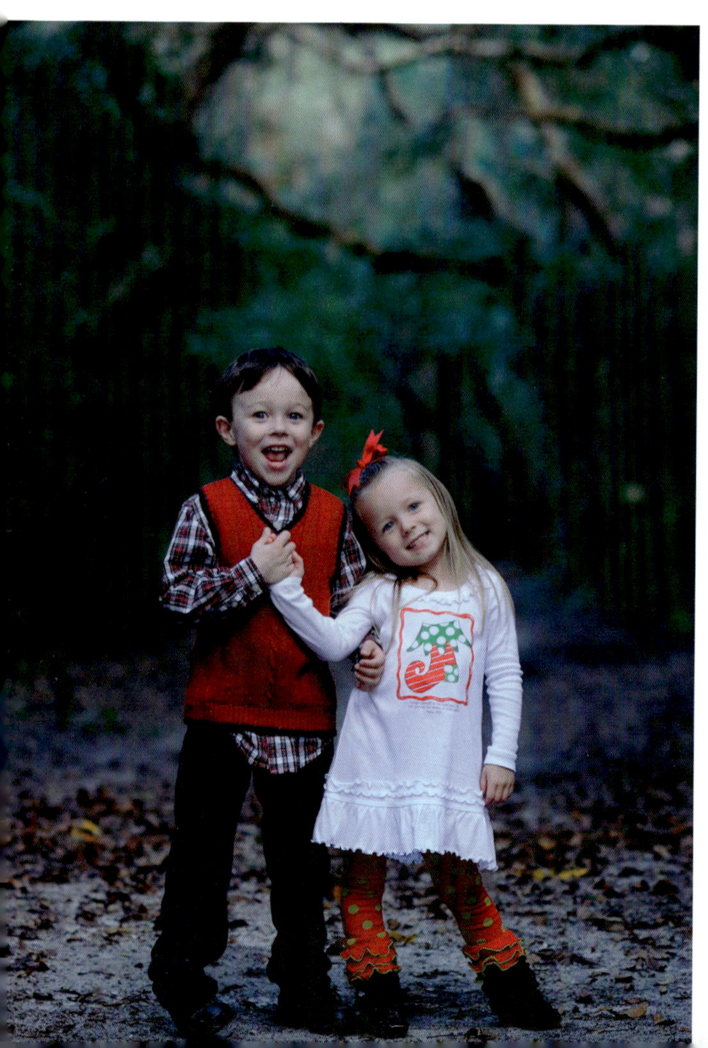

◄ These kids were not shy, and a great image was captured simply by following the process and taking a burst of exposures.
➤ With Mom and Dad in place, the family portrait was completed.

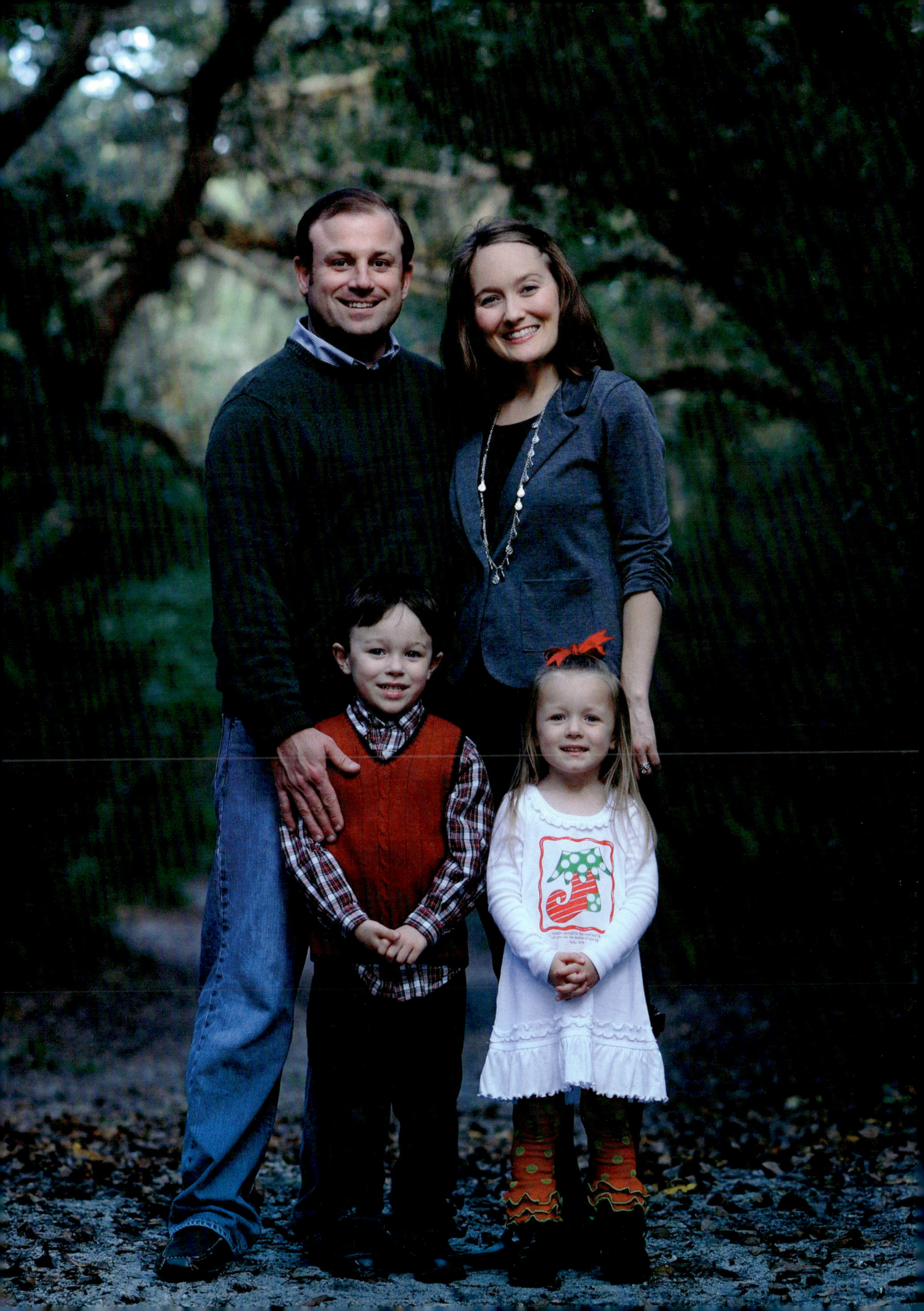

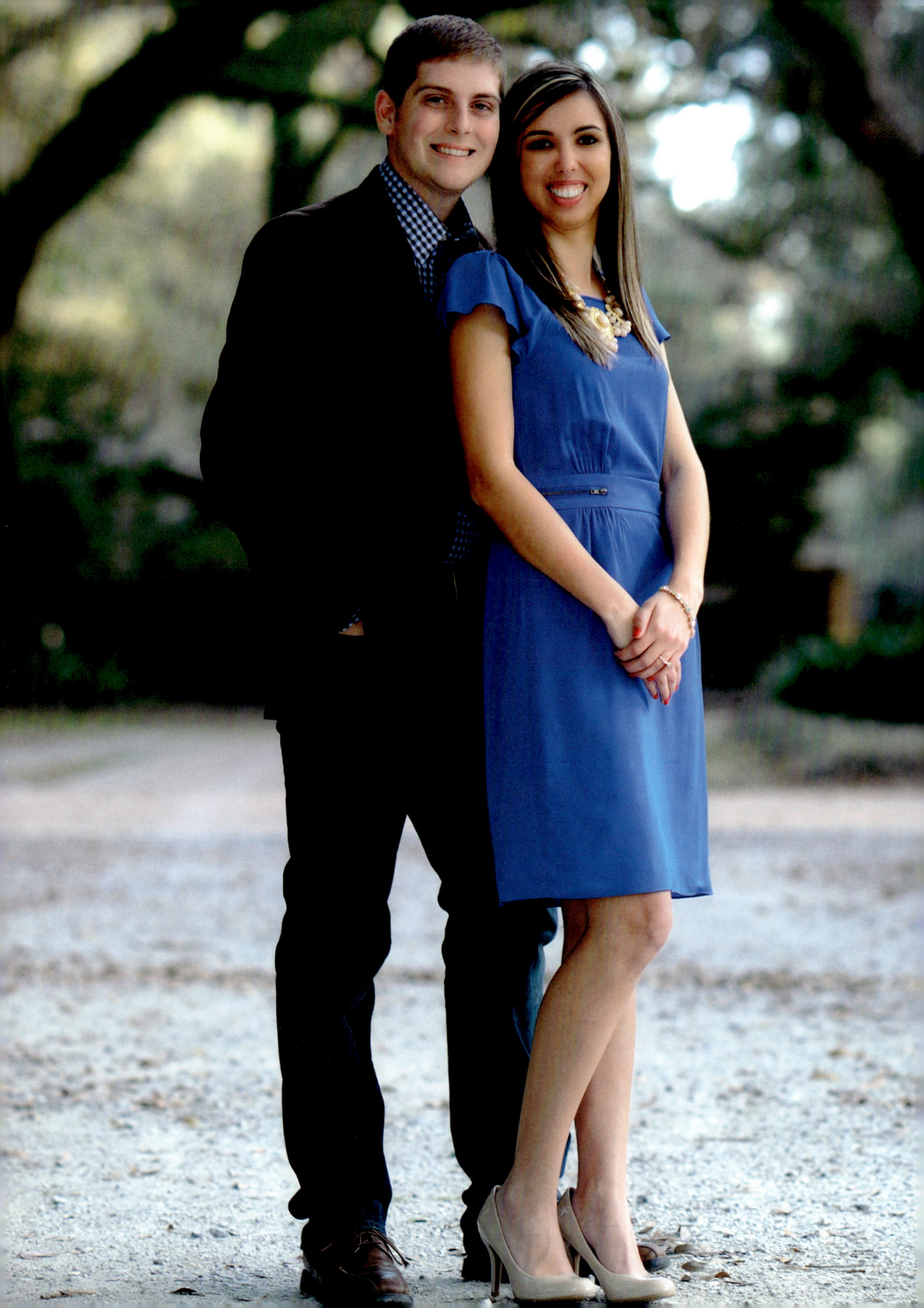

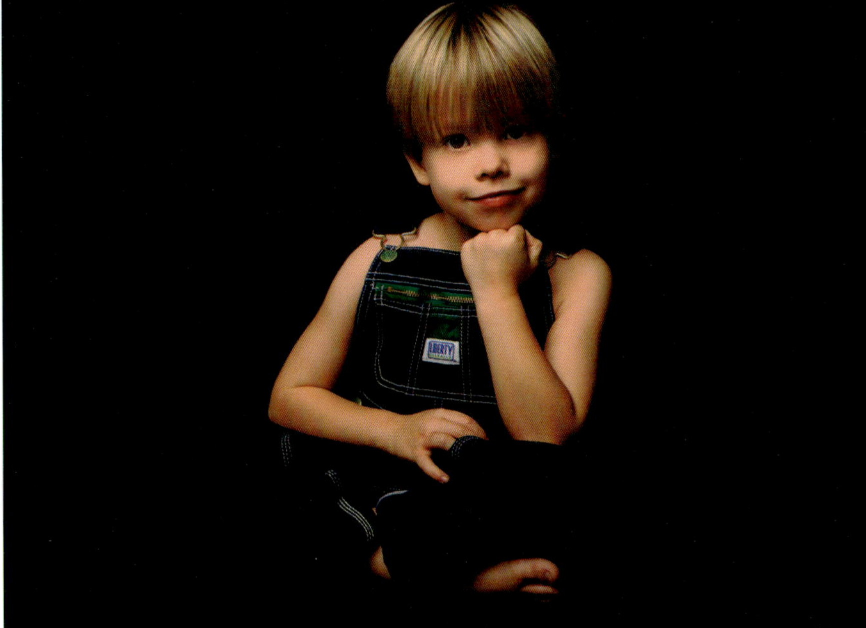

➤ This young lad was a natural in front of the lens. A 5-foot octabox served as the main light, and the resultant image produced from this low-key lighting arrangement won praise from his parents.

◄ Here's another example of how well simple poses work.

your communication skills. Whether you are working with a family, children, or top models, posing them properly is a function of your ability to communicate effectively. Work diligently toward achieving an exposure that idealizes your subject. The people in your photos should look terrific, with beauty, detail, and emotion. Avoid *acceptable* and push yourself toward *phenomenal!*

Review Your Work with a Critical Eye

It is difficult to see one's own works of art the way that others do. I believe this is true due to a built-in bias that we have prior to and during the creative process. The bias comes in the form of excitement, emotion, and varying degrees of experience both artistically and technically. For example, upon reviewing a photograph that you took a couple of years ago, you may find that it doesn't meet your current standards or expectations. Perhaps the composition is off, or the image is underexposed. Interestingly, you did not see any issues back then, but now that you do, you have a pretty good idea of what you might do to shoot that photograph differently. We all experience this form of dissonance with the past

to varying degrees. It's normal. The point to be made here is to try to avoid getting caught up in a photograph; rather, attempt to look at your own work as though it is produced by someone else. Give the image a thorough "scrubbing." Review the elements of composition, pose, lighting, and exposure critically. Ask yourself, "Is this photograph the best that it can be?" If the answer is yes, then hopefully, you have completed the task. If the answer is no, then strive to overcome the issue as you move forward with future projects and clients. The act of critically reviewing your work, evaluating what could have been done better, and then doing better is a form of continuous improvement which will result in you creating better and better portraits.

Editing the Digital Image

Photoshop, Lightroom, and NIK NK2 are just three of the outstanding, powerful editing tools available on the market. I use Photoshop to complete 100 percent of my portrait editing tasks. However, as a photographer, the majority of your time should be spent behind the camera. Editing should be kept to a minimum.

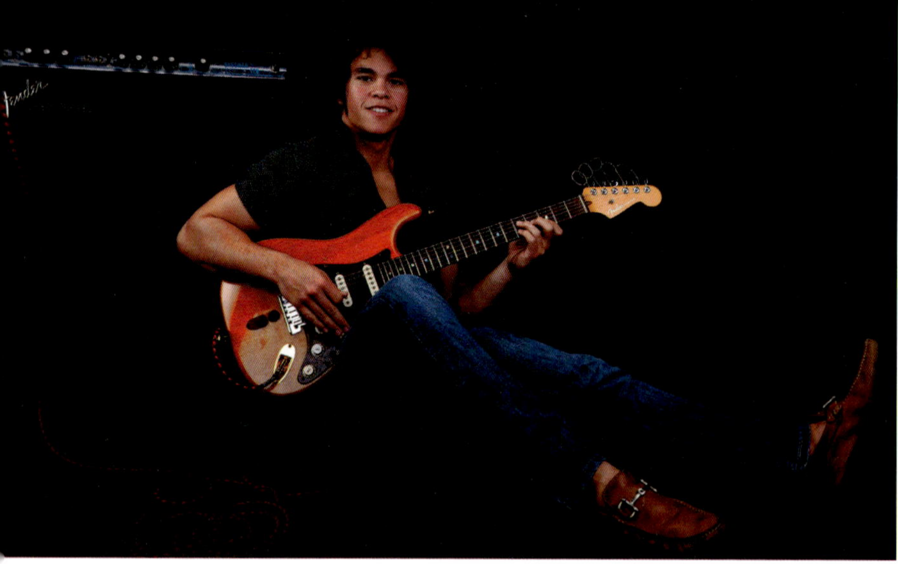

◄ This young and amazingly talented musician had so much personality that capturing it was easy.

The following is a short list of five functions that I preform when editing digital portraits:

1. I save my RAW file in TIFF format. TIFF is a lossless file format. This means there is little to no compression when the image is opened and resaved, so there is no notable impact on image quality. As TIFF files are not impacted by a compression algorithm, the files are large in size. I complete all of my editing, printing, and image archiving in TIFF format.

   JPEG files are much smaller than TIFFs, as a compression algorithm is used every time the image is saved. JPEG files are appropriate for Web/Internet media, e-mailing images to family and friends, and general printing. Bear in mind, however, that JPEG files do not contain all of the image information that TIFFs do.

2. My second step is to fine-tune the white balance in the portrait. For an image to look its best, white objects in the image must be rendered as pure white. Without a correct white balance, the white tones will have a reddish-orange or bluish color cast. Because

I shoot in RAW, making a final white balance adjustment is simple and easy. See the Tech Tip on white balance for additional information on this topic.

3. Step three entails making a local brightness/contrast adjustment. On a layer in Photoshop, I make adustments to local objects (i.e., background, subject's clothing, sky) by increasing or decreasing subject brightness—but only by a tiny amount. If more intensive changes are necessary, it is likely the image is improperly exposed and should be rejected.

4. Step four requires the retouching/removal of blemishes, stray hairs, and fine lines. When creating a photograph as described in this book, you the photographer have limited control over the person's facial attributes. Although careful attention should be paid to hair and makeup, often you have no control (e.g., sometimes the wind will disrupt your subject's hairstyle).

   When removing a blemish or stray hair, a light touch is required. Good retouching skills are acquired with practice. There are countless books, articles, workshops, and webinars devoted to the art of retouching. I recommend that you invest the time required to learn, practice, and master your technique.

5. Straightening and cropping the image are my final step. When photographing people, my intention is to perform an in-camera crop so that the captured image is the final image (aside from light white balance and retoching is concerned). Despite your best efforts, though, you will find that there are times when the lines of the image just are not perfectly level. Cropping can correct for this error.

One final point about editing: Don't overdo it. Be careful not to change the size or proportion of the subject. I personally and professionally feel that this is a big no-no.

Recall the point that I made early on in the book: The photographer's job is to idealize the subject—to make them look their very best. For me, it is imperative that the person appears absolutely authentic, real, and devoid of evidence that you performed any modifications.

Attend Workshops and Seminars by Great Photographers

If you had the opportunity to play tennis with a world-class tennis professional, the odds are you would become a much better tennis player. The corollary with photography and photographers holds true. Socialize with other photographers who are performing above your current level of performance. Observe how they conduct themselves, handle the equipment, and interact with people. Don't be afraid to ask questions—any and all questions—in order to gain a full and complete understanding of an issue that is important to you photographically. Money is often

involved in this scenario. Provided that the cost of admission is not harmful to you financially, may I suggest that you make the investment? By doing so, you can significantly accelerate your learning curve, hang out with people who share your passion, and raise the bar on your portrait photography skills.

A Short List of the Photographers Whom I Admire Most

Ansel Adams
Helmut Newton
Henri Cartier-Bresson
Saudek

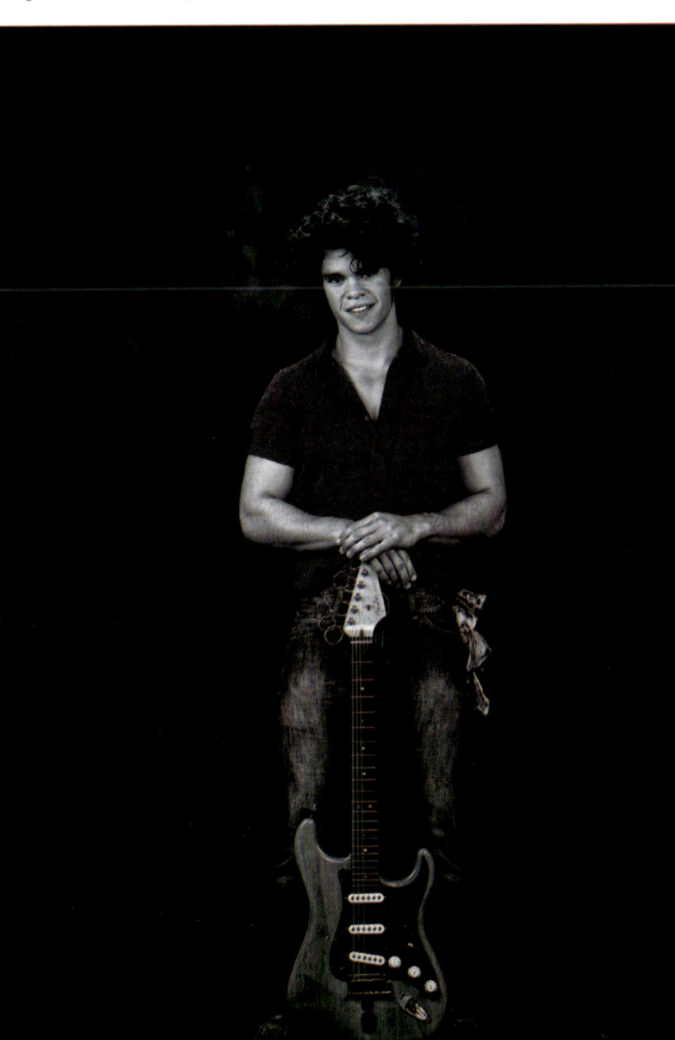

By converting this image to black & white, the textures of apparel, hair, and instrument are exemplified. The pose, again, is straightforward and simple.

Index